# Disruptive Behavior Disorders in Childhood

# Disruptive Behavior Disorders in Childhood

Edited by

## DONALD K. ROUTH

*University of Miami*
*Coral Gables, Florida*

PLENUM PRESS • NEW YORK AND LONDON

Library of Congress Cataloging-in-Publication Data

Disruptive behavior disorders in childhood / edited by Donald K.
Routh.
    p.    cm.
    Papers prepared in honor of Herbert C. Quay upon the occasion of
his retirement.
    Includes bibliographical references and index.
    ISBN 0-306-44695-2
    1. Behavior disorders in children.    I. Routh, Donald K.
    [DNLM: 1. Quay, Herbert C. (Herbert Callister), 1927-    .
    2. Child Behavior Disorders.    WS 350.6 D613 1994]
    RJ506.B44D57   1994
    618.92'858--dc20
    DNLM/DLC
    for Library of Congress                                94-16761
                                                              CIP

*/775972    //-21-94*

ISBN 0-306-44695-2

©1994 Plenum Press, New York
A Division of Plenum Publishing Corporation
233 Spring Street, New York, N.Y. 10013

Printed in the United States of America

**Herbert C. Quay**

# Contributors

RUSSELL A. BARKLEY • Departments of Psychiatry and Neurology, University of Massachusetts Medical Center, Worcester, Massachusetts 01655

DON C. FOWLES • Department of Psychology, University of Iowa, Iowa City, Iowa 15213

ANN M. FURUSETH • Department of Psychology, University of Iowa, Iowa City, Iowa 15213

EDWARD D. HAIGLER • Department of Psychology, University of Kentucky, Lexington, Kentucky 40506

SUSAN D. HAMBURGER • National Institute of Mental Health, Child Psychiatry Branch, Bethesda, Maryland 20892

CYNTHIA M. HARTUNG • Department of Psychology, University of Kentucky, Lexington, Kentucky 40506

LEAH A. HEROD • Department of Psychology, Auburn University, Auburn, Alabama 36849-5214

MARKUS J. P. KRUESI • Institute for Juvenile Research, Department of Psychiatry, University of Illinois at Chicago, Chicago, Illinois 60612

BENJAMIN B. LAHEY • Department of Psychiatry, University of Chicago, Chicago, Illinois 60637-1470

HENRIETTA L. LEONARD • National Institute of Mental Health, Child Psychiatry Branch, Bethesda, Maryland 20892

ROLF LOEBER • Western Psychiatric Institute and Clinic, University of Pittsburgh, Pittsburgh, Pennsylvania 15213

JAMES C. S. LIU • University of Medicine and Dentistry of New Jersey, Piscataway, New Jersey 40506

CATHERINE A. MARTIN • Department of Psychiatry, University of Kentucky, Lexington, Kentucky 40506

RICHARD MILICH • Department of Psychology, University of Kentucky, Lexington, Kentucky 40506

SUSAN N. NADI • National Institute of Neurological and Communicative Disorders and Stroke, Laboratory of Neurophysiology, Bethesda, Maryland 20892

JUDITH L. RAPOPORT • National Institute of Mental Health, Child Psychiatry Branch, Bethesda, Maryland 20892

DONALD K. ROUTH • Department of Psychology, University of Miami, Coral Gables, Florida 33124

JOSEPH A. SERGEANT • Department of Clinical Psychology, University of Amsterdam, 1018 WB Amsterdam, The Netherlands

STEVEN K. SHAPIRO • Department of Psychiatry, Auburn University, Auburn, Alabama 36849-5214

SUSAN E. SWEDO • National Institute of Mental Health, Child Psychiatry Branch, Bethesda, Maryland 20892

JAAP VAN DER MEERE • Laboratory of Experimental Psychology, University of Groningen, Groningen, The Netherlands

# Preface

*Disruptive Behavior Disorders in Childhood* honors Herbert C. Quay upon the occasion of his retirement. It consists of chapters written by his colleagues in the fields of psychology and psychiatry, most of whom are associated with the Society for Research in Child and Adolescent Psychopathology (SRCAP), an organization Quay founded. The initial chapter, written by the editor, provides a personal account of Herbert Quay and provides some details concerning his research activities related to the disruptive behavior disorders in childhood.

The other chapters are presentations of research and theory relating to one or another of the disruptive behavior disorders, which include oppositional defiant disorder (ODD), attention-deficit hyperactivity disorder (ADHD), and conduct disorder (CD). The chapter authors demonstrate their awareness of Quay's own recent research and theory applying Jeffrey Gray's hypotheses to child and adolescent psychopathology. Briefly, Quay has hypothesized that CD in children and adolescents and antisocial personality disorder in adults have a biological basis in an overactive Behavioral Activation System (BAS) involving excessive sensitivity to the effects of reward. Quay also has hypothesized that ADHD has a biological basis in an underactive Behavioral Inhibition System (BIS) involving decreased sensitivity to the effects of punishment. The chapter authors were also aware of Quay's strong commitment to empirical research in child and adolescent psychopathology. Thus, they were encouraged by the editor to pursue their own theoretical inclinations and to present the results of their own investigations, whether these were consonant with Quay's hypotheses or not. Indeed, the authors have followed these instructions to let the chips fall where they may. The result is a wide-ranging collection of essays that in part support Quay's hypotheses but also present a number of theoretical and research findings attempting to go beyond Quay's work. Knowing Herbert Quay as we do, we do not believe that he would want the book to be otherwise.

The first substantive chapter, by Russell A. Barkley, presents a new theory concerning ADHD that takes off from the work of Jacob Bronowski rather than that of Jeffrey Gray. Barkley hypothesizes that the fundamental deficit in ADHD is an inability to delay responding. Later in development, this deficit is considered to result in difficulty separating affect from the information accompanying it. Subsequent effects include a lack of foresight or hindsight, poor internalization of language, and poor analysis and synthesis. Barkley reviews a very large literature in relation to this conceptual framework and concludes that it may be a more promising approach than either his own previous theoretical formulations or those of Quay.

The next chapter, by Joseph Sergeant and Jaap van der Meere, presents an information-processing approach to research concerning ADHD. Much of Sergeant and van der Meere's recent research has studied ADHD children's performance in vigilance situations such as the continuous performance task. The authors have used this task as a theory-driven set of experimental procedures to investigate the child's underlying cognitive processes rather than as a fixed psychometric test. They argue for the superiority of this approach as compared to more superficial ones involving only the observation of behavior such as the direction of the child's gaze or a judgment of whether the child is "on task." Sergeant and van der Meere conclude that the principal deficit in ADHD may involve motor response processes rather than attention as such.

Shapiro and Herod, in the next chapter, also report research related to ADHD. They attempt to link it to central auditory-processing and academic-achievement problems. Although the outcome of this study in terms of auditory-processing deficits is not unequivocal, this type of approach is important because of the well-documented association of ADHD with academic deficits.

Richard Milich and his colleagues, in the following chapter, focus on the "impulsivity" component of disruptive behavior disorders, which was the subject of an important literature review they carried out a decade ago. In addition, they report research findings testing some of Quay's hypotheses with both a "go, no-go" task and the Newman card-playing task frequently used in Quay's previous research. Milich's study included children with both ADHD and CD. The research produced many significant findings, including some that had been predicted by Quay's theory and others that had not. It is clear that considerably more research will be needed before performance on even these particular experimental tasks is thoroughly understood in relation to the BAS and the BIS.

Lahey and Loeber, in the next chapter, present a developmental model that attempts to describe how ODD in young children can lead to "intermediate" and "advanced" CD (and finally to antisocial personality disorder in adulthood). This model is discussed both in terms of the relevant research literature and the research carried out by the authors themselves—for example, the Pittsburgh Youth Study and the recent DSM-IV field trials. The Lahey and Loeber chapter relates to Quay's extensive involvement in developing assessment procedures such as the Revised Behavior Problem Checklist and his well-known critical reviews of the factor-analytic literature on child psychopathology.

Fowles and Furuseth, in the following chapter, discuss electrodermal hyporeactivity in relation to antisocial behavior in children and adults. Beginning with a discussion of the electrophysiology of the dermal system, this methodologically and substantively sophisticated presentation deals with what aspects of this system are or are not of psychological interest. It also discusses how electrodermal responses are related to psychopathology, including anxiety and panic disorder as well as antisocial behavior. Then, Fowles and Furuseth review the electrodermal literature related to Quay's hypotheses concerning the relation of the BIS to disruptive behavior disorders.

The concluding chapter is highly biologically oriented, which is entirely appropriate to Quay's hypotheses of a biological substrate to child psychopathology. Kruesi and his colleagues report a study comparing children and adolescents with disruptive behavior disorders with another sample suffering from obsessive-compulsive disorder. As hypothesized, those with disruptive behavior disorders had significantly less guilt and higher levels of beta endorphins in their cerebrospinal fluid.

We hope that Herbert Quay, himself the founding editor of the *Journal of Abnormal Child Psychology*, the editor of numerous volumes of reviews of research on child and adolescent psychopathology, and the founder of SRCAP, where such presentations are made year after year, will find these chapters to be a rich sample of the kind of scientific activity he has spent his entire professional life encouraging. Other readers should also find that this material will add to their knowledge of the field and stimulate their wish to pursue these questions further.

DONALD K. ROUTH

# Contents

## Chapter 1

### A PERSONAL ACCOUNT OF HERBERT C. QUAY, AN ARCHITECT OF THE SCIENCE OF CHILD AND ADOLESCENT PSYCHOPATHOLOGY

*Donald K. Routh*

## Chapter 2

### IMPAIRED DELAYED RESPONDING: A UNIFIED THEORY OF ATTENTION-DEFICIT HYPERACTIVITY DISORDER

*Russell A. Barkley*

## Chapter 3

### TOWARD AN EMPIRICAL CHILD PSYCHOPATHOLOGY   59

*Joseph A. Sergeant and Jaap van der Meere*

## Chapter 4

### COMBINING VISUAL AND AUDITORY TASKS IN THE ASSESSMENT OF ATTENTION-DEFICIT HYPERACTIVITY DISORDER   87

*Steven K. Shapiro and Leah A. Herod*

## Chapter 5

### BEHAVIORAL DISINHIBITION AND UNDERLYING PROCESSES IN ADOLESCENTS WITH DISRUPTIVE BEHAVIORAL DISORDERS                                         109

*Richard Milich, Cynthia M. Hartung, Catherine A. Martin, and Edward D. Haigler*

## Chapter 6

### FRAMEWORK FOR A DEVELOPMENTAL MODEL OF OPPOSITIONAL DEFIANT DISORDER AND CONDUCT DISORDER

 139

#### Benjamin B. Lahey and Rolf Loeber

# Chapter 7

## Electrodermal Hyporeactivity and Antisocial Behavior 181

*Don C. Fowles and Ann M. Furuseth*

# Chapter 8

## Endogeneous Opioids, Childhood Psychopathology, and Quay's Interpretation of Jeffrey Gray 207

*Markus J. P. Kruesi, Henrietta L. Leonard, Susan E. Swedo, Susan N. Nadi, Susan D. Hamburger, James C. S. Liu and Judith L. Rapoport*

# A Personal Account of Herbert C. Quay, an Architect of the Science of Child and Adolescent Psychopathology

## DONALD K. ROUTH

This book is a *festschrift,* a collection of scholarly essays by colleagues honoring Herbert C. Quay upon the occasion of his retirement. A related symposium was presented at the 1992 meeting of the Society for Research in Child and Adolescent Psychopathology in Sarasota, Florida. Anyone who knows Herbert Quay knows his preference for a task-oriented, quantitative, empirical approach to his field. Thus he would doubtless prefer a volume such as this to focus upon research issues rather than upon his own accomplishments as such, or his professional biography. Yet, I believe it is essential in a volume such as this to convey some impression of the individual we are honoring and of his contributions. So I am going to go ahead and try to do so, even if it embarrasses him. In fact, it is my job here to embarrass him.

As the editor of the volume, I directed each of the chapter authors to write something that, above all, would facilitate the development of their own programmatic research efforts rather than feeling constrained

DONALD K. ROUTH • Department of Psychology, University of Miami, Coral Gables, Florida 33124.

*Disruptive Behavior Disorders in Childhood,* edited by Donald K. Routh. Plenum Press, New York, 1994.

to say much about Quay or his work. However, I was not personally in a position to write the kind of chapter I directed others to produce. My own research and that of my colleagues and students in recent years has focused upon child health psychology rather than on disruptive behavior disorders in childhood. Thus, I have chosen to introduce the volume with a more personal account of my interactions with Herb Quay over a period of time and to try to explain why those who work in the field of child psychopathology hold him in such high esteem.

The first person I encountered who had known Quay personally was another red-headed clinical psychologist, Thomas Borkovec. At the time I met him, Borkovec was being interviewed for a junior faculty position at the University of Iowa, and I was taking him over to meet the dean (who mistakenly thought he was some kind of "radical"). Borkovec had just completed his PhD at the University of Illinois, where he had done his dissertation using adolescent delinquents as subjects. He mentioned to me that his research supervisor at Illinois was Quay. Borkovec described his advisor as an expert on delinquency and antisocial behavior but also a remarkably kind person. Another friend of Quay's, Miami Juvenile Court Judge Seymour Gelber, later remarked to me that this kind of "hard outside, soft inside" personality is common among people who work effectively with delinquents. You must above all avoid being conned, but once it is clear that you are "wise" to the youngster, it helps to be sympathetic. After I came to know him well, I saw occasions where Quay had essentially zero tolerance for "crooks," who appear occasionally in academic life as they do anywhere in the world.

At about the same time I found myself in the position of supervising an Iowa PhD dissertation by Barbara J. Shea concerned with aggressive children. The theoretical framework she chose for her study was that of Albert Bandura. She observed the children trying to carry out a rather difficult task and compared their use of socially versus nonsocially mediated help in the task. As I recall, the results did not support Bandura's theory at all; instead, the findings were almost an exact fit for the sort of Hullian theory of social facilitation espoused by Nicholas Cottrell, another faculty colleague. When we came to write up the article based on this research for publication, I was in a quandary as to where we should send it. "Aggression" was not exactly the kind of psychopathology emphasized by conventional clinical psychology journals, and the theoretical framework adopted in the article did not seem to have mainstream appeal either. I soon came across an advertisement for a new peer-reviewed publication to be called the *Journal of Abnormal Child Psychology*, edited by Herbert C. Quay (at that time he was affiliated with Temple University in Philadelphia). Finding out about this journal seemed like an answer to my prayers, and indeed Quay and his reviewers liked our manuscript, and it was published in the first volume of the journal, in 1973 (Shea, Routh, Cottrell, & Brecht, 1973).

I moved to the University of North Carolina and became involved in another sort of ad hoc research project with a graduate student interestingly named Eric Errickson. I mentioned in class one day that it had proven very difficult to teach "impulsive" children to slow down their response times and reduce their error rates on Jerome Kagan's Matching Familiar Figures task. Errickson, who had had extensive experience with behavior modification in a Minnesota institution for persons with mental retardation, scoffed at this statement. He was willing to lay odds that any competent operant conditioner could teach children to do better on this task. We carried out a study with a mixed group of children in a special education class using "response cost" to try to reduce their errors on the Kagan task. It worked quite well, as Errickson had predicted. However, when we wrote up the study for publication, there was again the question of where to send it. This paper also received favorable review and was published in the *Journal of Abnormal Child Psychology* in its first, 1973, volume (Errickson, Wyne, & Routh, 1973). By that time, I was clearly hooked on Herbert Quay's journal. Over the years I published many other papers in it, mostly ones concerned with hyperactivity, distractibility, impulsivity, and related academic and social difficulties in children.

In 1977, I returned to the Psychology Department at the University of Iowa. One of the universities I visited during that year was the University of Miami in Coral Gables. I confess that one of the main attractions of Miami to me at the time was the presence of Quay on its faculty. Imagine my disappointment when I visited Coral Gables, talked to a large number of faculty members and gave my colloquium talk, and never got to meet the man. He happened to be out of town at the time. When I inquired about him, people said that although he had an appointment in the Psychology Department, he had been brought to the university by the President and directed a center for applied social science funded by grants. Many years later it was explained to me by faculty colleagues at the University of Miami that during his early years there, Quay was rather detached from the Psychology Department, happily "doing his own thing" mainly in the area of correctional psychology. He even received a bit of a cold shoulder from the Miami clinical psychology faculty, which at that time was more psychodynamically oriented than he and more interested in matters related to professional practice. It is interesting to note that within a decade after his arrival in Miami, Quay found himself the chair of the department and also had the task of seeking a replacement for the Director of Clinical Training.

Back in Iowa, a year or so later I had the opportunity to teach a graduate seminar in clinical psychology and decided to focus it on a challenging topic, interventions for youngsters with conduct disorders. One outcome of this seminar was that the students and I became very familiar with the literature. I therefore planned a symposium on this topic at the next convention of the American Psychological Association in Chicago. We asked Herbert Quay to be the discussant of the symposium, and thus it was that I finally got to meet him in person. Even after all of my correspondence with him, I was not quite ready for his physical appearance: Here was this big, tall fellow with reddish-blond hair and a sort of Irish-tenor voice. He was respectful of the speakers and courteous to them, but he was appropriately skeptical about the effectiveness of all existing treatments for conduct problems. I particularly remember his interchange with Milton Shore. Shore focused on the fact that these youngsters needed help (regardless of limitations in our knowledge about what might be helpful). Quay emphasized the need for solid scientific evidence. His knowledge of the research literature was indeed impressive, and as a discussant he easily dominated the symposium.

It was probably about this time that I must have seen Quay's curriculum vita. According to the information this document provides, Herbert C. Quay was born August 27, 1927, in Portland, Maine, although, I am told, he grew up mostly on the west coast of Florida, in the St. Petersburg area. After graduating from high school, he served in the U.S. Army from 1946 to 1948 in the immediate post–World War II era. He received his BS in psychology at Florida State University in 1951 and stayed on to complete a master's degree in psychology under the direction of A. Sweetland the next year. An article based on Quay's thesis was published in the *Journal of Abnormal and Social Psychology* in 1952 (Sweetland & Quay, 1952). It was on a topic very unlike Quay's present interests, the hypnotic dream.

In what may have been a very formative experience, Quay worked as a psychologist at the Florida School for Boys (Marianna, Florida) in 1952–1953. An early delinquency scale, developed during this time in collaboration with Donald Peterson, was published a few years later (Quay & Peterson, 1958). Then, before going back to graduate school, Quay worked from 1953 to 1955 as a psychologist at the Milledgeville, Georgia State Hospital and did a psychology internship during 1955–1956 at the Danville, Illinois Veterans Administration Hospital. Thus, before he began his academic career, Quay had five full years of clinical experience, including work with adults as well as children.

In 1956, Quay was admitted into the doctoral program in clinical psychology at the University of Illinois, where he worked under the direction of J. McV. Hunt. Many years later Quay was informed by Hunt that they were both intellectual descendants of one of the founders of scientific psychology in the United States, Edward Titchener, of Cornell University (Titchener, a student of Wilhelm Wundt of Leipzig, trained Madison Bentley, who in turn trained Hunt). Quay's PhD dissertation, completed in 1958 and published the next year, was *The Effect of Verbal Reinforcement on the Recall of Early Memories* (Quay, 1959). It was intended as a psychotherapy analog study of the kind that was popular in the days before many direct therapy outcome studies had been done. Like Quay's master's thesis, the dissertation contained no suggestion of the ultimate direction his interests took.

Like many of us, Quay was a bit of an academic gypsy. He began as an assistant professor at Vanderbilt, moved to Northwestern as an associate professor, and then moved back to Illinois in 1963 as director of the Children's Research Center, ultimately being promoted to professor there. After a summer as a visiting professor in Hawaii, he became chair of the Division of Educational Psychology at Temple University and finally moved to the University of Miami in 1974, becoming chair of psychology there in 1984.

Quay had a distinguished research career, with many notable publications including articles, book chapters, and edited books. Perhaps his single best-known article dealt with "psychopathic personality as pathological stimulation seeking" and was published in the *American Journal of Psychiatry* (Quay, 1965). His most frequently cited book chapter (Quay, 1979) was a tour de force on the classification of psychopathology, documenting the ubiquity of the factors of conduct disorder (externalizing), personality disorder (internalizing), and "inadequacy-immaturity" in factor-analytic studies of children and adolescents' behavior.

His awards include one for Distinguished Contribution to Correctional Psychology from the American Association of Correctional Psychologists in 1974, an Award for Outstanding Research Achievement from the Florida Psychological Association in 1986, and the Award for Distinguished Professional Contribution from the Section on Clinical Child Psychology in 1991. I heard him give an address on the occasion of the Section 1 award and recall that he modestly attributed it to his "longevity."

To return to my narrative, we invited Herb Quay to give a colloquium at the University of Iowa in the early 1980s. By that time I had been a journal editor for a few years and had certainly come to see him as a role model. Shortly before that time, I did a book review of his 1979 edited child psychopathology book and found it to be the most up to date and thorough in its coverage of the scientific literature of the several books I was discussing in my review. I also noted the thoroughness and the convincing nature of his chapter on "classification." The same three dimensions underlying child psychopathology kept turning up everywhere. I was very enthusiastic about this work. In fact, when I introduced Herb's colloquium talk, I recall he said if he ever decided to run for public office, he would ask for my help. As an invited speaker, Quay fit in very well among the self-consciously scientific psychologists at Iowa—he was used to that kind of interaction and seemed to enjoy it a lot. He and Harold Bechtoldt got into a serious dialogue about the need for higher reliabilities and hence more items on some scales of the Behavior Problem Checklist.

At that time I was also very involved in the activities of the Section on Clinical Child Psychology (Section 1 of Division 12 of the American Psychological Association) and was one of the people who talked Quay into coming to one of the section's social hours. Because of his research and his founding of the journal, Quay was already well known by reputation and was immediately welcomed by the members of the section. In fact, before long, he was elected its president. Unlike most of its other officers, he came in quickly as sort of an "outsider," and the section had to make more of an adjustment to him than it did to most new presidents. Quay was an experienced administrator. He carefully read the bylaws of the organization and began to run it "by the book." In contrast, most of its previous officers, including myself, had gotten involved in the group more slowly and picked up its informal norms very gradually before being elected to any office. Quay also helped get some other highly scientifically oriented psychologists such as Russell Barkley to be active in the section. I think it would be agreed that he generally strengthened its scientific backbone in the process. Quay's presidential address to Section 1 was the first occasion on which many of us heard about his adaptation of Jeffrey Gray's theory in the explanation of externalizing disorders in children. Research on the Quay–Gray theory has been his main theme in recent publications and is in fact the main focus of the present book.

When Quay was president of Section 1, it was convenient for him to plan for the midyear meeting of its executive committee to be in Coral Gables. We all stayed in a motel across U.S. 1 from the University of Miami campus and met in a conference room of the Department of Psychology at the university. Quay explained to us that he had now become chair of the department. As an aside, he told me that his move into that role had freed up a slot for a senior faculty member and encouraged me to send in my curriculum vitae. One thing led to another, and in 1985 I found myself moving to the University of Miami.

It is one thing to develop a professional relationship with a colleague several thousand miles away, but it is quite another to have the person as your boss. Obviously, I had the chance to get to know him a lot better. He seemed to think highly of me, but going to Miami was sort of like acquiring a new "advisor" again after years of being on my own in academic life. This was a mixed blessing. He was very supportive, but he also had very high expectations. Having feet of clay like anyone else, I met some of these but did not meet others. Certainly, I was happy to take over as director of clinical training at Miami and ultimately to serve as Herb's replacement as editor of the *Journal of Abnormal Child Psychology*.

Having lived through an era of conflict and changing leadership at Iowa (with many long faculty meetings), I was glad to learn that Quay was a forceful, "hands-on" department chair. Although he was very respectful of the democratic process, he had clear views about where he would like to see the department go, and in general his plans were fulfilled. He helped the university recruit its new provost. On occasion I watched him confront and overcome powerful opposition, both within the department and in the central administration of the university. I can remember his bringing a large university faculty meeting to a momentary standstill simply by asking the dean, in his rather dry, innocent way, what the evidence was for a statement the dean had just made. (The dean admitted there was no hard evidence for it, as Quay had surely thought when he asked the question.) Perhaps the greatest change to occur within Quay's time as department chair was the movement of a number of tenured developmental psychology faculty from the Mailman Center for Child Development and the Department of Pediatrics into the Department of Psychology. I can remember Herb saying that a certain faculty colleague who was opposing this change was just going to have to "shape up." This man indeed concluded that he did not want to be marching in one direction while the chair was marching in the other. When Quay retired, he was asked by the university to be its faculty marshall and lead the commencement procession.

Yet as a chair, Herb also was capable of compassion when it was called for. I will never forget how empathic and understanding he was on the occasion when my adult daughter was killed in an automobile accident. I was able to leave classes and other university obligations behind and go off to be with my family as long as necessary. And this was at a time when Herb was also suffering a family tragedy, the birth of a handicapped grandchild.

Of course, I had the opportunity to observe Quay interacting with several of his students. He was an experienced research supervisor, but students had to learn to deal with his rather formidable scholarly knowledge and his ingrained critical attitudes regarding research methods. Once I remember driving with Ana Calleja and her husband, who were going to a party in Miami celebrating her defense of her PhD dissertation under Quay's direction. She asked me casually what I thought of Herb, and I admitted I still found him formidable. Her response was, "You, too?" She could hardly believe that, despite my gray hair and bald head, my reaction to him was still much the same as hers.

Through knowing Herb Quay, I also got the chance to participate in the founding of what became the Society for Research in Child and Adolescent Psychopathology (SRCAP) by Quay and several colleagues in psychology and child psychiatry. The initial planning meeting occurred in Dennis Cantwell's room at the meeting of the American Academy of Child and Adolescent Psychiatry in Washington, DC, in 1987. This is an interdisciplinary international group focused solely upon the presentation of research. It has achieved harmony by staying strictly away from professional "guild" issues and was perhaps foreshadowed by Quay's productive long-term professional relationship with child psychiatrist John Werry, now in New Zealand. In fact, Werry attended the original meeting at which SRCAP was planned. Quay incorporated SRCAP in Florida, and it had its first annual meeting in 1989 in Miami. It subsequently met in Costa Mesa, California; Amsterdam, Holland; Sarasota, Florida; and Santa Fe, New Mexico, and will meet in London, England, in 1994.

Knowing how active Quay always had been as a scholar, I was a little surprised to hear of his plans to retire right at the conventional time to do so. Yet, upon reflection, I could see that he always appreciated the fact that there was much more to life than psychology. After all, he was raised in St. Petersburg and was a lifelong tennis player. He looked forward to taking a full month's vacation every year and could not understand people who did not do so. He was the only faculty member in the Miami Department of Psychology who lived on Key Biscayne, near its wonderful Atlantic beach. Let's admit it, Quay is a bon vivant. He drives a little sports car, appreciates an elegant meal, and knows a lot about wines. When the occasion demands, he can personally act as the chef, as he did at the many faculty parties he hosted as chair at Miami, celebrating the holidays or St. Patrick's Day. He also enjoys world travel. In fact, the last time I heard, Herb was in Paris. Eliot Werner, of Plenum Press, hosted a farewell luncheon for Herb and his wife Anne Hogan upon Herb's retirement as editor of the *Journal of Abnormal Child Psycholo-*

gy. At one point he called for a bottle of wine that Herb recognized as superb. Eliot looked across the table at me at the time and said something like, "Don, when you have completed 19 years with the journal, we will buy you a bottle of wine just like this."

ACKNOWLEDGMENTS. I would like to thank Annette M. LaGreca and Marion W. Routh for their comments on an early draft of this chapter.

# References

Errickson, E. A., Wyne, M. D., & Routh, D. K. (1973). A response-cost procedure for the reduction of impulsive behavior of academically handicapped children. *Journal of Abnormal Child Psychology, 1,* 350–357.

Quay, H. C. (1959). The effect of verbal reinforcement on the recall of early memories. *Journal of Abnormal and Social Psychology, 59,* 254–257.

Quay, H. C. (1965). Psychopathic personality as pathological stimulation seeking. *American Journal of Psychiatry, 122,* 180–183.

Quay, H. C. (1979). Classification. In H. C. Quay & J. S. Werry (Eds.), *Psychopathological disorders of childhood* (2nd ed., pp. 1–42) New York: Wiley.

Quay, H. C., & Peterson, D. R. (1958). A brief scale for juvenile delinquency. *Journal of Clinical Psychology, 14,* 139–142.

Shea, B. J., Routh, D. K., Cottrell, N. B., & Brecht, J. M. (1973). Help seeking in aggressive and nonaggressive boys as a function of social or mechanical mediation of assistance. *Journal of Abnormal Child Psychology, 1,* 214–224.

Sweetland, A., & Quay, H. C. (1952). An experimental investigation of the hypnotic dream. *Journal of Abnormal and Social Psychology, 47,* 678–82.

———————————— 2 ————————————

# Impaired Delayed Responding
## A Unified Theory of Attention-Deficit Hyperactivity Disorder

### Russell A. Barkley

Everything comes to those who can wait
—RABELAIS, *Gargantua*

Attention-deficit hyperactivity disorder (ADHD) (American Psychiatric Association, 1994) refers to children, adolescents, and adults who demonstrate a pattern of deficits in behavioral control and self-regulation comprising poor sustained attention, impulsivity, and hyperactivity (Barkley, 1990). This pattern of behavior commonly arises during the preschool or early childhood years, is significantly inappropriate for the child's developmental level, is relatively stable, and persists into adolescence in more than half of all cases diagnosed in childhood (Barkley, 1990; Barkley, Fischer, Edelbrock, & Smallish, 1990). As many as 30% to 60% of childhood cases may continue to have the disorder into their young adult years (Gittelman, Mannuzza, Shenker, & Bonagura, 1985; Weiss & Hechtman, 1986).

Throughout its long history, ADHD has been renamed frequently with terms such as defective moral control and volitional inhibition

RUSSELL A. BARKLEY • Departments of Psychiatry and Neurology, University of Massachusetts Medical Center, Worchester, Massachusetts 01655.
*Disruptive Behavior Disorders in Childhood,* edited by Donald K. Routh. Plenum Press, New York, 1994.

11

(Still, 1902), restlessness syndrome (Levin, 1938), postencephalitic behavior disorder, brain-injured child syndrome (Strauss & Lehtinen,
1947), minimal brain dysfunction (Clements, 1966), hyperkinetic reaction of childhood (American Psychiatric Association, 1968), hyperactive
child syndrome (Chess, 1960), and attention-deficit disorder with or
without hyperactivity (American Psychiatric Association, 1980). With
each change in terminology came a commensurate effort to reconcep-
tualize the disorder in order to account for the diverse deficits often seen
in such cases, to refine the understanding of its etiology, or to clarify the
underlying psychological nature, or essence, of the disorder. As often
occurs in a healthy science, each new theoretical conceptualization of
the disorder remained vibrant and useful only so long as it was able to
parsimoniously account for the extant research findings. Ultimately,
each was eclipsed by a new theory attempting to bring a more unified
view of the accumulating discrepancies between empirical research and
current theory. It is the purpose of this chapter to assert yet another
theory of this disorder, in keeping with this laudable tradition, in hopes
of providing a more simple, unifying, and heuristically valuable theoretical perspective of ADHD than existing theories can provide. Like any
such reconceptualization, the present theory predicts many new findings in areas not previously thought to be relevent to understanding
ADHD. Other areas that the theory suggests are promising have been
studied only tangentially or have received only cursory scientific attention. The theory points to a number of exciting areas for future scientific
investigation that should advance our understanding of the nature of
ADHD.

## Previous Theories of ADHD

As early as 1902, George Still described a group of 20 children seen
in his medical practice who displayed clinically significant degrees of
aggression, antisocial acts, hostile and defiant behavior, inattention, and
hyperactivity. He conjectured that they represented a unique disorder
apart from the developmental disorders, such as mental retardation, of
interest at the time. The children were of relatively normal intelligence
and had apparently received proper child rearing for the era but were
seriously delayed in their development of social conduct and moral behavior. Still postulated that these symptoms or behaviors stemmed from
a more fundamental defect in the "moral control of behavior" and in
"volitional inhibition." The defect was felt to arise from a dysfunction,
injury, or disorder of neurological development and to be chronic in

most cases. Despite the heavy emphasis on the nebulous constructs of morality and will in this conceptualization, the clinical descriptions, and the underlying ideas Still attempted to convey ring true with contemporary clinical scientists.

Rephrase Still's concepts into current psychological jargon and one could view it as a problem in the manner in which social rules exert control over behavior and in effortful inhibition of behavior to meet environmental demands. The contemporary concepts of rule-governed behavior, cognitive self-control, metacognition, executive function, and behavioral impulsivity or disinhibition would be areas suggested by Still's view for further exploration as potentially problematic in ADHD. All of these constructs have been noted by one or another author or authors as pertinent to understanding ADHD (Barkley, 1981, 1989, 1990; Benton, 1991; Conners & Wells, 1986; Douglas, 1972, 1983; Kendall & Braswell, 1985; Mattes, 1980; Quay, 1989). Thus, Still may have been close to the mark if my paraphrasing accurately reflects his intent.

Over the ensuing decades, theoretical writings have shifted their emphasis. They have ranged from distractibility (Strauss & Lehtinen, 1947), to restlessness (Levin, 1938), to hyperactivity (Chess, 1960; Werry & Sprague, 1970), and on to inattention combined with impulsivity and hyperactivity (Douglas, 1972; American Psychiatric Association, 1987). In 1981, I theorized that deficits in rule-governed behavior (compliance, self-control, and problem solving) were the central deficits in ADHD. By 1984, I modified this view to incorporate deficits in response to behavioral consequences, particularly reinforcement, and rapid extinction of behavior under partial reinforcement schedules (Barkley, 1984, 1989). Related views have been espoused by Haenlein and Caul (1987) regarding a diminished sensitivity to reinforcement and by Quay (1988, 1989) concerning a diminished sensitivity to punishment stemming from underactivity of the brain's Behavioral Inhibition System (BIS). Despite this effort to find a unifying theory of ADHD, current clinical conceptualizations still stress a triad of primary deficits even though the accumulating research does not now support such a view.

## ADHD as Impaired Delayed Responding

Within the past decade a number of findings from various laboratories using diverse methodologies have converged on a common conclusion akin to Still's. The central impairment in ADHD relative to other psychopathologies in children is one of response inhibition or behavioral impulsivity. Although Herbert Quay (1988, 1989) has been a recent proponent of a disinhibition model of ADHD, his use of Gray's neuro-psychological model (Gray, 1982) to posit deficits in the BIS as underly-ing ADHD does not go far enough in explaining the myriad cognitive and social problems seen in ADHD.

Impulsivity has come to be viewed as a multidimensional construct involving at least two different dimensions or components (Milich & Kramer, 1985). That component of impulsivity known as behavioral im-pulsivity, or what others have called motor disinhibition or delay aver-sion, has been most consistently found to be impaired in ADHD. Disin-hibition is the most distinguishing feature of ADHD as a disorder from other disorders, is most associated with impairments in the ongoing daily adaptive functioning associated with ADHD, and is the most pre-dictive of later adversities in the adolescent and young-adult outcomes of these children relative to the symptoms of inattention. Research also shows that hyperactivity is simply a further manifestation of disinhibi-tion. The evidence supporting these assertions is reviewed later.

I now believe that the manifold deficits witnessed in ADHD can be reduced to a single deficiency in the capacity to delay responding to a signal, event, or stimulus. ADHD children certainly have other deficits that stem from other disorders often associated with ADHD, such as learning disabilities or oppositional defiant and conduct disorder. The symptoms believed to reflect ADHD itself, however, can be reasonably accounted for by an impairment in the development of delayed respond-ing or response inhibition. This developmental incapacity is not absolute but is deficient relative to peers of similar mental age. The deficit will be found to improve with development but remain below that capacity seen in same-age peers.

The capacity for delayed responding is apparently mediated by the orbital frontal cortex and its rich connections with the limbic system. It is a commonly documented impairment in primates with experimentally induced lesions to these areas and in humans with accidental damage to these same areas (Benton, 1991; Gratten & Eslinger, 1991; Mateer & Williams, 1991; Smith, Kates, & Vriezen, 1992). But it seemingly arises in most individuals with ADHD more as a result of underfunctioning of this brain system rather than as a consequence of damage. This dimin-ished brain activity may have a genetic origin as the symptoms of ADHD, particularly impulsive-hyperactive behavior, have a high heri-tability (Edelbrock, Rende, Plomin, & Thompson, 1992; Faraone et al., in press; Gilger, Pennington, & DeFries, 1992; Gillis, Gilger, Pennington, & DeFries, 1992; Goodman & Stevenson, 1989; Gross-Tsur, Shalev, & Amir, 1991; Stevenson, 1992).

This impairment in delayed responding creates a hyperresponsivity to immediate signals or events. A lower-than-normal threshold seems to exist for compelling stimuli to elicit behavior in those with ADHD relative to normal peers. This leads to excessive action or behavior in children with ADHD—hence their hyperactivity. But this hyperactivity is better conceptualized as a hyperresponsivity to the setting and its immediate events. It is the easy elicitation of behavior that should be the focus of our attention, not the by-product of increased activity level. ADHD children are more stimulus-bound than are same-age individuals. Viewed as such, their hyperactivity is but one side of the same coin as impulsivity, that being impaired delayed responding or disinhibition. This suggests why research on ADHD has not been able to disentangle the constructs of impulsivity and hyperactivity.

The evidence for impaired delayed responding or motor disinhibition as the cornerstone of ADHD now seems irrefutable. It has been reflected in increased errors of commission on vigilance or continuous performance tests (CPT) relative to normal and non-ADHD clinical control groups (Barkley, 1991; Chee, Logan, Schachar, Lindsay, & Wachsmuth, 1989; Douglas, 1972, p. 83; Douglas & Peters, 1979; Kupietz, 1990; Robins, 1992; Swanson & Kinsbourne, 1978; Reeves, Werry, Elkind, & Zametkin, 1987; Werry, Reeves, & Elkind, 1987; Werry, Reeves, Elkind, & Smith, 1987). Similar errors are frequently found on paper-and-pencil versions of CPTs, such as the Children's Checking Task (Aman & Turbott, 1986; Brown & Wynne, 1982). The behavior of ADHD children observed and formally coded during the CPT task is also revealing of excessive responding to the task as well as increased rates of behavior away from the task (Barkley, DuPaul, & McMurray, 1990; Draeger, Prior, & Sanson, 1986). ADHD children display more movement in their seats and about the room, more looking away from the task apparatus, more play with furnishings in the room, and more vocal noises than non-ADHD subjects.

Similarly, studies using information-processing theory and related tasks by van der Meere, Sergeant, and colleagues have routinely found hyperactive or ADHD children to be deficient in motor response inhibition or "presetting" rather than on parameters of the task that measure attention (van der Meere, 1993; van der Meere, van Baal, & Sergeant, 1989; van der Meere & Sergeant, 1988a,b,c; van der Meere, Wekking, & Sergeant, 1991). Moreover, ADHD children do not slow down after making an error on such tasks when there is a high cognitive load to the task. Normal children do slow down following such errors to ensure that the subsequent response will be correct (Sergeant & van der Meere, 1988). The investigators concluded that ADHD technically does not represent an impairment in attention but in motor function. All of these laboratory findings are therefore consistent with an impairment in delayed responding or response inhibition in ADHD.

Direct observational studies of ADHD, or hyperactive, children in free field and task-performance in laboratory analog settings have repeatedly found high levels of response to stimuli (e.g., toys, furnishings, etc.) and diminished adherence to restrictions placed on behavior within these settings, especially in more structured task-performance situations (Barkley & Ullman, 1975; Campbell, Szumowski, Ewing, Gluck, & Breaux, 1982; Kalverboer, 1988; Luk, 1985; Routh & Schroeder, 1976; Ullman, Barkley, & Brown, 1978). Behavioral observations of ADHD children taken in classroom situations provide a similar profile of excessive behavior (both motor and vocal), poor response inhibition, limited persistence to tasks, and diminished compliance with rules and restrictions (Atkins, Pelham, & Licht, 1985; Prinz, Tarnowski, & Nay, 1984). ADHD children have been noted to opt for small rewards that were more immediately available in place of larger delayed rewards (Rapport, Tucker, DuPaul, Merlo, & Stoner, 1986) and to have been less able to tolerate delays to desirable rewards (Campbell et al., 1982; Gordon, 1979; McClure & Gordon, 1984). This is seen as further evidence of impaired behavioral inhibition or delayed responding in ADHD. That ADHD children have also been found to display excessive speech and vocal behavior more generally in interactions with parents (Barkley, Cunningham, & Karlsson, 1983), teachers (Atkins et al., 1985; Whalen, Henker, & Dotemoto, 1980), and peers (Cunningham & Siegel, 1987) is also in keeping with a hyperresponsivity to context and diminished delay of responding in social communication.

Studies using neuropsychological tests assessing response inhibition or delayed responding have likewise found deficits in ADHD cases compared to controls. Impaired inhibition on the Go/No-Go test, poor execution of the Hand Movements Task of the Kaufman Assessment Battery for Children, deficient performance on the interference part of the Stroop Word-Color Association task, excessive perseverative responses on the Wisconsin Card Sort Test, impaired maze performance, and poor ability to delay responses on a DRL task have all been found in ADHD relative to normal children (see Barkley, Grodzinsky, & DuPaul, 1992, for a review; Gordon, 1979; Kuehne, Kehle, & McMahon, 1987; Robins, 1992). Also, impaired response to punishment on the Card Playing Task (Milich, 1993) relative to control groups can be interpreted as arising from impaired delayed responding. The increased perseverative errors noted above on tests like the WCST may occur from a pattern of automatically responding to the immediate stimulus card consistent with previous reinforced similar responses without imposing a delay in the response pattern. This delay would permit a detection of a shift in the sorting rules associated with the task.

Further support for behavioral impulsivity being the hallmark of

ADHD comes from the recently completed field trials used in developing diagnostic criteria for the DSM-IV (Frick et al., 1993). This study of more than 440 children and adolescents found that (1) items pertaining to impulsive-hyperactive behavior form a separate factor or dimension of behavior than items pertaining to inattention—a finding found frequently in earlier, smaller studies of clinical and epidemiological samples of children (Achenbach & Edelbrock, 1983; DuPaul, 1992; Goyette, Conners, & Ulrich, 1976); (2) whether a child would be diagnosed as ADHD by the clinicians in the study was highly related to the severity of ratings on the impulsive-hyperactive item dimension but only weakly associated with inattention ratings; and (3) the degree of impairment found on other measures such as clinical ratings of impairment, teacher ratings of impaired school performance, and other indices were most highly associated with the number of impulsive-hyperactive items and less so or not at all with the number of inattention items. The DSM-III-R field trial (Spitzer, Davies, & Barkley, 1990) similarly found that symptoms of impulsivity–hyperactivity were the most discriminating of ADHD from other disorders.

In keeping with such findings, many follow-up studies of hyperactive or ADHD children have found that negative outcomes were more predicted by childhood ratings of impulsive–hyperactive behavior than of inattention (Fischer, Barkley, Edelbrock, & Smallish, 1993; Weiss & Hechtman, 1986). Even the persistence of the disorder over time has been most associated with the degree of early impulsivity–hyperactivity rather than early inattention (Campbell & Ewing, 1990; Fischer et al., 1994; Hart, Lahey, Loeber, & Frick, 1993). Such findings provide strong circumstantial evidence that behavioral impulsivity is the predominant feature in ADHD. These findings imply that a more accurate term for ADHD would be behavioral impulsivity or Behavioral-Inhibition Disorder (BID).

Further support for behavioral inhibition as the major impairment in ADHD are three recent studies on the effects of delay intervals on reward-choice and memory tasks in ADHD children (Sonuga-Barke, Taylor, & Heptinstall, 1992; Sonuga-Barke, Taylor, Sembi, & Smith, 1992). The results indicated that hyperactive and normal children both chose to maximize overall reward levels in the tasks but that hyperactive children were more delay averse, preferring to choose strategies in the task that reduced the delay intervals imposed during the trials. This was so regardless of whether the delays occurred between trial response and the reward or between the reward delivery and availability of the next trial. The results further suggest that ADHD children are not just trying to maximize immediate gratification (delay to the reward) but are delay averse as well, showing an unconditional sensitivity to overall level of delay within the task.

In summary, the most consistent findings in research on the nature of ADHD are those related to poor response inhibition or delayed responding rather than poor attention. Where difficulties with attention have been noted, they have been most reliably found on measures of sustained attention or persistence of responding and are highly correlated with the deficits in response inhibition. Numerous studies indicate that ADHD children are more likely to shift off-task, do so more often, and have difficulty persisting on tasks, particularly where behavioral consequences in task performance are of a low magnitude. It is possible to interpret such attentional problems as also reflecting poor response inhibition. The subject has difficulty inhibiting responses to parallel activities that compete with the performance of the assigned task, particularly where those parallel activities may be more stimulating or reinforcing than the assigned activity. For instance, Milich and his colleagues (Landau, Lorch, & Milich, 1992; Milich & Lorch, 1993) showed that ADHD and normal children displayed no differences in attending to television programs when no toys were present in the setting. However, when toys were available, ADHD children looked away, or attended less, to the television screen and were more likely to engage in play with the toys than control children. This tendency to shift away from the task so as to react to task-irrelevant but more reinforcing stimuli or signals, I believe, is what parents, teachers, and clinicians are referring to in describing ADHD children as being highly distractible (American Psychiatric Association, 1980, 1987; Barkley, 1990).

The three deficits or symptoms traditionally believed to be the core or essence of ADHD—poor sustained attention, impulsivity, and hyperactivity—can be reduced, I believe, to a single core impairment in delayed responding or response inhibition. Academic, occupational, or social situations as well as laboratory tasks that place a premium on delayed responding or motor response inhibition, particularly where the consequences associated with performance in the setting are weak, delayed, or relatively nonexistent, seem to be those in which individuals with ADHD will be found to be less successful in meeting the demands of the context than are their normal peers.

## Cognitive Capacities Derived from Delayed Responding

So far all I have shown is that impaired response inhibition or delayed responding is the cardinal feature of ADHD. I am not the first to make this claim. George Still (1902), Herbert Quay (1989), and more recently Jaap van der Meere (1993) and Sonuga-Barke et al. (1992) have made similar assertions. What they have failed to do, however, is explain just how such a deficit leads to the diverse impairments noted in the academic, social, occupational, cognitive, linguistic, and emotional domains of functioning of individuals with ADHD. How does this account for such findings as deficient use of warning stimuli in reaction time tasks (see Douglas & Peters, 1979; Douglas, 1983), immature self-directed speech (Berk & Potts, 1991; Copeland, 1979), and less efficient performance of mental arithmetic (Barkley, DuPaul, & McMurray, 1990)? And how might it explain less organized or mature social communication with peers (Whalen, Henker, Collins, McAuliffe, & Vaux, 1979) and delayed moral reasoning (Hinshaw, Herbsman, Melnick, Nigg, & Simmel, 1993), just to name a few disparate research findings? How does it explain the poor rule governance of behavior, particularly in that component called *tracking* (Hayes, 1989)? What does poor inhibition have to do with a seemingly limited capacity to take anothers' perspective in a situation, poor utilization of a sense of time in preparing for upcoming events, forgetfulness, deficient organization, and excessive emotional reactivity to events by ADHD children and adults relative to normal peers (Barkley, 1990; Chess, 1960; Kane, Mikulac, Benjamin, & Barkley, 1990; Shekim, 1989, Ratey et al., 1992; Still, 1902; Wender, 1971)? How does this impairment provide a unitary explanation for these numerous and diverse problems noted in the performance of adaptive or daily living tasks, social interactions and relations, performance of academic tasks, successful occupational performance, and even use of sound driving practices (see Barkley, 1981, 1990; Barkley et al., 1993; Ross & Ross, 1982, 1976; Weiss & Hechtman, 1986; Whalen & Henker, 1980)? Could not poor response inhibition simply be one of several equally primary yet interacting deficits that underlie ADHD as the current clinical consensus makes it out to be?

My reason for asserting that impaired delayed responding can provide a simple, unitary account of the myriad cognitive, behavioral, social, academic, and occupational deficits directly attributable to ADHD rests in my recent discovery of a theory advanced more than 25 years ago by Jacob Bronowski (1967), the late philosopher, physicist, and mathematician. In a brief yet profound essay in honor of Roman Jakobson, Bronowski discussed the evolution of this simple capacity to impose a delay between a signal or event and the organism's response to that event. He described the dramatic consequences that this simple ability would have for the development of more complex cognitive abilities that are distinctly human attributes. Bronowski argued that the delays imposed by humans between signals or messages and the response to those signals are substantially longer than any such delays witnessed in our closest evolutionary relatives:

Human language is remarkable because it is not only a means of communication. It also serves as a means of reflection, during which different lines of action are played through and tested. This can only happen if there is a delay between the arrival of the stimulus and the utterance of the message that it has provoked. I propose to treat this delay between receipt of the incoming signal and the sending of a signal out as the central and formative feature in the evolution of human language. (Bronowski, 1977, p. 113)

This dramatic increase in delayed responding, according to Bronowski, provides the basis for four uniquely human capabilities that distinguish human from animal languages. These consequences flow from our increased capacity for delayed responding and are considered to be fundamental executive functions that are critical to successful adaptive behavior in meeting the daily demands of human society. These four abilities, according to Bronowski, are those of *separation of affect, prolongation, internalization,* and *reconstitution.* A hypothetical developmental representation of them is depicted in Figure 1. Although Bronowski referred to these abilities, and that of delayed responding, within the context of distinctions between human and animal lan-

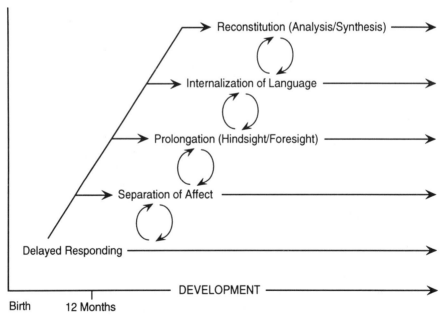

**FIGURE 1.** A schematic representation of Bronowski's theory of delayed responding, the four related cognitive processes, and their developmental staging.

guages, there seems little reason to limit their applicability only to linguistic functions and social communication. They may have a much larger meaning in understanding ADHD if extended to the broader arena of general stimulus–response functional events. Nevertheless, these four capabilities, whether restricted to language or applied more broadly to human environment-response functional relations, seems to me to have profound implications for our understanding of ADHD, as I hope to show later.

## Separation of Affect

Bronowski asserted that the imposition of a delay between the arrival of a stimulus and the response it precipitates permits humans to separate the message or informational content of the signal from its emotional charge for the individual.

> Most animal signals are total, and must be, because they are immediate. By contrast, we are conscious of the time that we take to frame a reply, particularly to a question that makes an emotional challenge. Many of us remember that we are advised as children to create a deliberate delay before we speak under emotional stress: to count to twenty, or to say paternoster. The separation of instruction from affect in human language depends on this delay in the brain. Without it, it would not be possible to make neutral statements: to keep silent when angry, or to write scientific prose. Indeed, it would not be possible to make purely cognitive statements at all. (Bronowski, 1977, p. 115)

This capacity permits the individual to evaluate events more objectively, rationally, and logically as if from the standpoint of an outside, neutral witness to the event. The response so informed by this process is more likely to be successful or adaptive than would be a more immediate and passionate reaction. To achieve this separation, the delay in responding must be used to refer the incoming signal to more than one brain center for processing of the content in parallel fashion, the most important property of a large brain, Bronowski contended.

## Prolongation

Bronowski reasoned that a second consequence of increased delay in responding was the ability to prolong the effect of the stimulus while using this prolongation to compare the signal with memory. Prolongation

> is the ability to refer backward or forward in time, and to exchange messages [with others] which propose action in the future. Human

beings can interpret these messages because they have a sense of the future: that is, they can recall the past and manipulate the imagery of recall to construct hypothetical situations. In one application, this is the gift of imagination; and in another application, it forms the concept of time—both of which are effectively absent in animals. In its application to language (Hebb & Thompson, 1954), it makes possible the prolongation of reference, and the postponement of the instruction, which we recognize as a characteristic in many human messages. (Bronowski, 1977, p. 116)

The term *prolongation* used by Bronowski may be comparable in some ways to the use of the term *working memory* in cognitive and neuropsychological literatures. It is the means by which a stimulus or signal is held or prolonged while parallel processing of the content of the signal takes place to extract information from the stimulus, to manipulate or act upon its content, to compare and contrast the signal and its content with information previously stored in human memory, and to conjecture hypothetical future events given the results of this reference to the past.

## Internalization of Language

A third effect of the increased capacity to delay responding in humans is the internalization of language. Bronowski contends that this internalization creates the most far-reaching and consequential differences between how humans and animals use language.

When language is internalized, it ceases to be only a means of social communication, and is thereby removed from the family of animal languages. It now becomes an instrument of reflection and exploration, with which the speaker constructs hypothetical messages before he chooses one to utter. In time, the sentences that he makes for himself lose the character of messages, and become experimental arrangements of the images of past experience into new and untested projections. . . . . Human beings therefore live with two languages, an inner one and an outer one. They constantly experiment with the inner language, and find arrangements which are more effective than those which have become standard in the outer language. In the inner language, these arrangements are information, that is cognitive assertions; and they are then transferred to the outer language in the form of practical instructions. (Bronowski, 1977, p. 118)

Bronowski's concept of internalized language as a means of forming rules and practical instructions that then inform subsequent behavior has its parallel in the literatures on rule-governed behavior (Hayes, 1989;

Skinner, 1953). This behavioral theory deals with the stimulus control of behavior by language and posits three developmental stages in its acquisition: (1) the control of behavior by the language of others (pliance); (2) the control of behavior by self-directed public speech that ultimately becomes subvocal or private to one's self; and (3) problem solving or the novel creation of new rules. Such rules are formed from the use of questions that interrogate one's sense of past and bring forth the novel combination of existing information within one's repertoire. Important in both Bronowski's and the behavioral conceptualizations is not just the power to reflect and create, but the capacity for practical instructions or messages formed thereby to feed forward in the planning, execution, control, and termination of motor responses. The individual's behavior is therefore no longer under the immediate and total control of the surrounding context but can be governed by hypothetical projections about the future translated into linguistic instructions that initiate motor programs in keeping with those instructions. In so doing, the ongoing behavior of the individual is brought under the control of plans, goals, directions, and anticipated future events conjectured in the various hypothetical futures. A sense of the past yields a sense of the future that controls behavior in the present. This control does not arise without the imposition of the delay between signal and response.

Hayes (1989, 1991) has articulated a number of effects that result from internalized speech and the rule-governed behavior it permits: (1) The variability of responses to a task is much less with rule-governed than contingency-shaped behavior; (2) the individual's behavior is less susceptible to control by immediate contingencies and their momentary and potentially spurious changes; (3) where rules and contingencies compete in a situation, the rule is typically more likely to control behavior; (4) responding under some conditions may be rigid because the rule extracted and used by the individual to control behavior is incorrect; (5) self-directed rules permit individuals to respond effectively under extreme delays in consequences; and (6) the development of rule-governed behavior will show a typical developmental growth trajectory in which infants respond more like primates to conditioning paradigms but become more rule-governed and less variable in their responding with maturation.

## Reconstitution

Bronowski states that the internalization of language has a special structure that allows for two processes that he calls *reconstitution*. The first of these is analysis or the decomposition of the signal, now prolonged, into components or parts rather than being treated as "inviolate wholes" as they are in other species. The second is the process of synthesis wherein these dissembled parts can be manipulated and used to reconstruct or reconstitute entirely new messages.

> The procedure of analysis must not be conceived as a simple breaking into parts. It is a progressive redistribution of the message, so that its cognitive content becomes more particularized, and its hortative content more generalized. . . . The effect is to progressively form in man a different picture of reality from that which animals have. The physical world is pictured as made up of units that can be matched in language, and human language thereby itself shifts its vocabulary from command to description or predication. (Bronowski, 1977, p. 121)

> It is the procedure of reconstitution as a whole, analysis as well as synthesis, which creates the potential for original productivity in human language. By this means human beings have provided themselves individually with a vocabulary roughly a hundred times larger than the rhesus monkey, and communally another hundred times larger again. The grammatical rules for the combination of so many words . . . are themselves a conceptual description of the world as we act on it and picture it, and it is this which makes it possible for us to recognize their right use at a glance. We experiment with these units in our inner language, and make original sentences for the outer language, by a total procedure of reconstitution. (Bronowski, 1977, p. 123)

The process of reconstitution can be seen to endow humans with tremendous powers of problem solving, imagination, and creativity. It greatly expands their capacity to generate numerous alternative messages and, from these motor responses, to reconstitute them in nearly infinite ways, and to select among them that which may be most adaptive, not only for the moment, but also in the hypothetical future.

Each of these capacities resembles to some degree ideas expressed by others as human executive abilities or those functions subserved by the prefrontal lobes (Luria, 1966; Smith et al., 1992; Stuss & Benson, 1986). Undoubtedly, each capacity informs the others, as when internalized language permits prolongation of the signal to be used for symbolic encoding of information about the event. This can be used later to reconstruct the cognitive representation of that event. Or, as when prolongation, which permits the construction of hypothetical futures, informs the internalized language such that messages can be exchanged with others about events that have a future reference.

## Neuroanatomical Considerations

As noted above, increasing evidence exists to show that ADHD is probably a disorder in the prefrontal lobes and more precisely in the orbital–frontal area and its associated pathways with the caudate nucleus, striatum, and other limbic system structures (Giedd et al., 1993; Heilman, Voeller, & Nadeau, 1990; Hynd, Marshall, & Gonzalez, 1993; Lou, Henriksen, Bruhn, 1984; Lou, Henriksen, Bruhn, Borner, & Nielsen, 1989; Zametkin et al., 1990). Much evidence also exists to show that delayed responding is mediated by these same structures, particularly the caudate in human and primate infants, and later the orbital–frontal cortex itself (Crowe, 1992). Hypothesizing a link between ADHD, delayed responding, and the prefrontal lobes, therefore, makes sense and seems well supported. Suffice it to say here that the orbital–frontal cortex mediates delayed responding and therefore regulates the four consequent processes noted here. It is surely the seat of our social intelligence, as Dimond (1980) stipulated. These processes, as Bronowski reasoned, are what make us most human. They are also what is so tragically disrupted in patients with orbital–frontal injuries or, to a lesser degree, those with ADHD whose orbital–frontal–limbic axis seems woefully underactive (Zametkin et al., 1990).

Bronowski hypothesized that human language certainly evolved from animal language, but that this process had two distinct components. The first was the physiological evolution of the capacity for delayed and more complex responses. "Somewhere near the level of the primates, a number of the direct response pathways of lower animals were lengthened by being switched through the new brain. . . . The effect was to delay and divide the response, and both of these are important" (p. 124). The cytoarchitecture of the orbital–frontal regions of the prefrontal lobes, their pathways to the limbic system, and their rich cortico–cortical interconnections to other brain systems would seem to provide the ideal mechanism for the lengthening of the time to respond, the referral of the signal to various brain centers for parallel processing, and the division of the response itself. The second component in the evolution of human language was the cultural selection for hindsight and foresight and the internalization of symbolism. This creates a means for language to express cognitive information and not just social communication. Bronowski speculated that this second component came later in evolution but with a strong and rapid selective influence.

## Developmental Considerations

It is not clear whether these four capacities become functionally mature at the same or different times in human development. The latter seems more likely given the other cognitive or neuropsychological functions that must mature in order to subserve these functions, such as language, memory, temporal perception, and possibly even visuospatial functions. It is also more likely if Bronowski's theory of the temporal arrangement of these capacities in evolution is correct. The capacity for delayed responding should emerge first in infant development, and we know that it does by approximately 12 months of age (Smith et al., 1992). This would seem to be followed by the capacity to separate content from affect in incoming signals. Whether the internalization of speech proceeds simultaneously with this process or is somewhat later in child development is not clear, though the latter is thought by Bronowski to be the sequence in human evolution. The capacity for reconstitution is thought to emerge last in evolution and so may it be in ontogenetic development. Although Figure 1 illustrates a hypothetical developmental staging of these capacities, I do not claim that this accurately represents the actual developmental pattern for their emergence, only their staging as might be inferred from Bronowski's theory.

## Implications of Bronowski's Theory for ADHD

Very compelling evidence exists for a deficit in delayed responding or response inhibition in ADHD. The extension of Bronowski's theory to an understanding of the additional problems seen in ADHD seems very profitable and exciting. Not only does it provide a simple, parsimonious, yet more comprehensive and unifying explanation of the deficits explicated in the extant literature attributed to ADHD than previous theories, but it suggests a number of fruitful avenues for further investigation. Thus, it provides a rich heuristic by which to proceed with further study of the nature of ADHD. I have organized these implications and research directions under the four consequential capacities described above that are said to flow from the capacity to delay responding.

This theory of ADHD does not mean that those with ADHD cannot engage in the consequent capacities permitted by delayed responding (i.e., separation of affect, etc.). It does mean that they will not engage these capacities as well or as often in daily adaptive behavior because of the impairment "upstream" from them in delayed responding. It also means that even when the processes are engaged, they will be less

efficiently used, and the resulting information is less likely to feed forward to influence subsequent responses in the situation as well as it
does in individuals without ADHD. It is not the individual capacities
that are directly impaired in ADHD. It is the preclusion of their adequate
use in governing behavior that occurs when responses are not delayed
as they are in normal peers.

I also see no reason why the impairment in delay should be restricted to external signals or events, or those outside the skin. There is
just as good a rationale for positing that it takes place in response to
internal events, such as thoughts or bodily sensations. Those with
ADHD might respond just as impulsively to these internal events without due reflection and modification by the four additional capacities
linked to delayed responding. Could this be why children with ADHD
report more somatic complaints (Barkley, DuPaul, & McMurray, 1990) or
why adolescents with ADHD have an increased incidence of somatiza-
tion disorders (Szatmari, Offord, & Boyle 1989)? It could certainly explain the reports of many adults with ADHD that they are more likely to
react impulsively to their own ideas without due deliberation (Kane et
al., 1990; Wender, 1987).

This theory of ADHD clearly states that the essence of ADHD is not
a deficit in skills or knowledge but one of inhibition or performance.
Kinsbourne (1989) has made this point nicely when he stresses that
ADHD is a dysregulation in ongoing behavior, not a deficit. ADHD is
not a problem of knowing what to do; it is a problem of doing what you
know. It is an impairment in delayed responding or response inhibition
that diminishes individuals' utilization of their capacities for separation
of affect, prolongation, internalization of language, and reconstitution
or, where these processes are engaged, diminishes their results from
feeding forward to influence ongoing or future responding. Although
these capacities are not themselves impaired, it is possible that over
years of such underutilization and practice, they, too, may become directly impaired or less proficient.

The resultant impact of the totality of these deficits on daily adaptive functioning can be devastating, as it clearly is in both those with
severe ADHD (Barkley, 1990; Weiss & Hechtman, 1986) as well as patients with orbital–frontal lobe injuries (Gratten & Eslinger, 1991; Smith
et al., 1992; Stuss & Benson, 1986). Yet despite its pervasive and per-
nicious impact on social conduct and adaptive functioning, the deficits
are very hard to detect on standard psychological and neuropsychological tests because such tests simply are not well designed to assess these
capacities. The implications of this conceptualization of ADHD for as-

sessment and treatment planning are substantial and radical relative to contemporary practices, but are not unexpected. I will first examine what reasons I have to believe that those with ADHD are impaired in the cognitive processes that arise from delayed responding. Then I review their implications for the assessment and treatment of ADHD.

## Separation of Affect and ADHD

Bronowski's model helps us to better understand the greater emotional reactivity often clinically noted in children and adults with ADHD. If individuals with ADHD cannot delay responding as well as normal peers, then we should see less separation of informational and affective components from incoming signals as well as greater use of affective signals in their social communication and responding to environmental events. The low frustration tolerance frequently described in such children as well as their greater tendency toward temper outbursts, silliness or giddiness, anxiety and sadness, as well as the whole panoply of emotional reactivity (Barkley, 1990) may well be explained by this diminished capacity to separate affect from informational content in both incoming signals and one's responses to them. The excitability in response to rewards given in conditioning experiments and the problems in modulating emotional arousal to situational demands noted by Douglas (1983) could be explained by this same process.

Such a deficit in the separation of affect could lead to a diminished capacity to remain objective in social situations, especially those that might be charged with affective signals from others. Embedded within this problem is the possibility that the individual with ADHD is less likely to distinguish the personal meanings and valences of events for themselves from the information being communicated in social exchanges. The result might be a greater display of narcissistic, self-centered, selfish, and generally less mature social conduct in situations and a reduced ability to evaluate the ongoing social events from the perspective of someone else. Events may simply be personalized more by the individual with ADHD than by others. An appreciation of the needs, feelings, and opinions of others might also be diminished in ADHD individuals given their difficulties in separating out the personalized emotional messages from their objective content. Clinical descriptions of individuals with ADHD, especially adults with the disorder, frequently include references to such deficits or limitations in their social conduct that lead others to judge them as immature, rude, inconsiderate, base, and insulting (Barkley, 1990; Kane et al., 1990; Ratey et al.,

1992; Shekim, 1989; Wender, 1987). If correct, this theory would predict that research conducting analyses of speech content of ADHD children and adults might reveal proportionally more references to self personal feelings, and expressed emotion in their narratives or explanations of the logic of their thinking than would be seen in normal peers. Certainly the analysis of affective tone in the speech and behavioral reactions of ADHD children to events should reveal a greater preponderance of emotion than in normal peers. Some findings do exist showing that ADHD children make more negative affect references during performance concept learning tasks, particularly when noncontingent negative feedback is provided (Rosenbaum & Baker, 1984).

The problem of separating affect might also lead to trouble in the ability of the individual with ADHD to objectively evaluate and respond to his or her own ongoing behavior. Again, research on speech content of individuals with ADHD might reveal a relative paucity of judgmental references about themselves and their own behavior and its rightness, fairness, or ethics and morality. Such references are not the same as those of personal feelings, emotions, or needs that might actually be more frequent in their speech than normal, as conjectured above. This reduced capacity for objective self-evaluation has been hinted at in some recent studies that have found teenagers with ADHD describing themselves as having fewer personal problems and less conflicts with others than others report for them (Fischer et al., 1993). Yet virtually no research exists that has formally explored these problems related to the separation of affect in any systematic or precise way. If correct, the theory provides a fascinating glimpse into how such problems with affective reactions and objectivity in ADHD may arise from the underlying impairment in delayed responding.

This theory may also help to explain one puzzling feature about the clinical presentation of some children with ADHD: their greater likelihood of displaying symptoms of anxiety. How can this be if they have a limited capacity to anticipate future events or to take them into account in managing current behavior as would be deduced from Bronowski's theory? It would seem as if such a deficit in conjecturing hypothetical futures, as described below (see the section on prolongation and ADHD), would preclude one from being especially anxious. Yet anxiety can be both reactive as well as anticipatory—the former occurring when the individual confronts an anxiety-eliciting event in the immediate stimulus context. It may be that ADHD children will be found to display more such reactive anxieties and fears as part of their hypothesized deficiency in the separation of affect. Yet they would display less anticipatory anxiety derived from fears or worries over future events whose premonition is not contained within signals in the immediate situation but must be conjectured from foresight (e.g., what may happen tomorrow, next week, or next month if school homework is not completed). In any case, scientific investigations into the capacity of ADHD children to separate affect from information in evaluating and responding to signals or events would seem to be a highly promising avenue of exploration.

## Prolongation and ADHD

Bronowski's theory predicts that we should see a diminished capacity for prolongation in individuals with ADHD. That is, people with ADHD should show more limited hindsight or a sense of past, more limited foresight or a sense of the future, and more limited control of their ongoing behavior by past events and the person's construction of hypothetical futures. Measuring such deficits would not be easy as it taxes the ability of psychology to assess these cognitive events that lie outside the realm of direct observation. The presence of the deficits may have to be inferred from differences between ADHD and normal groups in ongoing adaptive behavior that would be predicted from these reduced cognitive capacities for prolongation, hindsight, and foresight. That such investigations would be fruitful, however, is strongly intimated from clinical descriptions of individuals with ADHD. These descriptions frequently note that children and adults with ADHD seem to live more in the moment, are less organized, planful, and goal- or future-oriented. Even when such plans or goals are made, these plans have less influence on current behavior resulting in the person's being less likely to reach the goals that he or she set for himself or herself.

What is not clear is whether the reduction in prolongation results in a poorer reliance on memory of past events, less proficient utilization of memory, or in how memory is used to construct hypothetical alternative futures. It could also result in problems with the actual process of construction of such futures, in the feeding forward of such information into practical instructions used to control ongoing and subsequent behavior, or in the capacity of such instructions to actually initiate and govern ongoing behavior. Research clearly shows that memory storage and recall is generally not impaired in those with ADHD (Barkley, Grodzinsky, & DuPaul, 1991; Benezra & Douglas, 1988). It is the use to which memory is put in the service of goals or in constructing hypothetical futures (i.e., memory strategies and efficiency) and extracting from them the practical instructions that guide behavior, and in the actual governance of behavior by such instructions that may be more affected.

The problem with prolongation seems to explain why ADHD children have more difficulties with mental arithmetical computation than normal children (Barkley, DuPaul, & McMurray, 1990; Zentall & Smith, 1992). The diminished prolongation may be reflected in a restriction of working memory and a more rapid decay of the stimulus that must be encoded, held in working memory, scanned for information, and manipulated to produce the correct result. This is much more likely to be problematic in mental arithmetic rather than that done with pencil and paper as the latter allows stimuli related to the task to remain present in the context, thereby greatly reducing the need for prolongation to accomplish the problem. Such a problem with prolongation would be less likely to affect oral reading, spelling recognition, or even spelling to dictation as the demands in such tasks do not require the prolongation of the signal or use of working memory for manipulation of the information to the extent required by mental arithmetic. But the problem of prolongation would be expected to adversely affect other tasks besides math in which a sequence or complex set of stimuli must be held in short-term memory (i.e., prolonged) and acted upon. This would be especially so as the complexity of the manipulations required in memory by the task increased. Such an effect has been noted on tests of word order (Carter, Zelko, Oas, & Waltonen, 1990), tapping sequences (Homatidis & Konstantareas, 1981), and hand movements (Mariani, 1990) with ADHD children.

More generally, Bronowski's theory as applied to ADHD intimates that the sense of time, the scope or span of our awareness in time, and how that sense exerts an influence over ongoing behavior may be different or more limited in those with ADHD than in non-ADHD peers. Is this diminution seen in reduced temporal perception, or the attention to environmental cues that are related to a sense of time? Is it that those with ADHD are more attentive or responsive to spatial information within the immediate context (stimulus bound) and less attentive or responsive to temporal information about the rate of change within the context? If so, we should see inaccurate estimations of intervals of time in those with ADHD. Or is it that despite adequate time perception, information about time does not feed forward to adequately influence ongoing behavior or govern such behavior due to the impairment in the delay of responding?

The work of Zakay (1989, 1990) on the development of a sense of time in children seems relevant. Zakay (1992) found that normal 7- to 9-year-old children make shorter time estimations when asked to judge intervals retrospectively and longer time intervals when asked to judge time intervals prospectively—a finding also seen in adults. However, when distracted during the prospective estimation, they gave shorter time estimates than when not distracted. This implies that ADHD children might be more likely to give shorter time estimates on prospective time tasks than normal children given that the former will be distracted away more from such tasks by their problem of disinhibition than will same-age normal children. Introducing more salient distractors into the paradigm for both groups of children would likely shorten the time estimates of both groups but might more adversely affect those with ADHD. Research on time estimations in ADHD children relative to normal children seems most worthy of study.

Sonuga-Barke, Taylor, Sembi, and Smith (1992) discuss the possibility that ADHD children, because of being delay averse, perceive time as passing more slowly. They become inattentive as a means of helping time to pass more quickly in their subjective estimation of it. The former prediction is contrary to that expected from Zakay's (1990, 1992) work. Distracted, disinhibited children should make both shorter retrospective and prospective time estimations because their deficit disrupts their attention to temporal cues in both temporal directions. Thus, ADHD children should become impatient with delays because they underestimated the actual interval of the delay. They may even experience more frustrative nonreward at not being able to get on with the task or activity at the point where they subjectively estimated the delay should have ended.

Research does exist to show that children with ADHD do not benefit from warning stimuli meant to signal forthcoming events in the immediate future in improving their performance (see Douglas, 1983). The extent to which they must wait during preparatory intervals also adversely affects their performance on reaction time trials (Zahn, Krusei, & Rapoport, 1991). I doubt that the trouble is in perception or detection of the warning stimulus as no body of evidence exists to show that ADHD is a sensory or perceptual problem. More likely the problem is the child's greater responsivity to nontemporal stimuli than to temporally arranged signals, like warning stimuli. The warning signal carries no weight in determining subsequent performance. Such a stimulus could even prove disruptive to performance by eliciting inaccurate estimates of time to the event. In sum, children, like adults, provide longer time estimations when their attention is directed toward stimuli that signal the passage of time and away from nontemporal stimuli in the context. To the extent that children with ADHD are more stimulus bound or responsive to nontemporal events in the context, they will generate shorter and less-accurate time estimations and will be less prepared for impending events that actually occur later in real time than they had expected. Such differences between subjective expectations and real time could create a never-ending series of disappointments in ADHD children concerning the arrival of expected events and a higher level of impatience with delays in temporally arranged events.

Clinical descriptions of children and adults with ADHD are replete with references to the difficulties these people have with time. They are often late in meeting deadlines, appointments, and future commitments to others or to themselves, or simply fail to follow through on these commitments. They are often tardy for classes, meetings, or engagements with others, and are generally disorganized relative to time parameters of tasks. They are also less likely to employ sound time-management procedures. As noted above, they also seem to be more susceptible to immediate gratification, living more in the moment and giving less consideration to the future consequences of their acts. In adults, these hypothesized difficulties with the sense of time and its utilization in the ongoing governance of behavior might be further reflected in (1) poorer management of money; (2) poorer organization of household activities; (3) less ability to manage their children's activities and schedules as a parent; (4) less ability to work independently of supervision in one's occupation; and so (5) a commensurately slower upward progression in socioeconomic or occupational–educational status. Such problems have been reported in the adult outcomes of hyperactive children (Weiss & Hechtman, 1986) and in clinic-referred adults with ADHD (Barkley, 1990; Ratey et al., 1992; Wender, 1987).

It is interesting to speculate whether a reduced sense of the future and its governance over ongoing adaptive behavior might also make those with ADHD less health conscious. Are they more likely to engage in behaviors that have widely known and associated future health risks (i.e., smoking, alcohol use, limited regular exercise, poorer nutrition, etc.)? The answer seems to be yes. Those with ADHD have been shown to be more likely to engage in such health risks as smoking and excessive alcohol use (Barkley, Fischer et al., 1990; Kramer, 1993; Weiss & Hechtman, 1986), especially where co-morbid antisocial behavior exists. But the relationship of these behaviors to the impairment in delayed responding and, consequently, prolongation remains conjectural.

This impairment in prolongation could result in less-effective encoding of the signal or event, particularly if it is not especially salient to begin with, resulting in the often-heard complaint of ADHD children and adults that they are "forgetful." The problem is not one of storage (Benezra & Douglas, 1988) but one of less adequate use of strategies for encoding of the event or to aid with its later retrieval (Douglas & Benezra, 1990). This could be particularly problematic if the signal is somewhat incidental and competes with more rewarding ongoing parallel stimuli, such as telling a person with ADHD while they are watching TV to remember to do something later.

In future research, the impairment in prolongation might be detected in the self-reported future plans of those with ADHD as evidenced by proportionally more references to immediate circumstances and consequences and less to those arising in the future that would be predicted from such plans. The further into the future such events or consequences arise as a function of present behavior or plans, the less likely they are to be noted by those with ADHD. The priorities assigned by the ADHD individual to various alternative plans that they may describe or that are presented by others might also reflect this greater penchant for mindfulness of the present more than the future. Moreover, as noted earlier, one might expect to find less anticipatory emotional reactions to impending future events while finding more reactive emotions to immediate events in the behavior of those with ADHD (the latter due to the problem of separation of affect from immediate signals or events). The further into the future the anticipated consequent, the less likely it is to elicit anticipatory emotion in the moment.

I am aware of absolutely no research that has addressed this potential problem with prolongation. Certainly care must be taken in any future research on the matter not to contaminate the assessment of the problem with repeated descriptions of the future event or its consequences. This would immediately bring symbolic representations of that event to mind in the person with ADHD, thus assisting his or her foresight. This would defeat the assessment by having the examiner serving as a prompter of the behavior or cognitive events of interest. The assessment procedures must carefully probe for whether ADHD individuals anticipate and use this information about the past and future but should not provide it for them. This will prove no easy task as has been the case in the neuropsychological literature on testing frontal-lobe functions in human clinical cases. But it is where our work must take us if this extrapolation of Bronowski's theory to ADHD is correct.

## Internalization of Language and ADHD

Bronowski's theory posits that impaired response inhibition results in a reduced capacity to internalize and employ self-directed speech in ongoing adaptive behavior. If so, and if ADHD is such a problem with response inhibition, then by extension those with ADHD ought to show less developed and organized self-directed or private speech, less use of internal speech and greater use of public self-directed speech in the management of their own adaptive behavior, and less ongoing control of such behavior by self-speech, rules, and instructions. This hypothesized deficiency is very much akin to my earlier theorizing (Barkley, 1981, 1984, 1989, 1990) that ADHD seems to represent an impairment in rule-governed behavior, or the stimulus control of behavior by language, rules, and instructions. The problem may be less obvious in the response of the person with ADHD to directives or instructions given by others in the moment to be performed at that moment because the external instruction and consequences associated with it are immediately present. The problem arises when rules are given that have future references for performance and for the associated consequences. This would be especially so if the rule is to be followed in the absence of the rule-giver and rule at the future time (Hayes, 1989). Because the latter requires internalized speech and a self-directed repetition of the rule at some later time, ADHD children would be less able to comply with such rules. The problem with internalized speech and rule-governance will also be obvious if individuals with ADHD must generate their own rules (problem solving; Skinner, 1953).

As noted earlier, Hayes (1989, 1991) observed six effects on behavior that would be evident from internalized speech and rule-governed behavior. If correct, then ADHD children should differ from normal children in these effects. We could expect that ADHD children would (1) display greater variability of responses on tasks because their behavior is more contingency shaped and less rule-governed; (2) be more susceptible to control by immediate contingencies and their momentary and potentially spurious changes; (3) be more likely to respond to the immediate contingencies and less controlled by rules in situations where rules and contingencies compete; (4) show less rigidity in responding even when the rule they extract and try to use to control their behavior is incorrect; (5) perform less well under conditions involving extreme delays in consequences; and (6) display a delayed developmental growth trajectory in the development of progressively greater rule-governed behavior such that it resembles the performance of younger normal children to rule following. Some findings exist to support these predictions about rule-governed behavior, as in the greater variability of ADHD children in their responses to laboratory tasks or conditioning trials. The heightened sensitivity of ADHD children to immediate rewards, their greater and more rapid decline in task performance as contingencies change from continuous to intermittent, the greater disruption of their performance by noncontingent consequences, and the reduced control of their behavior by delayed consequences (see section on sensitivity to consequences below) are all consistent with the predictions of this theory. Other predictions simply have not been evaluated with ADHD children yet they would seem to be very promising areas for research.

The extant research on the more general issue of internalized language also has been limited. What exists indicates that ADHD children talk more and make more task-irrelevant comments than others during play, schoolwork, and interactions with others (Barkley, Cunningham, & Karlsson, 1983; Cunningham & Siegel, 1987; Copeland, 1979; Ludlow, Rapoport, Brown, & Mikkelson, 1979). They also have less mature self-directed or private speech than normal children (Berk & Potts, 1991; Copeland, 1979), appear delayed in the process of internalizing self-directed speech (Berk & Potts, 1991), are less able to adhere to inhibitory rules or instructions in play situations (Routh & Schroeder, 1976; Ullman et al., 1978), and are less compliant with parental instructions (Barkley, Karlsson, & Pollard, 1985; Cunningham & Barkley, 1979). ADHD children are also less adequate problem solvers (see Douglas, 1983), are less mature in their organization and efficiency in communicating information to others (Whalen et al., 1979), show deficient verbal fluency on demand, such as measured by the FAS test (Grodzinsky & Diamond, 1992) or in story narratives (Tannock, Purvis, & Schachar, 1992), and display less conceptual curiosity in describing play objects (Fiedler & Ullman, 1983). Their type of play is also less mature, less symbolic, and less organized than their peers and more sensorimotor and stereotyped in nature (Alessandri, 1992). They also are poorer at using organizational rules and strategies in memory tasks (August, 1987; Douglas & Benezra, 1990), particularly where effortful processing is required (Butterbaugh et al., 1989). All of these findings seem to me to reflect a delay in the internalization of speech and its integration with thought that is so important to guiding children's play and adaptive behavior (Berk & Potts, 1991).

Clinical descriptions of ADHD children have also noted their excessive speech, excessive task- or topic-irrelevant speech, poor compliance with instructions (i.e., don't seem to listen or don't follow through on rules and instructions; DSM-III-R), and diminished ability to problem-solve. Nevertheless, the issue of delayed internalization of speech in ADHD is far from being resolved. Greater research is to be encouraged on the potential problem of internalization of language in those with ADHD.

At a more general level, these difficulties with internal language could easily result in defects in the moral development of the individual. Consistent with this prediction is a recent study showing that children with ADHD were significantly delayed in moral reasoning (Hinshaw et al., 1993). Clinical descriptions of ADHD children dating back to Still's

(1902) initial report have remarked on the problem of defective moral regulation of behavior in this population. If the current theory is correct, then the degree of difficulties noted in moral development, reasoning, and problem solving should be a direct function of the degree of problems in internalized language and, indirectly, of the extent of the deficit in response inhibition. The total effect of these deficits would be a general delay and ultimately earlier arrest in social development in individuals with serious ADHD.

## Reconstitution and ADHD

The capacity for analysis and synthesis, the two related processes Bronowski calls *reconstitution,* that flow from the ability to inhibit responding similarly would be expected to be impaired in people with ADHD. Reconstitution, according to Bronowski, is closely linked and dependent upon the other three capacities that stem from delayed responding: internalization of language, separation of affect, and prolongation. Thus, we should find that those with ADHD are poorer at the dissembling of signals, messages, and events into components or units of analysis and in the recombination of such components into new responses. Creativity, in short, should be less well developed in those with ADHD as it is used to meet daily demands on adaptive behavior. Again, this is not to say that those with ADHD cannot engage in these processes; under environmental prompts and cues to use them or increased motivational consequences for doing so, those with ADHD should perform closer to, if not at, normal levels. It is to say that in everyday, garden-variety situations in society to which they must adapt, these processes will not be readily deployed because responses are not delayed sufficiently to permit their effective engagement. The results of such processing also may not feed forward to satisfactorily inform and govern subsequent ongoing responding in these situations. Future research in this area would be expected to show that ADHD children spend less time engaged in analysis during learning tasks due to poor response inhibition. They also may be less likely to decompose the results of their analysis into more meaningful components or units of analysis, and less likely to spontaneously generate more novel or reconstructed responses/answers to the task relative to children who are not ADHD.

Several research findings are in keeping with this hypothesis. Children with ADHD (1) are less adequate at problem solving (Douglas, 1983); (2) perform more poorly on verbal fluency tasks (Grodzinsky & Diamond, 1992); and (3) display less conceptual curiosity but more object curiosity (Fiedler & Ullman, 1983). *Conceptual curiosity* refers to the number of different conceptual dimensions a child verbally uses in describing an object. *Object curiosity* represents the number of manipulations of an object by a child that would be expected to yield new information about the object, overt meaningful questions the child asked about the object, as well as any spontaneous comments about the object that indicated curiosity (Fiedler & Ullman, 1983). The former may represent a more mature means or later developmental stage of obtaining information from the environment than the latter. The play of ADHD children has also been shown to be less mature, symbolic, and creative than normal children (Alessandri, 1992). All of these findings seem to reflect the possibility that reconstitution (analysis and synthesis) may be less well developed in ADHD.

Another expected result from an impairment in the use of reconstitution in ADHD would be a pattern of focal or selective memory impairments under certain task conditions. If the memory task involves trials in which the length of time available for memorizing the stimulus is self-determined, ADHD children will take less time, end the trial more quickly, and therefore derive less information from the time allotted to inspect the stimulus. This culminates in a poorer performance than normal on such a task. Where the task specifies a fixed period of time per trial to learn each new stimulus, they will again use less of the time for inspection or analysis than normals and, where possible, opt to terminate the trial earlier than normal. However, where an external prompt or behavioral consequence is provided to encourage inhibition of responding and to use the time allotted for more careful analysis of the stimulus, ADHD children will do so and thereby perform at normal levels. Finally, if the presentation rate of trials in such a task were to be increased to a point where delayed responding would not be adaptive, ADHD and normal children should not be found to differ in their results. Again, the deficit in ADHD is not one of memory but one of delayed responding that prematurely interrupts or terminates the period available for analysis (and synthesis) to take place such that performance is impaired relative to normal peers. This is precisely what was found by Sonuga-Barke, Taylor, and Hepinstall (1992) in their evaluation of delay intervals on the performance of ADHD and normal children on a picture memory task and by Chee et al. (1989) on the effects of stimulus presentation rate in reaction-time tasks.

As repeatedly noted above, the application of Bronowski's theory to ADHD provides a more unified theory of the widely diverse findings associated with the disorder and makes a number of fascinating predictions concerning potentially fruitful avenues for future exploration. This is certainly true regarding the possibility of a less functional process of reconstitution in ADHD.

## Sensitivity to Behavioral Consequences and ADHD

The clinical literature has repeatedly commented on the apparent reduced sensitivity of ADHD children to contingencies of consequences provided for their behavior. Even as far back as 1902, Still remarked on the apparent inability of such children to learn from their mistakes and to respond to rewards and punishments as well as normal children. In 1971, Wender also hypothesized that children with ADHD were less sensitive to reinforcement. Several reviews of the extant literature show differences between the sensitivity of ADHD and normal children to behavioral consequences (Barkley, 1989; Douglas, 1983, 1989; Haenlein & Caul, 1987; Quay, 1989). Suffice it to say here that ADHD children do not perform tasks as well as normal children under conditions of partial or delayed reinforcement or even noncontingent reinforcement (Douglas & Parry, 1983, 1994; Haenlein & Caul, 1987; Parry & Douglas, 1983; Sagvolden et al., 1989). It is less certain about their response to partial, delayed, or noncontingent punishment, but one study (Rosenbaum & Baker, 1984) found the latter to be highly disruptive to task performance in ADHD but not in normal children. When continuous consequences are provided in these tasks, the performance of ADHD children approximates that of normal children. The withdrawal of continuous consequences results in an immediate return to prior impaired levels of performance.

Douglas (1983) has argued that these results reflect a heightened sensitivity to immediate reward. Although I previously disagreed with this finding, I now believe that Douglas's observations are likely correct but that it is her interpretation of their meaning that is in error. ADHD children are not overly sensitive to immediate reinforcement so much as as they are not as governed by rules and internalized self-directed speech as are their normal peers. As normal children progressively acquire control over their behavior by internalized language and a sense of the future, there is a commensurate decline in their control by consequences in the immediate context. As noted earlier, ADHD children are delayed in this developmental sequence such that they remain under the control of immediate and momentary contingencies far longer into development than do normal children. Such children are less proficient than normal at extracting and following rules about the ongoing contingency arrangements and using them to govern their responding. Saying that they are more sensitive to the consequences distracts our focus from the real deficiency—the control of their behavior by rules and inter-nalized speech integrated with a sense of the future. The fact that they seem more sensitive to immediate reinforcement is a sign of devel-opmental delay in the progression from contingency-shaped to rule-governed behaviors (see Hayes, 1989, 1991; Skinner, 1953). Moreover, it is not just immediate reinforcement to which they seem more sensitive but also immediate punishment, for much the same reason. This is why noncontingent consequences of either valence have proven so much more disruptive of their task performance relative to normal children. It is also why immediate shifts in the schedule or arrangement of contin-gencies produce far more immediate shifts in the behavior of ADHD than of normal children—the former are remaining under the influence of the immediate contingencies, whereas the latter are more controlled by internal language and rules, especially those given by the experi-menter.

This also explains why Quay's (1988, 1989) analysis of ADHD as an insensitivity to signals of impending punishment (diminished behav-ioral inhibition system) may not be quite correct. To the consternation of Quay's theory, evidence shows that ADHD children are quite sensitive to punishment, such as response cost, when used in behavioral treat-ment programs (Pfiffner & O'Leary, 1987; Pfiffner, O'Leary, Rosen, & Sanderson, 1985). Even in laboratory paradigms designed to assess re-sponse inhibition to punishment, a large minority of ADHD children may stop responding in the task within a single or a few exposures to the punishment (Milich, 1993; Fischer, personal communication, Febru-ary 20, 1993). It is when prior responding has been reinforced and then there is a gradual increase in the ratio of punishments to rewards that ADHD children continue to respond to the task longer than do normal children, thus experiencing more punished trials than normals. It is most likely *the arrangement of the contingencies* that account for the diverse findings in this literature and not a greater or lesser sensitivity to a consequence. This likely results from ADHD children being more gov-erned by the immediate contingencies and reinforcement history than their normal peers who analyze or read the contingency shift and formu-late a rule that guides their responding. Again, it is the greater delay in prolongation (foresight and hindsight), internalized use of self-directed language, and analysis/synthesis of the ADHD children that is being witnessed in these paradigms; not their greater sensitivity to reward or lower sensitivity to punishment.

The previous impairments in delay and the four consequent pro-cesses could also be predicted to result in a deficient response of the person with ADHD to social feedback. Such use of corrective feedback in the form of reprimands, praise, attention, rejection, censure, and criticism, to name but a few, would likely appear to go unheeded by the individual with ADHD. This is not because the feedback was not attended to or even stored in memory but because it was not an effective consequence as it is for others. It is also possible that in subsequent situations the individual would once again respond quickly without permitting adequate time for delay that would have resulted in the previous social feedback informing the subsequent response. A further problem that might be predicted to arise from such feedback stems from the hypothetical problem with separation of affect in ADHD noted above. The person with ADHD might respond more impulsively to the social feedback, and especially its affective charge, with an excessively emotional reaction resulting in a worsening of the social encounter. Again, the theoretical connection here is conjectural but worth greater study.

One additional corollary of the impairment in delayed responding vis-à-vis sensitivity to consequences is the possible impact response inhibition would have on learning under passive versus active avoidance paradigms (Cunningham, personal communication, February 20, 1993). Where an individual must make an active response to terminate, escape from, or avoid punishment, people with ADHD should do as well or possibly better than normal given their disinhibited response pattern. However, where passivity or inhibiting a response is required to terminate, escape, or avoid the punishment, those with ADHD will experience more such punished trials than normal. Just such a finding has been observed in a study of ADHD children during a passive avoidance paradigm with the deficient performance being normalized by stimulant medication (Freeman & Kinsbourne, 1990). This problem with passive avoidance may be what is meant in the clinical and parental descriptions of ADHD children that they do not seem to learn as well from their mistakes.

Many, including myself (1989), have interpreted these research findings to suggest that a deficit exists in the brain's reward (Haenlein & Caul, 1987) or punishment centers (Quay, 1989) in ADHD that results in a reduced sensitivity to these consequences. These theories also stipulated that the impulsivity, inattention, and hyperactivity arose as a result of these brain-system insensitivities. Unlike these theories, the present conceptualization argues the opposite point of view—that the reduced sensitivity to behavioral consequences derives from the impairment in delayed responding.

Such brain centers as those for reward and punishment are quite old in an evolutionary or phylogenetic sense and should be less prone to disruption by genetic or environmental influences than are more recently evolved or evolving brain structures, such as the orbital prefrontal cortex. It seems more likely that the reduced sensitivity to consequences arises from an impairment elsewhere in a more recently evolved brain system than those limbic-system centers subserving reward and punishment. A good candidate for this other center is a higher cortical one that regulates the lower reward and punishment centers to bring them under the control of hindsight, foresight, and internalized language. This would provide a substantial increase in the effectiveness of these motivational centers for regulating behavior. The most likely candidate for such a late evolving center or ability, it seems to me, is the orbital–frontal cortex. This cortical structure is believed to have evolved out of lower limbic system structures and likely exerts a powerful regulatory influence over them (Stuss & Benson, 1986). It is also, as noted earlier, the most likely substrate moderating delayed responding.

## Developmental Considerations and ADHD

Research on the components of this theory as applied to ADHD is likely to find that delayed responding and its consequent processes shown in Figure 1 are delayed in their development, or shifted to the right in Figure 1, in children with ADHD. It is not certain just how delayed or shifted the development and integration with adaptive responding these processes will be. A figure of 30% to 40% delay would not be surprising given that this seems to be the level of delay in their degree of impulse control in some research. It is also likely that once these processes are fully functional and "on-line" or integrated with other prefrontally regulated functions, they will not be as proficient in ADHD as in normal children. My educated guess is that the relative proficiency of these processes as they emerge will remain at a 30% to 40% delay relative to same-age normal children.

Past studies on the development of delayed responding in human infants has shown that delays of 2 to 5 seconds can be mastered by 12 months and that some rudimentary self-control and planning abilities are evident by this age as well (Diamond, 1990; Diamond & Doar, 1989; Diamond & Goldman-Rakic, 1986). If correct, the present theory would predict that ADHD children master particular delay intervals later than do normal children, always lagging behind the delay durations that normal children are able to master by particular mental ages. Thus, very young children who show impairments when tested for their ability to engage in delayed responding or response inhibition ought to be predictive of an increased risk for ADHD behaviors later in development. Silverman and Ragusa (1992) found just these results when 24-month-old children were tested on a measure of delayed responding. This measure proved to be highly predictive of behaviors at age 4 years related to ADHD.

In a similar vein, Levin et al. (1991) have shown significant increases in sensitivity to feedback, problem solving, concept formation, and response inhibition between 7- to 8-year-old and 9- to 12-year-old age groups of normal children. Further significant developmental advances were noted in memory strategies, memory efficiency, planning time, problem solving, and hypothesis seeking between 9- to 12-year old and 13- to 15-year-old age groups of normal children. These abilities fit well within the conceptual schema developed by Bronowski. Were such a battery to be given to ADHD children, I would hypothesize from this schema a delay in the development of these abilities such that at each age level, ADHD children would perform like younger normal children but would show a pattern of development otherwise similar to that of normal children in shape and trajectory. Using a somewhat different neuropsychological test battery of presumed frontal-lobe functions in children, Grodzinsky and Diamond (1992) found just such a stable pattern of differential delay between her 6- to 8-year-old and 9- to 11-year-old groups of ADHD and normal children on measures of response inhibition, verbal fluency, problem solving, and response planning. Both groups displayed age-related advances, but the ADHD children remained significantly behind the normal children at each age level. The cross-sectional nature of the design in both of these studies of prefrontal tests limits the degree to which inferences about true developmental processes can be made. But they do provide indirect evidence consistent with such developmental patterns.

From Bronowski's model of delayed responding, it is relatively easy to see why ADHD children would be at such a high risk for later oppositional and conduct problems and difficulties with their school performance. Disinhibited individuals who, as a consequence, are more stimulus bound to the immediate context, are more affectively reactive to situations, are less adequately rule-governed and task-persistent, have a more delimited sense of past and future, are less able to engage in analysis and synthesis (reconstitution), and perform more poorly under conditions of delayed or partial consequences should have a much greater probability for later oppositional defiant and conduct disorder. That disinhibited and ADHD-related behaviors emerge first, preceding these later antisocial behaviors, was nicely demonstrated in a study by Loeber, Green, Lahey, Christ, and Frick (1992), using parents' retrospective reports of ages of onset for various symptoms of ADHD, ODD, and CD from the DSM-III and DSM-III-R.

## Implications of the Theory for the Assessment of ADHD

If, as has been exposited here, ADHD is not a deficit in skills, knowledge, or general intelligence, then it is not likely to be easily, if at all, detected by contemporary psychometric tests routinely employed in clinical practice. These tests or batteries simply do not readily assess in any reliable way the cognitive processes described here that flow from the ability to delay and inhibit responding. Clinical standardized measures of separation of affect, prolongation, internalization of language, and reconstitution simply do not exist, nor do those that assess sensitivity to consequences. Some measures of frontal-lobe functions may assess these capacities in tangential ways, such as the Wisconsin Card Sort Test for rule formation and sensitivity to informational consequences that is, perhaps, related to internalized language. Measures such as the continuous performance tests, Go/No-Go test, Card Playing Test, and Stroop Word-Color Test (see Barkley, Grodzinsky, & DuPaul, 1992) may assess response inhibition, but as currently designed they become insensitive with development in individuals with ADHD. This would argue for an adjustment in their time limits or ceilings to accomodate different ages of children. The work by Levin et al. (1991) in attempting to establish the developmental sensitivities and factor structure of various measures of presumed frontal-lobe functions in children is a step in the right direction. Tests or tasks that incorporate measures of response variability over repeated trials would also be a useful addition to the assessment of ADHD and prefrontal-lobe functions in children.

But surely the most reliable and valid indicator of these processes lies in the day-to-day adaptive behavior of the individual in response to routine and recurring demands for their deployment in organizing behavior and directing it toward the future. Because, as Kinsbourne (1989) argued, ADHD is a dysregulatory phenomenon and not a skill deficit, it is not likely to be reliably detected by assessments that occur at single, relatively brief points in time. Moreover, it will be more likely to appear in the standard deviation of the individual around his/her own mean performance of tasks than in the mean score itself. The presence of the deficits will most definitively emerge from an analysis of how the person's adaptive behavior unfolds over time in response to the numerous challenges of daily life for someone of that developmental level. This is certainly true for patients with prefrontal-lobe injuries, especially those of the orbital–frontal cortex, and it is equally true of individuals with ADHD. Consequently, the observations of others collapsed across much longer time intervals and captured through ratings of behavior or measures of adaptive functioning, as was done by Stein (personal communication, October 15, 1992), may be far more indicative of the deficits in ADHD, and certainly their impact on daily life, than is the case with standard psychometric instruments.

## Implications of the Theory for the Treatment of ADHD

The present theory of delayed responding and ADHD posits that the disorder arises from a deficit in the performance of motor or response inhibition. I see this as a fundamental and automatic process that arises early in development and occurs, at least routinely, outside of conscious or volitional control. I do not see it as a skill that is trained or acquired, but it certainly can be partially or temporarily overridden by conscious effort. The four process impairments that derive from impaired delayed responding (i.e., prolongation, etc.) are, themselves, not necessarily directly impaired. Instead, they function far less proficiently and usefully in guiding ongoing adaptive behavior and social conduct due to the impairment in response inhibition. This is because the response has already been released before their functions can fully and effectively occur and feed forward to influence responding. Thus, the person with ADHD thinks after acting rather than before, if at all. But the deficit is not in thinking but in waiting long enough to give thinking a chance to occur and to then affect responding. Consequently, those with ADHD are more often in a position of reacting to unexpected events that sweep over them in the rush of time than in being more functionally proactive in anticipating and preparing for these future events. The key to treatment, however, is not so much to teach skills or to address the "downstream" processes that are partially precluded by not delaying the response. This has been the mistake of cognitive approaches to ADHD that attempt to train persons to think before and while they are responding. Admirable as their intent may be, such approaches do not address the fundamental impairment in the relatively automatic delay or inhibition process but instead work through the downstream process of internalized language. From this analysis, cognitive therapies would be predicted to be a failure in treating ADHD, which they have been (Abikoff, 1985, 1987; Kendall & Braswell, 1993).

The proper perspective on treatment is to view ADHD as a developmentally handicapping condition for which, at present, there is no cure. The use of stimulant medications has proven highly effective in the temporary amelioration and normalization of symptoms in most children, probably because of the direct effects of these medications on activating the motor inhibitory system of the orbital–frontal–limbic axis.

In keeping with the theory described here, such an improvement upstream in delayed responding should result in a normalization of the
four cognitive processes downstream that are permitted to occur by
delaying the response. There is every reason to think that such a temporary normalization takes place. ADHD children on stimulants behave
very much like their normal peers in meeting the daily challenges placed
upon them (Barkley, 1977; Barkley, DuPaul, & Costello, 1993; Berk &
Potts, 1991; Rapport & Kelly, 1992; Rapport, DuPaul, & Denney, 1993).
Unfortunately, they revert back to previous levels of impaired performance when the medication effects wear off, usually within a few hours.
The effects of stimulant medications in normalizing the processes of
prolongation, separation of affect, and reconstitution, however, remain
somewhat conjectural at this point and are most deserving of future
research. That normalizing effects on these processes likely will be
found is suggested by the findings of Berk and Potts (1991) that such
normalization occurred on measures of private speech in ADHD children when placed on stimulant medication. If so, ADHD children
should start on stimulant medication earlier than is now the case, and
treatment should be maintained over many yeas, perhaps allowing for
the normal development of proficiency in these four downstream cognitive processes.

This theory suggests that psychosocial treatments such as behavior
modification in the classroom (classroom management) and in the home
(via parent training) are palliative measures that result in only temporary management of the symptoms of ADHD so long as they are applied.
Such treatments probably work because they take advantage of the fact
that ADHD children are governed more by immediate contingency arrangements, whereas their normal peers are more controlled by rules
and internalized language. Where such immediate contingencies can be
intensively and artificially arranged to increase rewards and punishments in the immediate context, they will be very effective at behavior
management. What is striking here from a theoretical standpoint is that
their normal contemporaries do not require such systematically, artificially, and intensively arranged contingencies to behave well. These
artificially arranged contingencies also provide external prompts, cues,
and consequences for inhibited behavior that substitute for the deficient
internal ones associated with prolongation, internalization, and so forth.
These efforts by parents and teachers provide a prosthetic environment
around the child. This environment diminishes the impact of the child's
disability in delayed responding on performance while attempting to
increase the child's conscious use of inhibitory controls. Because these
methods cannot directly influence the underlying neurological substrate
that gives rise to the impairment in delayed responding as well as can

medication, however, their degree of control over behavior is considerably less effective. It is, however, better than nothing. Once the prosthetic environment is removed, though, behavior reverts to its formerly impaired range.

The answer to the problem of treatment at present is to arrange these artificial prosthetic environments in the *natural settings* of the child's daily life (home and school) as much as is feasible and to maintain these changes for considerable periods of time, often years. This view of psychosocial treatments fits very well with the extant literature on their effects (Barkley, 1989, 1990; Pelham et al., 1989). Based on this theory, the effects of any traditional clinic-based therapies for the child, such as play therapy, psychotherapy, group therapy, or the skills-oriented behavioral therapies, such as self-control or social skills training, also would be expected to be virtually useless in altering the core deficit of the disorder. The prevailing literature, again, supports this view (Abikoff, 1985, 1987; Barkley, 1990; Guevremont, 1990; Ross & Ross, 1976, 1982). The cognitive and social skill therapies, in particular, attempt to train the child in a skill that typically is not deficient but is not as mature or proficient because of the impairment in response inhibition (Berk & Potts, 1991). This seems especially so in the cognitive therapies. These therapies rely heavily on internalized and self-directed language that as noted above, is not necessarily impaired but is governing behavior less in daily situations due to the failure to delay responding (Berk & Potts, 1991). This impairment precludes the adequate use of internalized language and the recall and implementation of the skill in the settings where it is most useful. Further training of skills will not address the problem. The response of the ADHD child is simply too automatic and stimulus bound to the immediate context to permit the downstream cognitive processes that would have elicited the proper skill from the child's repertoire and effected its display. The child may be able to bring conscious and effortful control to improve their response inhibition when prompted to and reinforced for doing so, but such conscious control will be temporary.

The treatment philosophy for ADHD, then, is one similar to that used in dealing with patients with prefrontal-lobe injuries that have created permanent impairments in the functioning of that substrate. Such patients require a combination of treatments designed to provide some symptomatic management of the impairments in adaptive behavior. These include the use of the stimulants where feasible (see Gualtieri, 1992). But these patients also require (1) the arrangement of artificial external structure such as prompts, cues, and consequences within the natural environment; (2) the provision of greater supervision and external management of the patient's daily needs by others; (3) a reduction in the demands placed on the patient for normal levels of adaptive functioning and productivity; and (4) the maintenance of these adjustments for prolonged periods if not indefinitely.

## Conclusion

Bronowski's theory predicts that delayed responding or response inhibition permits four uniquely human capacities to unfold: separation of affect, prolongation, internalization of speech, and reconstitution. These capacities result in a reduced sensitivity to immediate behavioral consequences and a greater sensitivity to control by rules and internal speech in the regulation of behavior. Substantial evidence points to an impairment in response inhibition as a central feature of ADHD. By extrapolating Bronowski's elegant theory to ADHD, the theory predicts that these four capacities linked to delayed responding should also be impaired. The theory beautifully matches findings in a variety of areas of functioning in ADHD children. These findings appear to fall neatly within these four domains of cognitive processes outlined by Bronowski that previously seemed conceptually unrelated. The harmony of the theory with the extant literature is most impressive. Moreover, the hypothesized impairments in these four capacities point to a large number of additional avenues for future investigation that should yield significant information on the nature of ADHD. Much more research is certainly needed to evaluate the validity of the theory, the relationship among its component processes, their developmental staging and trajectories, and how these processes are delayed in ADHD. Present findings are encouraging of such theory-driven research in ADHD and suggest that the contribution to understanding, assessing, and treating ADHD may be substantial.

ACKNOWLEDGMENTS. This chapter is a much-expanded version of an article currently under review for publication. I wish to thank Charles Cunningham and Eric Mash for their enlightening discussions with me of the theory contained in this paper. While preparing this chapter, I was supported by grants MH45714 and MH42181 from the National Institute of Mental Health.

## References

Abikoff, H. (1985). Efficacy of cognitive training intervention in hyperactive children: A critical review. *Clinical Psychology Review, 5,* 479–512.

Abikoff, H. (1987). An evaluation of cognitive behavior therapy for hyperactive children. In B. Lahey & A. Kazdin (Eds.), *Advances in clinical child psychology* (Vol. 10, pp. 171–216). New York: Plenum Press.

Achenbach, T. M., & Edelbrock, C. (1983). *Manual for the Child Behavior Checklist and Revised Child Behavior Profile*. Burlington, VT: Thomas Achenbach.

Alessandri, S. M. (1992). Attention, play, and social behavior in ADHD preschoolers. *Journal of Abnormal Child Psychology, 20*, 289–302.

Aman, M. G., & Turbott, S. H. (1986). Incidental learning, distraction, and sustained attention in hyperactive and control subjects. *Journal of Abnormal Child Psychology, 14*, 441–455.

American Psychological Association. (1968). *Diagnostic and statistical manual of mental disorders* (2nd ed.). Washington, DC: Author.

American Psychiatric Association. (1980). *Diagnostic and statistical manual of mental disorders* (3rd ed.) Washington, DC: Author.

American Psychiatric Association. (1994). *Diagnostic and statistical manual of mental disorders* (4th ed.). Washington, DC: Author.

Atkins, M. S., Pelham, W. E., & Licht, M. H. (1985). A comparison of objective classroom measures and teacher ratings of attention deficit disorder. *Journal of Abnormal Child Psychology, 13*, 155–167.

August, G. J. (1987). Production deficiencies in free recall: A comparison of hyperactive, learning-disabled, and normal children. *Journal of Abnormal Child Psychology, 15*, 429–440.

Barkley, R. A. (1977). A review of stimulant drug research with hyperactive children. *Journal of Child Psychology and Psychiatry, 18*, 137–165.

Barkley, R. A. (1981). *Hyperactive children: A handbook for diagnosis and treatment*. New York: Guilford.

Barkley, R. A. (1984). *Do as we say, not as we do: The problem of stimulus control and rule-governed behavior in children with Attention Deficit Disorder with Hyperactivity*. Paper presented at the Highpoint Conference, Toronto, Canada.

Barkley, R. A. (1989). The problem of stimulus control and rule-governed behavior in children with Attention Deficit Disorder with Hyperactivity. In J. Swanson & L. Bloomingdale (Eds.), *Attention Deficit Disorders* (pp. 203–228). New York: Pergamon.

Barkley, R. A. (1990). *Attention deficit hyperactivity disorder: A handbook for diagnosis and treatment*. New York: Guilford.

Barkley, R. A. (1991). The ecological validity of laboratory and analogue assessments of ADHD Symptoms. *Journal of Abnormal Child Psychology, 19*, 149–178.

Barkley, R. & Ullman, D. G. (1975). A comparison of objective measures of activity and distractibility in hyperactive and nonhyperactive children. *Journal of Abnormal Child Psychology, 3*, 213–244.

Barkley, R., Cunningham, C., & Karlsson, J. (1983). The speech of hyperactive children and their mothers: Comparisons with normal children and stimulant drug effects. *Journal of Learning Disabilities, 16*, 105–110.

Barkley, R. A., Karlsson, J. & Pollard, S. (1985). Effects of age on the mother-child interactions of hyepractive children. *Journal of Abnormal Child Psychology, 13*, 631–38.

Barkley, R. A., DuPaul, G. J., & McMurray, M. B. (1990). A comprehensive evaluation of attention deficit disorder with and without hyperactivity. *Journal of Consulting and Clinical Psychology, 58*, 775–789.

Barkley, R. A., Fischer, M., Edelbrock, C. S., & Smallish, L. (1990). The adolescent outcome of hyperactive children diagnosed by research criteria, I: An 8 year prospective follow-up study. *Journal of the American Academy of Child and Adolescent Psychiatry, 29*, 546–557.

Barkley, R. A. Grodzinsky, G., & DuPaul, G. J. (1992). Frontal lobe functions in attention deficit disorder with and without hyperactivity: A review and research report. *Journal of Abnormal Child Psychology, 20,* 163–188.

Barkley, R. A., DuPaul, G. J., & Costello, A. J. (1993). Stimulant medications. In J. Werry & M. Aman (Eds.), *Handbook of pediatric psychopharmacology* (pp. 205–237). New York: Plenum Press.

Barkley, R. A., Guevremont, D., Anastopoulos, A., DuPaul, G., & Shelton, T. (1993). Driving related risks and outcomes in adolescents and young adults with attention deficit hyperactivity disorder: A 3–5 year follow-up survey. *Pediatrics, 92,* 212–218.

Benezra, E. & Douglas, V. I. (1988). Short-term serial recall in ADDH, normal, and reading-disabled boys. *Journal of Abnormal Child Psychology, 16,* 511–525.

Benton, A. (1991). Prefrontal injury and behavior in children. *Developmental Neuropsychology, 7,* 275–282.

Berk, L. E., & Potts, M. K. (1991). Development and functional significance of private speech among attention-deficit hyperactivity disorder and normal boys. *Journal of Abnormal Child Psychology, 19,* 357–377.

Bronowski, J. (1967). Human and animal languages. *To honor Roman Jakobson* (Vol. 1). The Hague, Netherlands: Mouton & Co.

Bronowski, J. (1977). Human and animal languages. *A sense of the future* (pp. 104–131). Cambridge, MA: MIT Press.

Brown, R. T., & Wynne, M. E. (1982). Correlates of teacher ratings, sustained attention, and impulsivity in hyperactive and normal boys. *Journal of Clinical Child Psychology, 11,* 262–267.

Butterbaugh, G., Giordani, B., Dillon, J., Alessi, N., Breen, M., & Berent, S. (1989). *Effortful learning in children with hyperactivity and/or depressive disorders.* Paper presented at the American Academy of Child and Adolescent Psychiatry, New York, October.

Campbell, S. B., & Ewing, L. J. (1990). Follow-up of hard-to-manage preschoolers: Adjustment at age nine years and predictors of continuing symptoms. *Journal of Child Psychology and Psychiatry, 31,* 891–910.

Campbell, S. B., Szumowski, E. K., Ewing, L. J., Gluck, D. S., & Breaux, A. M. (1982). A multidimensional assessment of parent-identified behavior problem toddlers. *Journal of Abnormal Child Psychology, 10,* 569–592.

Carter, B. D., Zelko, F. A., Oas, P. T., & Waltonen, S. (1990). *Journal of Psychoeducational Assessment, 8,* 155–164.

Chee, P., Logan, G., Schachar, R., Lindsay, P., & Wachsmuth, R. (1989). Effects of event rate and display time on sustained attention in hyperactive, normal, and control children. *Journal of Abnormal Child Psychology, 17,* 371–391.

Chess, S. (1960). Diagnosis and treatment of the hyperactive child. *New York State Journal of Medicine, 60,* 2379–2385.

Clements, S. D. (1966). *Task Force One: Minimal brain dysfunction in children.* National Institute of Neurological Diseases and Blindness, Monograph No. 3, U. S. Department of Health, Education, and Welfare.

Conners, C. K., & Wells, K. C. (1986). *Hyperactive children: A neuropsychosocial approach.* Beverly Hills, CA: Sage.

Copeland, A. P. (1979). Types of private speech produced by hyperactive and nonhyperactive boys. *Journal of Abnormal Child Psychology, 7,* 169–177.

Crowe, S. F. (1992). Dissociation of two frontal lobe syndromes by a test of verbal fluency. *Journal of Clinical and Experimental Neuropsychology, 14,* 327–339.

Cunningham, C. E., & Barkley, R. A. (1979). The interactions of hyperactive and normal children with their mothers during free play and structured task. *Child Development*, *50*, 217–224.

Cunningham, C. E., & Siegel, L. S. (1987). Peer interactions of normal and attention-deficit disordered boys during free-play, cooperative task, and simulated classroom situations. *Journal of Abnormal Child Psychology*, *15*, 247–268.

Dimond, S. J. (1980). *Neuropsychology.* Boston: Buttersworth.

Diamond, A. (1990). The development and neural bases of memory functions as indexed by the AB and delayed response task in human infants and infant monkeys. In A. Diamond (Ed.), *The development and neuronal bases of higher cognitive functions. Annals of the New York Academy of Science*, *608*, 276–317.

Diamond, A., & Doar, B. (1989). The performance of human infants on a measure of frontal cortex function, the Delayed Response task. *Developmental Psychobiology*, *22*, 271–294.

Diamond, A., & Goldman-Rakic, P. S. (1986). Comparative development in human infants and infant rhesus monkeys of cognitive functions that depend on prefrontal cortex. *Social and Neuroscience Abstracts*, *12*, 742.

Douglas, V. I. (1972). Stop, look, and listen: The problem of sustained attention and impulse control in hyperactive and normal children. *Canadian Journal of Behavioural Science*, *4*, 259–282.

Douglas, V. I. (1983). Attention and cognitive problems. In M. Rutter (Ed.), *Developmental neuropsychiatry* (pp. 280–329). New York: Guilford.

Douglas, V. I. (1985). The response of ADD children to reinforcement: Theoretical and clinical implications. In L. M. Bloomingdale (Ed.), *Attention deficit disorder: Identification, course, and treatment rationale.* New York: Spectrum Publications, Inc.

Douglas, V. I. (1990). Can Skinnerian psychology account for the deficits in attention deficit disorder? A reply to Barkley. In L. Bloomingdale & J. Swanson (Eds.), *Attention deficit disorder* (Vol. 4). New York: Pergamon.

Douglas, V. I., & Benezra, E. (1990). Supraspan verbal memory in attention deficit disorder with hyperactivity, normal, and reading disabled boys. *Journal of Abnormal Child Psychology*, *18*, 617–638.

Douglas, V. I., & Parry, P. A. (1983). Effects of reward on delayed reaction time task performance of hyperactive children. *Journal of Abnormal Child Psychology*, *11*, 313–326.

Douglas, V. I., & Parry, P. A. (in press). Effects of reward and non-reward on attention and frustration in attention deficit disorder. *Journal of Abnormal Child Psychology.*

Douglas, V. I., & Peters, K. G. (1979). Toward a clearer definition of the attentional deficit of hyperactive children. In G. A. Hale & M. Lewis (Eds.), *Attention and the development of cognitive skills* (pp. 173–248). New York: Plenum Press.

Draeger, S., Prior, M., & Sanson, A. (1986). Visual and auditory attention performance in hyperactive children: Competence or compliance. *Journal of Abnormal Child Psychology*, *14*, 411–424.

DuPaul, G. J. (1992). Parent and teacher ratings of ADHD symptoms: Psychometric properties in a community-based sample. *Journal of Clinical Child Psychology*, *20*, 245–253.

Edelbrock, C., Rende, R., Plomin, R., & Thompson, L. A. (1992). *A twin study of competence and problem behavior in childhood and early adolescence.* Submitted for publication, The Pennsylvania State University.

Faraone, S. V., Biederman, J., Chen, W. J., Krifcher, B., Keenan, K., Moore, C., Sprich, S., & Tsuang, M. T. (in press). *Segregation of attention deficit hyperactivity disorder: Evidence for single gene transmission. Archives of General Psychiatry.*

52 RUSSELL A. BARKLEY

Fiedler, N. L., & Ullman, D. G. (1983). The effects of stimulant drugs on curiosity behaviors of hyperactive boys. *Journal of Abnormal Child Psychology, 11,* 193–206.

Fischer, M., Barkley, R. A., Fletcher, K., & Smallish, L. (1993). The adolescent outcome of hyperactive children: Predictors of psychiatric, academic, social, and emotional adjustment. *Journal of the American Academy of child and Adolescent Psychiatry, 32,* 324–332.

Freeman, R. J., & Kinsbourne, M. (1990). *A stimulant-correctible incidental passive avoidance deficit in attention deficit hyperactivity disorder.* Unpublished manuscript, Simon Fraser University.

Frick, P. J., Lahey, B. B., Applegate, B., Kerdick, G., & Ollendick, T. (1993). *DSM-IV field trials for the disruptive and attention deficit disorder: Diagnostic utility of symptoms.* Submitted for publication. University of Miami School of Medicine.

Giedd, J., Castellanos, F., Kozuch, P., Vaituzis, C., Hamburger, S., & Rapoport, J. (1993). *Quantitative morphology of the corpus callosum in attention deficit hyperactivity disorder.* Paper presented at the Society for Research in Child and Adolescent Psychopathology, Santa Fe, NM, February.

Gilger, J. W., Pennington, B. F., & DeFries, J. C. (1992). A twin study of the etiology of comorbidity: Attention-deficit hyperactivity disorder and dyslexia. *Journal of the American Academy of Child and Adolescent Psychiatry, 31,* 343–348.

Gillis, J. J., Gilger, J. W., Pennington, B. F., & DeFries, J. C. (1992). Attention deficit disorder in reading-disabled twins: Evidence for a genetic etiology. *Journal of Abnormal Child Psychology, 20,* 303–315.

Gittelman, R., Mannuzza, S., Shenker, R., & Bonagura, N. (1985). Hyperactive boys almost grown up. *Archives of General Psychiatry, 42,* 937–947.

Goodman, R., & Stevenson, J. (1989). A twin study of hyperactivity—II. The aetiological role of genes, family relationships, and perinatal adversity. *Journal of Child Psychology and Psychiatry, 30,* 691–709.

Gordon, M. (1979). The assessment of impulsivity and mediating behaviors in hyperactive and non-hyperactive children. *Journal of Abnormal Child Psychology, 7,* 317–326.

Goyette, C. H., Conners, C. K., & Ulrich, R. F. (1978). Normative data on Revised Conners Parent and Teacher Rating Scales. *Journal of Abnormal Child Psychology, 6,* 221–236.

Gratten, L. M., & Eslinger, P. J. (1991). Frontal lobe damage in children and adults: A comparative review. *Developmental Neuropsychology, 7,* 283–326.

Gray, J. A. (1982). *The neuropsychology of anxiety.* New York: Oxford Press.

Grodzinsky, G. M., & Diamond, R. (1992). Frontal lobe functioning in boys with attention-deficit hyperactivity disorder. *Developmental Neuropsychology, 8,* 427–445.

Gross-Tsur, V., Shalev, R. S., & Amir, N. (1991). Attention deficit disorder: Association with familial-genetic factors. *Pediatric Neurology, 7,* 258–261.

Gualtieri, T. (1992). Psychostimulants in traumatic brain injury. In L. L. Greenhill & B. B. Osmon (Eds.), *Ritalin: Theory and patient management* (pp. 171–176). New York: Mary Ann Liebert.

Guevremont, D. (1990). Social skills and peer relationship training. In R. A. Barkley (Ed.), *Attention deficit hyperactivity disorder: A handbook for diagnosis and treatment* (pp. 540–572). New York: Guilford.

Haenlein, M., & Caul, W. F. (1987). Attention deficit disorder with hyperactivity: A specific hypothesis of reward dysfunction. *Journal of the American Academy of Child and Adolescent Psychiatry, 26,* 356–362.

Hart, E. L., Lahey, B. B., Loeber, R., & Frick, P. J. (1993). *Developmental change in attention-deficit hyperactivity disorder in boys.* Paper presented at the Society for Research in Child and Adolescent Psychopathology, Santa Fe, NM, February.

Hayes, S. (1989). *Rule-governed behavior.* New York: Plenum Press.

Hayes, S. (1991). *Rule-governed behavior.* Invited address for the Association for the Advancement of Behavior Therapy, New York, November.

Heilman, K. M., Voeller, K. K. S., & Nadeau, S. E. (1991). A possible pathophysiological substrate of Attention Deficit Hyperactivity Disorder. *Journal of Child Neurology, 6,* 74–79.

Hinshaw, S. P., Herbsman, C., Melnick, S., Nigg, J., & Simmel, C. (1993). *Psychological and familial processes in ADHD: Continuous or discontinuous with those in normal comparison children?.* Paper presented at the Society for Research in Child and Adolescent Psychopathology, Santa Fe, NM, February.

Homatidis, S., & Konstantareas, M. (1981). Assessment of hyperactivity: Isolating measures of high discriminant ability. *Journal of Consulting and Clinical Psychology, 49,* 533–541.

Hynd, G. W., Marshall, R., & Gonzalez, J. J. (1993). *Asymmetry of the caudate nucleus in ADHD: An exploratory study of gender and handedness effects.* Paper presented at the Society for Research in Child and Adolescent Psychopathology, Santa Fe, NM, February.

Kalverboer, A. F. (1988). Hyperactivity and obserational studies. In L. Bloomingdale & J. Sergeant (Eds.), *Attention deficit disorders: Criteria, cognition, and intervention* (pp. 29–42). New York: Pergamon.

Kane, R., Mikulac, C., Benjamin, S., & Barkley, R. (1990). Assessment and treatment of adults with ADHD. In R. A. Barkley (Ed.), *Attention deficit hyperactivity disorder: A handbook for diagnosis and treatment* (pp. 613–654). New York: Guilford.

Kendall, P. C., & Braswell, L. (1985). *Cognitive-behavioral therapy for impulsive children.* New York: Guilford.

Kendall, P. C., & Braswell, L. (1993). *Cognitive-behavioral therapy for impulsive children* (2nd ed.). New York: Guilford.

Kinsbourne, M. (1989). Control system instability in hyperactive children. In L. M. Bloomingdale (Ed.), *Attention deficit disorder* (Vol. 3; pp. 104–106). New York: Pergamon.

Kramer, J. (1993). *Childhood hyperactivity and aggression as differential predictors of adolescent progression to alcoholism vs. drug abuse.* Paper presented at the Society for Research in Child and Adolescent Psychopathology, Santa Fe, NM, February.

Kuehne, C., Kehle, T. J., & McMahon, W. (1987). Differences between children with attention deficit disorder, children with specific learning disabilities, and normal children. *Journal of School Psychology, 25,* 161–166.

Kupietz, S. S. (1990). Sustained attention in normal and in reading-disabled youngsters with and without ADDH. *Journal of Abnormal Child Psychology, 18,* 357–372.

Lahey, B. B., Pelham, W. E., Schaughency, E. A., Atkins, M. S., Murphy, H. A., Hynd, G. W., Russo, M., Hartdagen, S., & Lorys-Vernon, A. (1988). Dimensions and types of attention deficit disorder with hyperactivity in children: A factor and cluster analytic approach. *Journal of the American Academy of Child and Adolescent Psychiatry, 27,* 330–335.

Landau, S., Lorch, E. P., & Milich, R. (1992). Visual attention to and comprehension of television in attention-deficit hyperactivity disordered and normal boys. *Child Development, 63,* 928–937.

Levin, H. S., Culhane, K. A., Hartmann, J., Evankovitch, K., Mattson, A. J., Harward H., Ringholz, G., Ewing-Cobbs, L., & Fletcher, J. (1991). Developmental changes in performance on tests of purported frontal lobe functions. *Developmental Neuropsychology, 7,* 377–396.

Levin, P. M. (1938). Restlessness in children. *Archives of Neurology and Psychiatry, 39,* 764–770.

Loeber, R., Green, S. M., Lahey, B. B., Christ, M. A. G., & Frick, P. J. (1992). Developmental sequences in thet age of onset of disruptive child behaviors. *Journal of Child and Family Studies, 1,* 21–41.

Lou, H. C., Henriksen, L., & Bruhn, P. (1984). Focal cerebral hypoperfusion in children with dysphasia and/or Attention Deficit Disorder. *Archives of Neurology, 41,* 825–829.

Lou, H. C., Henriksen, L., Bruhn, P., Borner, H., & Nielsen, J. B. (1989). *Archives of Neurology, 46,* 48–52.

Ludlow, C., Rapoport, J., Brown, G., & Mikkelson, E. (1979). The differential effects of dextroamphetamine on the language and communication skills of hyperactive and normal children. In R. Knights & D. Bakker (Eds.), *Rehabilitation, treatment, and management of learning disorders.* Baltimore: University Park Press.

Luk, S. (1985). Direct observations studies of hyperactive behaviors. *Journal of the American Academy of Child Psychiatry, 24,* 338–344.

Luria, A. R. (1966). *Higher cortical functions in man.* New York: Basic Books.

Mariani, M. A. (1990). *The nature of neuropsychological functioning in preschool-age children with attention-deficit hyperactivity disorder.* Unpublished dissertation, Boston College, Boston, MA.

Mateer, C. A., & Williams, D. (1991). Effects of frontal lobe injury in childhood. *Developmental neuropsychology, 7,* 359–376.

Mattes, J. A. (1980). The role of frontal lobe dysfunction in childhood hyperkinesis. *Comprehensive Psychiatry, 21,* 358–369.

McClure, F. D., & Gordon, M. (1984). Performance of disturbed hyperactive and non-hyperactive children on an objective measure of hyperactivity. *Journal of Abnormal Child Psychology, 12,* 561–572.

Milich, R. (1993). *Disinhibition and underlying processes in hyperactive and aggressive adolescents.* Paper presented at the Society for Research in Child and Adolescent Psychopathology, Santa Fe, NM, February.

Milich, R., & Kramer, J. (1985). Reflections on impulsivity: An empirical investigation of impulsivity as a construct. In K. Gadow & I. Bialer (Eds.), *Advances in learning and behavioral disabilities* (Vol. 3). Greenwich, CT: JAI.

Milich, R., & Lorch, E. P. (1994). Television viewing methodology to understand cognitive processing of ADHD children. In T. Ollendick & R. J. Prinz (Eds.), *Advances in clinical child psychology, Volume 16* (pp. 177–202). New York: Plenum.

Parry, P. A., & Douglas, V. I. (1983). Effects of reinforcement on concept identification in hyperactive children. *Journal of Abnormal Child Psychology, 11,* 327–340.

Pelham, W. W., Schnedler, R. W., Bender, M. E., Nilsson, D. E., Miller, J., Budrow, M. S., Ronnel, M., Paluchowski, C. & Marks, D. A. (1989). The combination of behavior therapy and methylphenidate in the treatment of Attention Deficit Disorders: A therapy outcome study. In L. Bloomingdale (Ed.), *Attention Deficit Disorders* (Vol. 3, pp. 29–48). New York: Pergamon.

Pfiffner, L. J. & O'Leary, S. G. (1987). The efficacy of an all-positive management as a function of the prior use of negative consequences. *Journal of Applied Behavior Analysis, 20,* 265–271.

Pfiffner, L. J., O'Leary, S. G., Rosen, L. A., & Sanderson, Jr., W. C. (1985). A comparison of the effects of continuous and intermittent response cost and reprimands in the classroom. *Journal of Clinical Child Psychology, 14,* 348–352.

Prinz, R. J., Tarnowski, K. J., & Nay, S. M. (1984). Assessment of sustained attention and distraction in children using a classroom analogue task. *Journal of Clinical Child Psychology, 13,* 250–256.

Quay, H. C. (1988). Attention deficit disorder and the behavioral inhibition system: The relevance of the neuropsychological theory of Jeffrey A. Gray. In L. Bloomingdale &

J. Sergeant (Eds.), *Attention deficit disorders: Criteria, cognition, and intervention* (pp. 117–126). New York: Pergamon.

Quay, H. C. (1989). The behavioral reward and inhibition systems in childhood behavior disorder. In L. M. Bloomingdale (Ed.), *Attention Deficit Disorder III: New research in treatment, psychopharmacology, and attention* (pp. 176–186). New York: Pergamon.

Rapport, M. D., & DuPaul, G. J., & Denney, C. (1993). *Methylphenidate effects on behavior and academic functioning in children with ADDH: An empirical examination of dosage effects, outcome probabilities, and normalization rates in 76 children.* Paper presented at the Society for Research in Child and Adolescent Psychopathology, Santa Fe, NM, February.

Rapport, M. D., & Kelly, K. L. (1993). Psychostimulant effects on learning and cognitive function in children with attention deficit hyperactivity disorder: Findings and implications. In J. L. Matson (Ed.), *Hyperactivity in children: A handbook.* New York: Allyn & Bacon.

Rapport, M. D., Tucker, S. B., DuPaul, G. J., Merlo, M., & Stoner, G. (1986). Hyperactivity and frustration: The influence of control over and size of rewards in delaying gratification. *Journal of Abnormal Child Psychology, 14,* 191–204.

Ratey, J. J., Greenberg, M. S., Bemporad, J. R., & Lindem, K. J. (1992). Unrecognized attention-deficit hyperactivity disorder in adults presenting for outpatient psychotherapy. *Journal of Child and Adolescent Psychopharmacology, 2,* 267–278.

Reeves, J. C., Werry, J., Elkind, G. S., & Zametkin, A. (1987). Attention deficit, conduct, oppositional, and anxiety disorders in children: II. Clinical characteristics. *Journal of the American Academy of Child Psychiatry, 26,* 133–143.

Robins, P. M. (1992). A comparison of behavioral and attentional functioning in children diagnosed as hyperactive or learning-disabled. *Journal of Abnormal Child Psychology, 20,* 65–82.

Rosenbaum, M. & Baker, E. (1984). Self-control behavior in hyperactive and nonhyperactive children. *Journal of Abnormal Child Psychology, 12,* 303–318.

Ross, D. M., & Ross, S. A. (1976). *Hyperactivity: Research theory, and action.* New York: Wiley.

Ross, D. M., & Ross, S. A. (1982). *Hyperactivity: Current issues, research, and theory* (2nd ed.). New York: Wiley.

Routh, D. K., & Schroeder, C. S. (1976). Standardized playroom measures as indices of hyperactivity. *Journal of Abnormal Child Psychology, 4,* 199–207.

Sagvolden, T., Wultz, B., Moser, E. I., Moser, M., & Morkrid, L. (1989). Results from a comparative neuropsychological research program indicate altered reinforcement mechanisms in children with ADD. In T. Sagvolden & T. Archer (Eds.), *Attention deficit disorder: Clinical and basic research* (pp. 261–286). Hillsdale, NJ: Lawrence Erlbaum Associates.

Sergeant, J. A., & van der Meere, J. (1988). What happens after a hyperactive child commits an error. *Psychiatry Research, 24,* 157–164.

Shekim, W. (1989). Comprehensive evaluation of attention deficit disorder—residual type. *Comprehensive Psychiatry, 31,* 416–425.

Silverman, I. W., & Ragusa, D. M. (1992). A short-term longitudinal study of the early development of self-regulation. *Journal of Abnormal Child Psychology, 20,* 415–435.

Skinner, B. F. (1953). *Science and human behavior.* New York: Macmillan.

Smith, M. L., Kates, M. H., & Vriezen, E. R. (1992). The development of frontal lobe functions. In S. J. Segalowitz & I. Rapin (Eds.), *Handbook of neuropsychology: Volume 7, Section 10: Child Neuropsychology (Part 2)* (pp. 309–330). New York: Elsevier.

Sonuga-Barke, E. J. S., Taylor, E., & Hepinstall, E. (1992). Hyperactivity and delay aversion—II. The effect of self versus externally imposed stimulus presentation periods on memory. *Journal of Child Psychology and Psychiatry, 33,* 399–409.

Sonuga-Barke, E. J. S., Taylor, E., Sembi, S., & Smith, J. (1992). Hyperactivity and delay aversion—I. The effect of delay on choice. *Journal of Child Psychology and Psychiatry, 33,* 387–398.

Spitzer, R. L., Davies, M., & Barkley, R. A. (1990). The DSM-III-R field trial for the Disruptive Behavior Disorders. *Journal of the American Academy of Child and Adolescent Psychiatry 29,* 690–697.

Stevenson, J. (1992). Evidence for a genetic etiology in hyperactivity in children. *Behavior Genetics, 22,* 337–343.

Still, G. F. (1902). Some abnormal psychical conditions in children. *Lancet, 1,* 1008–1012, 1077–1082, 1163–1168.

Strauss, A. A., & Lehtinen, L. E. (1947). *Psychopathology and education of the brain-injured child.* New York: Grune & Stratton.

Stuss, D. T., & Benson, D. F. (1986). *The frontal lobes.* New York: Raven.

Szatmari, P., Offord, D. R., & Boyle, M. H. (1989). Correlates, associated impairments, and patterns of service utilization of children with attention deficit disorders: Findings from the Ontario child health study. *Journal of Child Psychology and Psychiatry, 30,* 205–217.

Tannock, R., Purvis, K. L., & Schachar, R. J. (1992). *Narrative abilities in children with attention deficit hyperactivity disorder and normal peers.* Unpublished manuscript, Hospital for Sick Children, Toronto.

Ullman, D. G., Barkley, R. A., & Brown, H. W. (1978). The behavioral symptoms of hyperkinetic children who successfully responded to stimulant drug treatment. *American Journal of Orthopsychiatry, 48,* 425–437.

van der Meere, J. (1993). *CPT and recent sustained attention data of ADHD children.* Paper presented at the Society for Research in Child and Adolescent Psychopathology, Santa Fe, NM, February.

van der Meere, J., & Sergeant, J. (1988a). Focused attention in pervasively hyperactive children. *Journal of Abnormal Child Psychology, 16,* 627–640.

van der Meere, J., & Sergeant, J. (1988b). Controlled processing and vigilance in hyperactivity: Time will tell. *Journal of Abnormal Child Psychology, 16,* 641–656.

van der Meere, J., & Sergeant, J. (1988c). Acquisition of attention skill in pervasively hyperactive children. *Journal of Child Psychology and Psychiatry, 29,* 301–310.

van der Meere, J., van Baal, M., & Sergeant, J. (1989). The additive factor method: A differential diagnostic tool in hyperactivity and learning disability. *Journal of Abnormal Child Psychology, 17,* 409–422.

van der Meere, J., Wekking, E., & Sergeant, J. (1991). Sustained attention and pervasive hyperactivity. *Journal of Child Psychology and Psychiatry, 32,* 275–284.

Weiss, G., & Hechtman, L. (1986). *Hyperactive children grown up.* New York: Guilford.

Wender, P. H. (1971). *Minimal brain dysfunction in children.* New York: Wiley.

Wender, P. H. (1987). *The hyperactive child, adolescent, and adult.* New York: Oxford Press.

Werry, J. S., & Sprague, R. L. (1970). Hyperactivity. In C. G. Costello (Ed.), *Symptoms of psychopathology* (pp. 397–417). New York: Wiley.

Werry, J. S., Elkind, G. S., & Reeves, J. C. (1987). Attention Deficit, Conduct, Oppositional, and Anxiety Disorders in children: III. Laboratory differences. *Journal of Abnormal Child Psychology, 15,* 409–428.

Werry, J. S., Reeves, J. C., & Elkind, G. S. (1987). Attention deficit, conduct, oppositional, and anxiety disorders in children. I. A review of research on differentiating characteristics. *Journal of the American Academy of Child and Adolescent Psychiatry, 26,* 133–143.

Whalen, C. K., & Henker, B. (1980). *Hyperactive children: The social ecology of identification and treatment.* New York: Academic Press.

Whalen, C. K., Henker, B., Collins, B. E., McAuliffe, S., & Vaux, A. (1979). Peer interaction in structured communication task: Comparisons of normal and hyperactive boys and of methylphenidate (Ritalin) and placebo effects. *Child Development, 50,* 388–401.

Whalen, C. K., Henker, B., & Dotemoto, S. (1980). Methylphenidate and hyperactivity: Effects on teacher behaviors. *Science, 208,* 1280–1282.

Zahn, T. P., Kruesi, M. J. P., & Rapoport, J. L. (1991). Reaction time indices of attention deficits in boys with disruptive behavior disorders. *Journal of Abnormal Child Psychology, 19,* 233–252.

Zakay, D. (1989). Subjective time and attentional resource allocation: An integrated model of time estimation. In I. Levin & D. Zakay (Eds.), *Time and human cognition: A life span perspective* (pp. 365–395). Amsterdam: Elsevier/North Holland.

Zakay, D. (1990). The evasive art of subjective time estimation: Some methodological dilemmas. In R. A. Block (Ed.), *Cognitive models of psychological time* (pp. 59–84). Hillsdale, NJ: Lawrence Erlbaum.

Zakay, D. (1992). The role of attention in children's time perception. *Journal of Experimental Child Psychology, 54,* 355–371.

Zametkin, A. J., Nordahl, T. E., Grass, M., King, A. C., Semple, W., Rumsey, J., Hamburger, M. S., & Cohen, R. M. (1990). Cerebral glucose metabolism in adults with hyperactivity of childhood onset. *The New England Journal of Medicine, 323,* 1361–1366.

Zentall, S. S., & Smith, Y. S. (1992). *Mathematical performance and behavior of children with hyperactivity with and without coexisting aggression.* Unpublished manuscript, Zentall University.

# 3

# Toward an Empirical Child Psychopathology

## JOSEPH A. SERGEANT and JAAP VAN DER MEERE

## Introduction

In the course of the last 20 years, the clinical term used to describe overactive, distractible, and impulsive children has changed from hyperactive to attention-deficit disorder with hyperactivity (ADDH) of Diagnostic and Statistical Manual of Mental Disorders, Third Edition (DSM-III) to attention-deficit hyperactivity disorder (ADHD) of DSM-III-R. DSM-IV will use the term attention-deficit hyperactivity disorder and subdistinguishes attention-deficit hyperactivity disorder, predominantly inattentive type, predominantly hyperactive-Impulsive type, and a combined type, if both inattention and impulsivity criteria are met for the past six months. The changes in diagnostic taxonomy have been arrived at by clinical opinion and are not based upon empirical findings. Quay (1988) argued that clinical child psychology needs a strong hypothetico–deductive approach in order to base taxonomies on empirical evidence. In this spirit, we have researched ADDH from a theoretical model of

JOSEPH A. SERGEANT • Department of Clinical Psychology, University of Amsterdam, 1018 WB Amsterdam, The Netherlands,     JAAP VAN DER MEERE • Laboratory of Experimental Clinical Psychology, University of Groningen, Groningen, The Netherlands.
*Disruptive Behavior Disorders in Childhood*, edited by Donald K. Routh. Plenum Press, New York, 1994.

attention that has well-established paradigms and lawful relations. The conclusion of this work has led us to suggest that children with attention deficit with hyperactivity are not attentional deficient (Sergeant, 1981), and that this is a misconception (van der Meere, 1988). This conclusion is counterintuitive. Indeed, Barkley (1991) has raised the issue of whether such experimental paradigms, such as the continuous performance task, have ecological validity for ADDH.

In reaction to the widespread application of ecologically unvalidated experimental cognitive tasks, Barkley (1991) observed that there was a low correlation between parent and teacher ratings of distractibility with task performance. He advocated that ecological validity be used as the criterion in the field. He argued that, in view of the poor ecological validity of many laboratory measures of attention, "one should certainly not try to exalt the lab measure as the actual ecological criterion and claim that it, more than ratings or observations of behavior in the natural setting, represents the true 'gold standard' for measuring attention" (p. 172). Against this background, two views on how the field should further develop appear; one using a strong hypothetico–deductive model, the other emphasizing the predictive role of research in daily, clinical practice. In this chapter we will address the relevance of an information-processing model for clinical child psychology.

There seem to be four issues in this discussion: first the discrepancy between levels of scientific enquiry of which the differences in observation and experimental tasks in hyperactivity research is but one example of many. Second, what is the rationale and validity of cognitive tasks in hyperactivity. Third, what have cognitive paradigms informed us of in hyperactivity research. Fourth, what are the uses and abuses of cognitive paradigms in hyperactivity research? Fifth we will consider the complementary role of observational and cognitive paradigms.

The conclusions we reach are, first, that discordance between daily life observations and experimental research is not new in psychology nor particular to the field of clinical child psychology; and second, that low correlation between tasks and daily life observations of hyperactive children is not in itself an argument to exalt observation data above task data. We will advocate the fruitfulness of a combined approach from ethology and experimental psychology.

## Discordance in Levels of Inquiry

For some time it has been known that there is a discrepancy between observation measures and information-processing measures of attention. On the one hand, there is a vast array of studies that have used observation methods or rating scales to evaluate attentional difficulties of hyperactive children. The results of this research point to a disregulation in hyperactive children of what, in common parlance, is called *distraction* or *inattention*. On the other hand, on the basis of information-processing measures of attention, we have suggested that inattention is not *the* problem of hyperactive children. Such discrepancy between levels of inquiry is not new in hyperactivity research. An early example was that of Satterfield and Dawson (1971). They hypothesized, on the basis of observing the overactivity of hyperactive children, that they would be physiologically overaroused. Following an orienting experiment with electrodermal measures, Satterfield and Dawson were forced to conclude that, contrary to observational data, hyperactives were physiologically underaroused.

Likewise, in other clinical and applied fields, a discordance between observation and performance has been noted and should not be considered unusual or specific to clinical child psychology. More recent theoretical work in the field of emotions and especially in anxiety and affective disorders has also found that the relation between self-rating scales or questionnaires with task performance is also poorly correlated (Frijda, 1986; Lang, 1970). In an earlier article on fear in parachutists, Fenz and Epstein (1967) noted that there was concordance and discordance between measures. Concordance between subjective ratings and physiological measures was found in novice parachutists. Discordance between subjective rating and physiological measures was obtained in experienced parachutists. Following research in phobics, Lang (1970) concluded that research in anxiety was forced to recognize discordance between measurement systems.

The divergence of what one measures by observational methods and task performance can be best illustrated by a more recent study that simulated aircraft controllers in a realistic task situation. Wiener (1987) noted survivors of aircraft accidents remarked that a crucial signal was missed. It was found during the simulation study that the proportion of missed targets was 97% despite the fact that controllers had their eyes open and observed the screen. Observational indices suggested that the controllers were performing optimally. Vigilance measures, however, told a different story. There is a clear practical need with tangible ecological consequences for vigilance research. This example demonstrates in a nutshell why observational measures can never be the "golden standard" by which to judge human performance. The radar operators were observed to work during their watch, but they failed to detect highly significant stimuli.

In summary, it can be stated that discordance between levels of psychological inquiry is part of a more general issue, namely, the relation between the levels of scientific enquiry. With respect to this issue, Rose (1976) pointed out that extrapolating from one level of scientific inquiry to another is a hazardous affair. When one descends in the levels of inquiry, one passes from the general to the particular. Thus lower levels of inquiry tend to be reductionistic. Study of cognitive dysfunctions has a lower level of inquiry than does ethology. It infers through input–output relations the nature of normal and abnormal human information processing. Thus finding a discrepancy between levels of inquiry does not in itself argue the validity of one level of inquiry above another. In fact, the criteria to make such a decision are absent and not obvious.

## Observation Studies in Childhood Disorders

For many years in European psychology, there has been a discussion about using laboratory measures as a means of predicting behavior in natural settings (so-called concurrent or ecological validity). Ounsted (1955) remarked that there is a problem of extrapolating from the "cage" of the scientific laboratory to the real world. This encouraged psychologists both in North America and Europe to study childhood disorders by observational methods (Barkley & Ullman, 1975; Hutt, Hutt, & Ounsted, 1963; Kalverboer, 1978; Routh & Schroeder, 1976). It was argued, that by placing restrictions upon a subject in a task environment of the laboratory psychologists obtained results that could not be extrapolated to the real world. The obvious face value of ethological measures is evident: One actually sees a child running around, throwing a book, or looking out the window. Seeing what is happening and transcribing observations into data is not, however, a self-evident process. There are several issues that we will address concerning ethological research.

First, ethologists have made it clear that there is considerable difficulty in the definition and measurement of the observational units, and this has been emphasized for hyperactivity research (Dienske & Sanders-Woustra, 1988). Cognitive biases of the investigators play a role in the definition decision rules of to-be-observed behavior. The observational categories are defined as accurately as possible, but exceptions to the definition confront the ethological psychologist with the problem of expanding definitions to accommodate variation in behavior. With respect to this issue, ethologists have long recognized the situational specificity of behavior. This has consequences for the relevance of the definition. For example, looking around may be an item in the category *distractibility,* only when the child is in a task situation that requires fixed gaze. Looking around in a game may be considered a useful search strategy and in that situation is not an index of "distractibility." Likewise, a useful ethogram for classroom observation may be highly inappropriate in the playyard. Consequently, definitions of what belongs to a category are situational dependent and require adjustment to the current task situation. We illustrate this point with a few examples from the literature.

What behaviors have been defined as critical indices of *distractibility* by ethologists? Hutt et al. (1963) employed the concept *attention span* and defined it in two ways: "duration of continuous engagement with the same stimulus," and second, with a view to operationalizing "distractibility," they used "running, jumping, hitting, and looking at." Others have defined attention span as "length of sustained watching of TV" (Anderson & Levin, 1976) or frequency of switching behaviors (Rapoport & Benoit, 1975). What behaviors fall into the same category is heterogeneous (Milich, Loney, & Landau, 1982). It should be noted that there is no criterion or theoretical model that enables one to choose one operationalization rather another. Merely to state that these are the critical behaviors considered by parents and teachers to be problematic is not a guarantee that these descriptions have more than face value. Consequently, in addition to face value, observational researchers might offer more hypothetical support for their choice of critical behaviors.

A second difficulty with the ethological approach in studying child psychopathology is that it lacks clear guidelines on what evidence may be used to support or reject a hypothesis. If we return to an issue addressed above, situational specificity, the same observational unit is valid in one situation but invalid in another as a measure of "attention." There is currently not a hypothetico–deductive model of child psychopathology guiding observational research. This leads to the choice of observational categories to the researcher but gives no indication of which dependent variables should be used. This may ensure ecological validity in some studies but does not lead to a systematic methods of hypothesis testing.

A third issue is in how far is the observed object influenced by being observed? Merely giving subjects attention through observation, the Hawthorne effect, could be the Achilles' heel of ethological studies. Draeger, Prior, and Sanson (1985) demonstrated that task performance became lower and activity level higher in hyperactives when the experimenter was absent rather than present and could give attention to the child. They observed that the activity level of hyperactives is higher when the experimenter is absent than when present.

A fourth problem is that using the observational method does not release the observer from the cage. Originally, Ounsted (1955), in addressing the problem of the cage, did not restrict his remarks only to formal testing situations. Ounsted questioned the ecological validity of free-field observations in laboratory settings, because they were, according to him, intrinsically different from real-life activities. Therefore, Kalverboer (1978) argued that the free-field laboratory study is at its best a *simulation* of possible daily-life environments. To observe behavior in laboratory conditions does not in itself have added ecological validity over cognitive paradigms. Both approaches, therefore, have to bridge the same gap between real life and the laboratory. Observational methods are no better a "golden criterion" than any other methods.

An argument in favor of observational research in hyperactivity has been that it brings the researcher closer to what parents and teachers see. Even allowing for the effects of the laboratory, one may wonder how desirable this advantage is. Schachar (1991) and Rutter (1989) noted that in the last 30 years of research in hyperactivity only a modest correlation (around 0.3) between parent and teacher ratings of inattention, overactivity, and impulsivity has remained. Both the DSM-III and DSM-III-R were confronted with the problem of when the parents and teacher differ in their opinion (Mattison, Bagnato, & Strickler, 1987), which one should be used to arrive at a diagnosis. As Schachar cogently argued, the discrepancy is not merely measurement error because it can be shown that there are meaningful differences between pervasive and situational hyperactives. Teacher-rated hyperactives seem to have a more cognitive problem (McGee & Share, 1988), whereas parent-rated hyperactives may have more psychological disadvantages. Pervasive hyperactives were suggested as having a generalized neurodevelopmental disorder. In our research with pervasive hyperactives, we have found that pervasiveness, as defined by concordance between parents and teacher, does not necessarily extrapolate to the laboratory situation. However, those children who were also hyperactive in the laboratory were more impaired in an information-processing task than moderately pervasive hyperactives (van der Meere, Wekking, & Sergeant, 1991). Because there is a discrepancy between the informants, it seems unlikely that a single observational study could be ecologically valid for both parents and teachers.

When multiple informants are required to be concordant before selecting children, there seems to be a greater chance of detecting information-processing deficits (van der Meere et al., 1991). We suggest that it would be useful in itself for the field to be able to indicate the degree and nature of cognitive impairments as related to the situational–pervasive distinction. Given that the observational approach has its limitations, what is the contribution of an attention-paradigm approach to child psychopathology?

## Why Use an Attentional Model?

It could be argued that by being able to clinically classify on the basis of observation that there is little use for experimental tasks in studying child psychopathology. Furthermore, if such tasks and models are designed to investigate questions of no concern to clinicians, they have little to contribute to the clinical management and treatment of hyperactive children. This argument assumes that research into the mechanisms of a disorder is fruitless. However, one of the reasons for experimental psychopathology is to understand the mechanisms that are disordered in order to develop models of classification and treatment that are based on substantiative knowledge rather than opinion.

In using cognitive tasks, what can we expect to predict concurrently and in the future from them? Should performance on cognitive tasks be regarded as a snapshot that when placed in a new frame (laboratory vs. school) should be considered an interesting academic datum of no relevance to clinical reality? Similarly, can laboratory, cognitive snapshots of 6- to 8-year-old children inform us in any way of their future adult performance and even risk for psychopathology?

Historically, one area of cognitive psychology, vigilance research, was developed to answer a practical question: why observers faithfully at work were no guarantee that the work performed was optimal. During World War II, radar operators were observed by their officers to monitor their screens. Nevertheless, they failed to detect incoming enemy aircraft and enemy submarines (Drew, 1940; Mackworth, 1950). This led to the development of vigilance measures: sensitivity (d') and response bias ($\beta$) (Mackworth, 1950). This work was the seedbed for the Continuous Performance Task (CPT). The CPT was originally developed for clinical neuropsychological assessment of the brain damaged (Rosvold et al., 1956).

In contrast to these practical requirements, earlier use of performance tasks in clinical psychology was motivated by a more theoretical sense to understand *mental* processes in dysfunctions such as schizophrenia. In the 1940s, the Worcester group (and others) used reaction time tasks to infer the cognitive dysfunctioning of schizophrenics (Cameron, 1939; Garmezy, 1959; Rodnick & Shakow, 1940; Sutton, Hakarem, Zubin, & Portnoy, 1961; Venables & Tizard, 1958). This worked branched into cognitive psychophysiology of clinical disorders (Callaway & Dembo, 1958), cognitive psychopharmacology of hyperactivity (Sprague, Barnes, & Werry, 1970), and cognitive performance of at-risk children (Friedman, Cornblatt, Vaughan, & Erlenmeyer-Kimling, 1986; Nuechterlein, 1983).

Although cognitive tasks have been developed in part to answer practical clinical questions, it is undoubtedly the case that model building has been the forté of experimental psychologists. It is often claimed that such models, because they were developed in the laboratory, are by definition irrelevant for psychopathology. This point does not seem consistent with the general acceptance of psychopharmacological models of psychopathology that were also developed in the laboratory. We emphasize that cognitive models of human information processing have been developed in the laboratory, but the processes that they describe are believed not to be restricted to the laboratory. There is no evidence that memory processes, vigilance, or attentional skills in or out of the laboratory are or should be different. An axiom of cognitive psychology is that cognitive processes, while modifiable according to circumstances, retain the same basic function and address the same brain areas in or out of the laboratory. We offer a rationale for employing attentional models in child psychopathology.

The rationale for using attentional paradigms begins with the fact that both clinical and common experience suggest that hyperactive children are more distractible than control children. DSM-III and DSM-III-R indicate that failures in distraction and sustained attention are symptoms of this disorder. This definition reflected the first phase of attention research in hyperactivity, the output model (concerned only with the measurement of total errors and mean reaction times), in contrast to the second phase of attentional research in hyperactivity, the process model, which is concerned with localizing the energetic-cognitive dysfunction of such children.

In the classic report by Sykes, Douglas, and Morgenstern (1973), a considerable effort was made to define the precise nature of the hypothesized attentional deficit. In the first phase, an output such as the number of errors was considered as a sufficient index of attentional performance. A lower score on the CPT by the hyperactive group compared with the control group was considered in itself sufficient evidence of an *attentional* deficit. The fact that the CPT has been found repeatedly (but not always) to discriminate between hyperactives and controls does offer some validity for the CPT. A more recent manner of tackling the issue of CPT validity has been conducted by Halperin, Newcorn, Sharma, Healey, Wolf, Pascualvaca, and Schwartz (1990). The CPT was administered to a large sample of nonreferred children and teachers, and parents were requested to complete the Conners Parent and Teacher Rating Scales. Although attentional performance was poorer in the hyperactive children, only half of them showed a performance deficit. One interpretation of these findings is that the CPT has questionable validity for assessing hyperactivity. A second interpretation is that there is an "attentional" deficit and an intact group in hyperactives. A third interpretation is that "attentional deficits" will be found mostly in referred clinical samples. Each of these interpretations rests upon the assumption that errors are a sufficient evidence of an "attention deficit."

We have argued on several occasions that the CPT is at best a heterogeneous measure of information processing and that its validity in measuring attention is questionable (van der Meere & Sergeant, 1988a; 1990). A higher or lower score on the CPT indicates a difference between two groups. Due to the multiplicity of processes required in the CPT, it is not possible to state which process is deficient on the basis of only the total number of false positives or false negatives observed between the two groups (see, for extensive discussion, Sergeant & van der Meere, 1990a). Greater vigilance decrement effects have been found when degraded rather than when intact stimuli are used (Nuechterlein, Parasuraman, & Jiang, 1983). In order to adequately interpret the CPT results, one needs to manipulate various task variables that are known to influence its effect and employ sensitive dependent variables (Halperin, et al., 1990). Because the CPT is the product of multiple processes, a correlation between the CPT with an observation variable does not inform us which of the processes employed in the CPT are actually responsible for the correlation.

To be able to have greater insight into the processes employed in the CPT, one needs a model of attention, which explicitly defines what attention is, the varieties of attention and their common information processes, and the type of tasks and variables by which attention can be measured. For this purpose, the second phase of studying cognitive dysfunctioning has been used, the so-called, fast-process approach (Sergeant, 1981).

In the fast-process model of Schneider and Shiffrin (1977) and Shiffrin and Schneider (1977), attention is subdivided into divided, focused, and sustained attention. Attention is defined as a limitation in the rate of controlled processing. It relies upon the assumption that the rate of processing is determined by independent stages of information processing (Sternberg, 1969). This additive factor model has been extended to incorporate energetic variables such as arousal, activation, and effort by Sanders (1983). This is the cognitive-energetic model. A feature of such models is that they are not simple output models. The models describe processes. Until now, discussions concerning the ecological validity of information-processing tasks have centered around output tasks such as the CPT. In the case of the additive-factor-method research, no correlations have been calculated between ratings and processes. Even if correlations were calculated, they would be of less interest because the correlation does not inform us which specific process is disturbed. The contribution of the additive factor method is that it attempts to locate the deficit rather than describe a global dysfunction.

In order to demonstrate the ecological validity of tasks derived from the additive-factor method, we suggest first that when degrees of clinical impairment are varied from low to high not only a task difference between high- and low-impaired subjects would be found but that the impairment would be localized at a specific process.

Second, we have argued that, if an attentional deficit is present in the clinical group and not in another group (hyperactive compared with controls), the difference between the two groups in attentional performance should *increase* with attentional demands. This means that to state that demand effects were present for both groups, both the hyperactive and the control groups should show a performance deterioration as demands increase. Three published studies Sykes et al., 1973; Dykman, Ackerman, & Oglesby, 1979; Seidel & Joschko, 1990) have claimed a sustained attention deficit with this performance characteristic. This contrasts with eight studies reviewed by Sergeant and van der Meere (1990a) that, although there was a sustained attention effect reported, did not find a group-by-block interaction. Furthermore, because the control group did not exhibit a performance decrement with time in the three previously mentioned studies, we argue that these studies employed tasks that exerted insufficient or no attentional demands and are, therefore, inconclusive. When either error rate or speed of processing do not increase with demand, it can be concluded that the task failed to require attentional processing, with the exception of a ceiling effect. In the vast majority of articles published on attentional processing in child psychopathology, and hyperactivity in particular, this premise is seldom put to the test. Consequently, citation of such studies in defense of an attentional-deficit hypothesis is misplaced because these studies are open to multiple interpretations. Equally, CPT studies cannot be used as ammunition to shoot down attentional paradigms as a criterion for evaluating attention in clinical groups because they failed to demonstrate that they measured attention in the first place.

In cognitive research, results from a study can be shown to be ambiguous when there is evidence that rather than simply measuring an attentional process the data are also determined by attentional strategy.

In interpreting, for example, a search task by Dykman et al. (1979), we pointed out that in this task the hyperactive group exhibited a speed-accuracy trade off (Sergeant & van der Meere, 1990a). Similarly, in other work (Sergeant & Scholten, 1985a), an apparent divided attention deficit in a distractible normoactive group had to be rejected because that group showed a tradeoff. These examples illustrate that apparent *process* deficits are in fact strategy or resource effects. This apparent fine tuning of attentional data is important because it rejects claims of *structural* attentional deficits and points to other attentional factors as being better constructs of the hyperactivity deficit.

In the second phase of attentional research in hyperactivity, several advantages may be noted by using paradigms developed in this tradition. The first is that the clinical researcher knows prior to commencing a study with a particular variable or combination of variables what task effects should be observed. If the task does not meet well-replicated findings, the experimental psychopathologist can conclude that the task as used in their laboratory did not meet specifications. A new task can be developed that does meet the paradigm's expectations. This has a clear advantage to the field as a whole: Wild speculation concerning the task is avoided, and the integrative ability of the field as a whole is enhanced. When a task meets paradigm expectations, for example, as shown recently by Zahn, Kruesi, and Rapoport (1991) using the prior preparatory-interval paradigm with boys fulfilling diagnoses in the disruptive behavior, the results can be interpreted within a tradition (Rodnick & Shakow, 1940) and other converging paradigms.

An advantage of the additive-factor model of attention for experimental child psychopathology is that it can indicate the specificity of a finding within the design model. We have indicated, in several articles, the attentional model we use, and only a brief outline is provided here (Sergeant & van der Meere, 1988, 1990a,b, 1991). Briefly, the model contains two levels: a computational level with four stages—encoding, search, decision, and motor organization. These stages are coupled to task variables. For example, in a degradation of stimuli, letters versus words can be placed within a stage referred to as *encoding*. The number of memory comparisons to be made (the task variable load) may be placed in a memory search stage. Decisions concerning targets present or absent occur at the decision stage. Compatible versus incompatible responding may be placed in the motor stage of processing. This provides order to a wide variety of variables. The second level of the model is the energetic level. Sanders (1983) coupled arousal to encoding, activation to motor organization, and effort to both arousal and activation. The terms *arousal, activation,* and *effort* are referred to as "energetic pools" to distinguish them from computational processes. Such a model also indicates which variables measure a process in common or are specific to a particular stage of information processing (Sanders, 1990).

An objection that has been raised against laboratory measures of cognitive processing has been the dissociation of motivation with cognition (Reitman, 1970). Here one argument is that cognitive performance is dependent upon the motivation of the subject. Laboratory tasks are said to bring the subject into a state of overperforming, possibly due to a Hawthorne effect. Another argument has been that the cognitive models that had been developed had no place for motivation. This latter objection is met in Sanders's model by the concept of effort and evaluation. The former argument will be considered below.

## Results Obtained from an Attentional Model Approach

The literature suggesting at what part of the model the hyperactivity deficit is localized was summarized by us recently (Sergeant & van der Meere, 1991). Briefly, there is no evidence of an encoding deficit (Benezra & Douglas, 1988; Borcherding, Thompson, Kruesi, Bartko, Rapoport, & Weingartner, 1981; Sergeant & Scholten, 1985a). It is interesting that psychopharmacological studies have demonstrated that methylphenidate and amphetamine do not have their effect at encoding (Frowein, 1981; Malone, Kershner, & Siegel, 1988; Peeke, Halliday, Callaway, Prael, & Reks, 1984). The central processes of search and decision have been demonstrated repeatedly to be intact in hyperactives (Fitzpatrick, Klorman, Brumaghim, & Keefover, 1988; Peloquin & Klorman, 1986; Sergeant & Scholten, 1983, 1985a; van der Meere & Sergeant, 1987; van der Meere, van Baal, & Sergeant, 1989). This finding has ruled out a divided and a focused attention deficit (van der Meere & Sergeant, 1988b) but has also helped in establishing discriminative validity (see below). In addition, study of central processing has found no support for an increased difficulty in acquisition of automatic processing in hyperactives compared with controls (van der Meere & Sergeant, 1988c). Because the relation or independence of performance with age is obviously relevant in the assessment of children, we will briefly note the relationship between the model and development.

There is evidence that encoding is age related (Maisto & Baumeister, 1975) but the search and decision stages are not (Herrman & Landis, 1977). Of greater importance for the interpretation of information-processing results is the finding that processing strategy and efficiency of the subject is age-dependent (Case, 1978; Chi, 1978). The development of information processing in children seems more to be related to which strategy is used and the efficiency with which a cognitive process can be used rather than the development of the process per se. However, Kail (1988) has found that central processing becomes swifter with development.

For discriminative validity to be justified, an interaction between group(s) and task is required, as argued before. A stronger test of discriminative validity is to demonstrate an interaction in performance between two independent stages with two clinical groups. This test has been performed by several teams with mixed results using the CPT or product approach. Klorman, Brumaghim, Salzman, Strauss, Borgstedt, McBride, and Loeb (1988) found no difference in CPT performance between hyperactives with and without aggressive–noncompliant features. Likewise, two studies, Kupietz and Balka (1978) and Lovejoy and Rasmussen (1990), found little or no relation between the CPT and parent and teacher ratings. On the other hand, O'Dougherty, Nuechterlein, and Drew (1984) were able to distinguish hyperactive from hypoxic children in a CPT. Further, Chee, Logan, Schachar, Lindsay, and Wachsmuth (1989) were able to distinguish children with ICD-9 hyperkinetic syndrome from conduct-disordered children with a CPT. Kupietz (1990) used a CPT and was able to differentiate between hyperactives with and without a learning disability, although he failed to demonstrate a group by time-on-task interaction. Halperin et al. (1990) concluded that hyperactives with manifest poorer performance, compared with those without poor performance on a CPT, were less conduct disordered. Using the process approach, van der Meere et al. (1989) have shown that hyperactives were specifically defective in stimulus–response compatibility, whereas learning-disabled children were defective in memory comparison. This result, in combination with the findings concerning the adequate functioning of the encoding, search, and decision stages, has led us to hypothesize that the locus of the hyperactive dysfunction is to be sought in an output stage or a related energetical pool.

In itself, discriminative validity only becomes interesting when replication, preferably by others, is achieved. The stimulus–response compatibility effect has been replicated in adolescents previously diagnosed as hyperactive by Klorman, Brumaghim, Fitzpatrick, and Borgstedt (1991). Zahn et al. (1991) manipulated response preparation in a mixed group of conduct-disordered and hyperactive boys. They reported that the clinical group had greater difficulty in preparing responses during long preparatory intervals, a finding supporting the motor hypothesis of van der Meere et al. (1989). These authors failed to find an interaction

between modality response mapping and groups. Zahn et al. interpreted this failure as not supporting the motor hypothesis. However,
due to the fact that the authors used a between-group design for
compatible–incompatible, whereas stimulus–response compatibility requires a *within*-subject design, this study actually failed to test the motor
hypothesis. This example indicates an advantage of using a well-defined
attentional model: Task manipulations are specific enough for investigators to compare whether the same or a different process is being measured. This avoids discussion of apparent rather than real differences
between reports. We will now proceed to consider a feature of attentional tasks that we consider essential to research in the area, namely, the
ability to *infer* mental processing in a manner that cannot be derived
from observational studies.

## What Can Attentional Paradigms Tell Us That Observations Do Not?

It is a common observation that when a subject makes an error, the
next time he or she is required to respond, more time is used to process
the information, and therefore the response is slower than what would
usually be required to process the stimulus correctly. Rabbitt and Rogers
(1977) showed that the reaction time following an error was substantially
longer than the time usually required to respond to the same signal but
not following an error. This phenomenon is known as RTE + 1. One
assumption of cognitive paradigms is that the required task behavior
(looking at the display, fingers on the response buttons) be exhibited
before interpreting results in terms of attentional processes. Using observational methods, Sergeant and Scholten (1985a) observed no difference in the off-task behavior of hyperactives compared with distractible
normoactives and control children. The ability to correct an error can be
observed, and at this point there is no difference between ethological
and cognitive measures. The difference between observational and cognitive methodology appears when the difference score of RTE + 1 trials
are studied. Hyperactives can be shown in low-task-demand conditions
to be far slower than controls. In contrast, in high-load demands, RTE +
1 was too fast in hyperactives compared with controls (Sergeant & van
der Meere, 1988). The ability to adjust resource allocation according to
task demands was *inferred* to be restricted in hyperactives. This finding
confirmed an earlier report by Sergeant and Scholten (1985b) in which
the ability to adjust to speed and accuracy instructions was demonstrated to be highly reduced in hyperactives compared with distractible

normoactives and controls. The failure to adequately allocate resources in hyperactives has also been argued by Carlson, Pelham, Swanson, and Wagner (1991).

These findings have led to the question whether the output dysfunction is in fact an energetical dysfunction. Because resource allocation is related to effort and stimulus–response compatibility is coupled to activation (which in turn is coupled to effort), the findings obtained in diverse studies may reflect a deficiency in effort/activation. This inference was put to the test by employing the task-variable event rate. This variable is known to influence the processing state of the organism (Boiten, Sergeant, & Geuze, 1992; Broadbent, 1971; Sergeant, van Winsum, & Geuze, 1987; van Winsum, Sergeant, & Geuze, 1984). Event rate was manipulated in a task with hyperactive and control children by van der Meere, Vreeling, and Sergeant (1992). It was found that hyperactives and controls were in the fast event rate (under influence presumably from arousal) indistinguishable from controls. In a slow event rate (hypothesized as under the influence of activation), both controls and hyperactives had poorer performance, but hyperactives had appreciably more than controls (van der Meere, Gunning, & Stemerding, 1991). These results, in combination with others (Chee et al., 1989; Conte, Kinsbourne, Swanson, Zirk, & Samuels, 1986; Dalby, Kinsbourne, Swanson, & Sobel, 1977), suggest an energetic dysfunction in hyperactivity that is related to output motor processing.

Two lines of evidence would favor the energetic hypothesis. One would be to show that an activating drug such as methylphenidate interacts with motor processing. A second line of evidence would be to show that an apparent sustained attention deficit in a hyperactive group could be modified by using a compensatory energetic variable. With respect to the first, there is evidence that methylphenidate has its locus in motor-output processing (Fitzpatrick et al., 1988). Klorman's group has consistently shown that the locus of the effect of methylphenidate must be at a stage succeeding memory search because an index of stimulus evaluation, the P300, is uninfluenced by methylphenidate, whereas reaction time and errors are modified by this drug (Brumaghim, Klorman, Strauss, Lewine, & Goldstein, 1987; Coons et al., 1981). Additional support can be found in the finding that motor inhibition in hyperactives is poorer than in controls (Schachar & Logan, 1990). Furthermore, methylphenidate improves the inhibition function of hyperactives (Tannoch, Schachar, Carr, Chajczyk, & Logan, 1989).

With respect to the second line of evidence, the disappearance of a time deficit with reinforcement, a recent unpublished study has shown that hyperactives with conduct disorder in a slow, continuous event task can be induced to exhibit a sustained attention deficit that is greater than that shown by controls (van der Meere, Hughes, Broekhaar, & Salee, 1992). When subjects were financially rewarded, the sustained attention deficit disappeared. This suggests that the time-on-task effect is related to energetical factors rather than a process dysfunction.

Other evidence of an energetic dysfunction that is linked to response inhibition stems from the finding that hyperactives with conduct disorder perserverate in a response to a gain reward (Daugherty & Quay, 1991). However, differential reinforcement effects have not been observed between hyperactives and controls in reaction time or delayed reaction time tasks (Firestone & Douglas, 1975; Solanto, 1990). Sonuga-Barke, Taylor, Sembi, and Smith (1992) and Sonuga-Barke, Taylor, and Heptinstall (1992) have shown that hyperactive children were more concerned with reduction of delay levels rather than either maximizing the amount or immediacy of reward. Thus the observed perseveration may reflect possible temporal relations in reward delay rather than the quantity of reinforcement.

Taken together, these findings suggest that an energetic-related dysfunction that is associated with long event rate, temporal timing, and response delay is crucial to the hyperactivity deficit, rather than "attentional" structural processes. These findings suggest to us that an issue that has long been discussed in the vigilance literature, namely, the beneficial/detrimental effects of motivation upon performance and its relation to real-world tasks be reconsidered. Motivation effects have been claimed to explain the time deficit of sustained attention. One argument is that subjects begin a task in a highly motivated state but lose motivation during the task. The opposite argument has been used, when no time deficits have been found in tasks. This is explained as using a too-boring task that elicited little interest in the subject at the beginning of the experiment; thus an initial poor performance at the beginning of a task remains constant throughout the task. In both of these cases, the lack of prediction to real-life tasks has been explained as that real-world tasks are more interesting, and thus no deficit appears, or that the subject can regroup resources by choosing to pause or talk with a colleague, while performing the task. The first two cases are examples of the allocation or lack of resources given to the task. The last argument is precisely the opposite of that found in teacher descriptions of hyperactives: Such children are described as lacking motivation in the classroom. When an adult experimenter provides attention and reward, the performance decay with time does not appear. It was precisely this point that van der Meere and Sergeant (1988a) addressed in a vigilance task—to demonstrate both in hyperactives and controls a time-on-task effect that failed to interact with the difference in group performance. We now address the complementary role of observational methods and experimental cognitive research in the area.

## Observation and Cognitive Paradigms: Complementary Approaches

Although it is evident that observational methods would not have been able to demonstrate many of the findings reported above, simply because gross observational units are not sensitive to processes that have a duration of several hundred msecs, observation can be useful in tandem with cognitive tasks. The number of studies with both methods is sparse. Nevertheless, they indicate some of the advantages to employing both methods.

One may begin by noting that observational methods are an essential feature to information-processing studies in that through observational data, a study can demonstrate that a primary assumption of cognitive research is met, namely, that the child had the required task behavior. If a child is looking away when an imperative signal appears or does not have his or her hands on the switches or has removed the earphones in a dichotic listening task, one can hardly interpret the dependent variables as indices of information processing. Sergeant and Scholten (1983, 1985a) and Sykes, Douglas, Weiss, and Minde (1971) observed hyperactives and found that they were more restless in a second session than in the first in a CPT. Recently, Alberts and van der Meere (1992) used a long CPT and observed hyperactive and control children. Activity tended to be more pronounced in hyperactives than controls, and looking away from the display was observed more frequently in the hyperactives than controls. However, the controls also increased at the same rate as hyperactives in their bodily activity during the course of the task. Thus the decline in cognitive performance reported by van der Meere and Sergeant (1988a) was not due to a differential increase in bodily activity in the hyperactives. Similarly, Alberts and van der Meere reported, as found by Sergeant and Scholten (1985a), that looking away occurred during the period succeeding response emission and the next stimulus. Hence, performance decrement could not be explained as due to inadequate task behavior. As such, these reports are useful in bolstering confidence that the task assumptions were met. However, they can hardly be said to demonstrate the ecological validity of such tasks with hyperactive children.

If one means by ecological validity that a task has to be performed in real-life conditions, the only study to our knowledge that meets this requirement is one performed by Vaessen (1988). Vaessen employed two tasks. Both tasks were based on dual-task methodology (Wickens, 1984). Vaessen used, for his first experiment, a balance beam and required the children to perform a choice reaction time. The results of this experiment (which was conducted in the laboratory) showed that hyperactives were slower walking along the balance beam than controls while performing the reaction-time task. A second task was used in which the children were placed in a traffic situation. The experiment was conducted on a road with medium to high traffic density (400 to 700 vehicles per hour). The child was required to cross a distance of 9 meters from one curb to another. The second curb was actually 4 meters away from the actual road. The child, however, could see the actual traffic at all times. The child was instructed to cross the 9-meter road in the same manner and at the same speed as the road on which the traffic was traveling. While observing the oncoming traffic, the children were required to memorize a set of digits and to detect a traffic gap at which it was safe to cross the road (Lee, Young, & McLaughlin, 1984). When the children reached the other side of the road, they were required to repeat the digits that they had been instructed to memorize. Vaessen found that hyperactives showed the greater variance in crossing time compared with control children. Further, he found that as the number of digits to be recalled increased, traffic performance of the hyperactive group significantly deteriorated compared with controls. These results suggest that the information-processing restrictions of hyperactives is not restricted to the laboratory and can be found in ecologically valid circumstances. Although this study is singular in its nature, it concurs with longitudinal follow-up reports of hyperactives being more prone to traffic accidents as adults (Weiss, Hechtman, Perlman, Hopkins, & Wener, 1979). This raises the issue of the predictive validity of information-processing tasks for hyperactive children as adults.

## Concluding Remarks

The enrichment of child psychopathology through well-controlled follow-up studies, has been seen in recent years. Schachar (1991) concluded that the results of these studies indicate that the diagnosis of hyperactivity is a strong predictor of adult outcome. In contrast to earlier opinion, the primary symptoms of overactivity, inattention, and impulsivity are stable, suggesting that they may be traitlike features. Clearly, it is desirable to be able to predict outcome for hyperactive children. To achieve this goal, two complications require solution. First, the high association of hyperactivity with conduct disorder and the failure (or impossibility) to distinguish between the two disorders make it difficult to assess whether the follow-up is more of the one than the other (Szatmari, Offord, Siegel et al. 1990). In addition, the persistence or development of socially inappropriate behavior of conduct-disordered children (Lahey, Loeber, & Thomas, 1991) suggests transitions in the phenomenon that is being studied. These transitions need not be entirely situational or be statelike factors but reflect changes with persistence over several years. Consequently, sampling such behavior to evaluate current functioning and assessing the predictive performance of a test or questionnaire will be dependent upon the time at which the sampling is conducted in the development of the disorder. This raises the question of whether it is possible to evaluate at a particular point in the pathological process the predictive power of the instrument because it is not clear at what point in the process the hyperactive is currently. To answer this, life-time follow-up is required. Here again the methodological issue (already present in the available follow-up studies) can be raised of whether one may extrapolate from a follow-up cohort to the general sample of hyperactives.

A second issue concerning follow-up cohorts is the fact that outcome is currently thought to be related to the predisposing familial factors, although an association with cognitive deficits remains (see, for review, Rutter, 1989). Poor familial relations, maternal deprivation, parental divorce, and paternal antisocial behavior are factors cited to influence outcome (Schachar, 1990). In addition to temperamental factors, follow-up research has shown that the degree of hyperactivity (and thus potential risk) is associated with dysfunction in attentional tasks (Taylor, Sandberg, & Thorley, 1991). Both the Dunedin and Quebec studies have indicated that there is an association between both hyperactivity and reading difficulties (Anderson, Williams, McGee, & Silva, 1989; Boudreault, Thivierge, Cote, Julien, Boutin, & Bergson, 1988; McGee & Share, 1988). Hyperactives followed up at adolescence have been found to be poorer than controls on a CPT (Fischer, Barkley, Edelbrook, & Smallish, 1990). Follow-up research has shown that hyperactives in adulthood may predisposed to accidents that may be associated with the style of information processing (Weiss, Hechtman, Perlmann, Hopkins, & Wenner, 1979). Klorman's group have found in a laboratory study that young adults diagnosed in childhood as hyperactive show motor-related deficits of information processing in adulthood (Fitzpatrick et al., 1988). These findings are suggestive (and only that) of a continued involvement of information processing (or style) in the adult hyperactive. It is our belief that information-processing measures will have only modest explanatory power and should be considered as only one of several indicators of adult dysfunctioning.

From the foregoing, we conclude with Rose (1976) that it is to be expected that there will be differences in findings between the levels of psychological inquiry. If human behavior could be translated from one level to another on a one-to-one basis, observation would be sufficient for science because what we see would indeed be what we get. Unfortunately (but what is more interesting), the systems of human behavior—subjective ratings, performance tasks, and psychophysiology, are, as Lang suggested, "loosely coupled" systems. Loosely coupled systems give rise to concordance at some times and situations but also to discordance in others.

Low correlation between two levels of study is not in itself a fatal blow to the validity of either level. Both can express a valid finding; they are merely uncoupled. Therefore, search for high correlations between levels is not necessarily the best approach to achieving ecological or any other form of validity. We suspect that when dynamic and fluctuating systems are being studied, correlations at a specific point in time will perhaps say something about that particular point but little about the nature of the process itself. This would mean that research that shows low to modest correlations at a particular point in time would take on a greater scientific significance than the size of their correlation. To achieve this purpose, research using time-series methods is required (van Geert, 1991). We believe that by applying a well-defined model of cognitive processing to hyperactivity not only will the hypothetico–deductive process be enhanced, but clear indications will be given of inadmissible findings. Furthermore, a well-defined model will enable deficit(s) to be localized and, in some cases, confirmed by using convergent measures. On this basis, we believe a sound empirical taxonomy of childhood psychopathology can be developed. At this stage of inquiry, one might prefer replication of findings as a standard, such as noted by Quay (1986) in his review of 60 factorial studies, rather than the mirages of human observation.

# References

Alberts, E., & van der Meere, J. J. (1992). Observations of hyperactive behaviour during vigilance. *Journal of Child Psychology and Psychiatry, 33*, 1355–1364.

Anderson, D. R. & Levin, S. R. (1976). Young children's attention to "Sesame Street." *Child Development, 47*, 806–811.

Anderson, J. C., Williams, S., McGee, R., & Silva, P. A. (1989). DSM-III disorders in preadolescent children: Prevalence in a large sample from the general population. *Archives of General Psychiatry, 44,* 69–76.

Atkins, M. S., Pelham, W. E., & Licht, M. H. (1989). The differential validity of teacher ratings of inattention/overactivity and aggression. *Journal of Abnormal Child Psychology, 17,* 423–436.

Barkley, R. A. (1991). The ecological validity of laboratory and analogue assessment methods of ADHD symptoms. *Journal of Abnormal Child Psychology, 19,* 149–178.

Barkley, R. A. & Ullman, D. G. (1975). A comparison of objective measures of activity and distractibility in hyperactive and nonhyperactive children. *Journal of Abnormal Child Psychology, 3,* 231–244.

Benezra, E., & Douglas, V. I. (1988). Short term serial recall in ADDH, normal, and reading disabled boys. *Journal of Abnormal Child Psychology, 16,* 511–526.

Boiten, F., Sergeant, J. A., & Geuze, R. (1992). Event-related desynchronization: The effects of energetic and computational demands. *Electroencephalography & Clinical Neurophysiology, 82,* 302–309.

Borcherding, B., Thompson, K., Kruesi, M., Bartko, J., Rapoport, J. L., & Weingartner, H. (1981). Automatic and effortful processing in attention deficit hyperactivity disorder. *Journal of Abnormal Child Psychology, 16,* 333–346.

Boudreault, M., Thivierge, J., Cote, R., Boutin, Y., Julien, Y., & Bergson, S. (1988). Cognitive development and reading achievement in pervasive-ADD and control children. *Journal of Child Psychology and Psychiatry, 29,* 611–619.

Broadbent, D. E. (1971). *Decision and stress.* New York: Academic Press.

Brumaghim, J. T., Klorman, R., Strauss, J., Lewine, J. D., & Goldstein, M. G. (1987). Does methylphenidate affect information processing? Findings from two studies on performance and P300 latency. *Psychophysiology, 24,* 361–373.

Callaway, E., and Dembo, R. (1958). Narrowed attention: A psychological phenomenon that accompanies a certain physiological change. *Archives of Neurology and Psychiatry, 79,* 74–90.

Cameron, N. (1939). Schizophrenic thinking in a problem-solving situation. *Journal of Mental Science, 85,* 1012–1035.

Carlson, C. L., Pelham, W. E., Swanson, J., & Wagner, J. L. (1991). A divided attention analysis of the effects of methylphenidate on the arithmetic performance of children with attention-deficit hyperactivity disorder. *Journal of Child Psychology and Psychiatry, 32,* 463–472.

Case, R. (1978). Intellectual development from birth to adulthood: A neo-Piagetian interpretation. In R. S. Siegler (Ed.), *Children's thinking: What develops?* Hillsdale, NJ: Lawrence Erlbaum Associates.

Chee, P., Logan, G., Schachar, R., Lindsay, P., & Wachsmuth, R. (1989). Effects of event rate and display time on sustained attention in hyperactive, normal and control children. *Journal of Abnormal Child Psychology, 17,* 371–391.

Chi, M. P. H. (1978). Age differences in speed of processing. *Developmental Psychology, 13,* 543–544.

Conte, R., Kinsbourne, M., Swanson, J., Zirk, H., & Samuels, M. (1986). Presentation rate effects on paired associate learning by attention deficit disordered children. *Child Development, 57,* 681–687.

Coons, H. W., Peloquin, L. J., Klorman, R., Bauer, L. O., Ryan, R. M., Perlmutter, R. A., & Salzman, L. F. (1981). Effects of methylphenidate on young adults vigilance and event-related potentials. *Electroencephalography and Clinical Neurophysiology, 51,* 373–387.

Dalby, J. I., Kinsbourne, M., Swanson, J. M., & Sobel, M. P. (1977). Hyperactive children's underuse of learning time: Correction by stimulant treatment. *Child Development, 48,* 1448–1453.

Daugherty, T. K., & Quay, H. C. (1991). Response pervasiveness and delayed responding in childhood behavior disorders. *Journal of Child Psychology and Psychiatry, 32,* 453–461.

Dienske, H. & Sanders-Woustra, J. M. R. (1988). A critical and conceptual consideration of attention deficit and hyperactivity from an ethological point of view. In L. F. Bloomingdale & J. Sergeant (Eds.), *Attention Deficit Disorder V* (pp. 43–64). Oxford: Pergamon Press.

Draeger, S., Prior, M., & Sanson, A. (1985). Visual and auditory performance in hyperactive children: Competence or compliance? *Journal of Abnormal Child Psychology, 14,* 411–424.

Drew, G. C. (1940). An experimental study of mental fatigue. Air Ministry. FPRC/227. London.

Dunn, L. M., & Markwardt, F. C. (1988). *Peabody Individual Achievement Test-Revised* Circle Pines, MN: American Guidance Service.

Dykman, R. A., Ackerman, P. T., & Oglesby, D. M. (1979). Selective and sustained attention in hyperactive learning disabled and normal boys. *Journal of Nervous and Mental Disease, 167,* 228–297.

Fenz, W., & Epstein, S. (1967). Gradients of physiological arousal in parachutists. *Psychosomatic Medicine, 29,* 33–51.

Firestone, P., & Douglas, V. I. (1975). The effects of reward and punishment on reaction times and autonomic activity in hyperactive and normal children. *Journal of Abnormal Child Psychology, 3,* 201–215.

Fischer, M., Barkley, R. A., Edelbrook, C. S., & Smallish, L. (1990). The adolescent outcome of hyperactive children diagnosed by research criteria: II. Academic, attentional and neuropsychological status. *Journal of Consulting and Clinical Psychology, 58,* 580–588.

Fitzpatrick, P., Klorman, R., Brumaghim, J. T., & Keefover, R. W. (1988). Effects of methylphenidate on stimulus evaluation and response processes: Evidence from performance and event-related potentials. *Psychophysiology, 25,* 292–304.

Friedman, D., Cornblatt, B., Vaughan, H., & Erlenmeyer-Kimling, L. (1986). Event-related potentials in children at risk for schizophrenia during two versions of the continuous performance test. *Psychiatric Research, 18,* 161–177.

Frijda, N. F. (1986). *The emotions.* Cambridge: Cambridge University Press.

Frowein, H. W. (1981). *Selective drug effects on information processing.* Enschede: Sneldruk Boulevard.

Garmezy, N. (1959). Stimulus differentiation by schizophrenic and normal subjects under conditions of reward and punishment. *Journal of Personality, 20,* 253–276.

Halperin, J. M., Newcorn, J. J., Sharma, V., Healey, J. M., Wolf, L. E., Pascualvaca, D. M., & Schwartz, S. (1990). Inattentive and nonattentive ADHD children: Do they constitute a unitary group. *Journal Abnormal Child Psychology, 18,* 437–449.

Herrman, D. J., & Landis, T. Y. (1977). Differences in search rate of children and adults in short term memory. *Journal of Experimental Child Psychology, 22,* 151–161.

Hutt, C., Hutt, S. J., & Ounsted, C. (1963). The behaviour of children with and without upper CNS lesions. *Behaviour, 24,* 246–268.

Kail, R. (1988). Developmental functions for speeds of cognitive processes. *Journal of Experimental Psychology, 45,* 339–364.

Kálverboer, A. F. (1978). MBD: Discussion of the concept. In A. F. Kalverboer, H. M. van Praag, & J. Mendelwicz (Eds), *Minimal brain dysfunction: Fact or fiction.* Basel: Karger.

Kaufman, A. S. *Intelligent testing with the WISC-R*. New York: Wiley Interscience.

Klorman, R., Brumaghim, J. T., Fitzpatrick, P. A., & Borgstedt, A. D. (1991). Methylphenidate speeds evaluation processes of attention-deficit disorder during a continuous performance test. *Journal of Abnormal Psychology, 19*, 263–284.

Klorman, R., Brumaghim, J. L., Salzman, L. F., Strauss, J., Borgstedt, A. D., McBride, M. C., & Loeb, S. (1988). *Journal of Abnormal Child Psychology, 16*, 413–422.

Kupietz, S. S., & Balka, E. B. (1978). Alterations in the vigilance performance of children receiving amitriptyline and methylphenidate placebo therapy. *Psychopharmacology, 50*, 29–33.

Kupietz, S. S. (1990). Sustained attention in normal and in reading-disabled youngsters with and without ADDH. *Journal of Abnormal Child Psychology, 18*, 357–372.

Lahey, B. B., Shaughency, E. A., Strauss, C. C., & Frame, C. L. (1984). Are attention deficit disorders with and without hyperactivity similar or dissimilar disorders? *Journal of the American Academy of Child Psychiatry, 23*, 302–309.

Lahey, B. B., Loeber, R., & Thomas, C. (1991). Diagnostic conundrum of oppositional defiant disorder and conduct disorder. *Journal of Abnormal Psychology, 100*, 379–390.

Lang, P. (1970). Stimulus control, response control and desensitization of fear. In D. Levis (Ed.), *Learning approaches to therapeutic behavior change*. Chicago: Aldine Press.

Lee, D. N., Young, D. S., & McLaughlin, C. M. (1984). A roadside simulation of road crossing for children. *Ergonomics, 27*, 1271–1281.

Lovejoy, M. C., & Rasmussen, N. H. (1990). The validity of vigilance tasks in differential diagnosis of children referred for attention and learning problems. *Journal of Abnormal Child Psychology, 18*, 671–682.

Mackworth, N. H. (1950). Researches on the measurement of human performance. MRC special report No. 268. Reprinted in H. W. Sinaiko (Ed.), *Selected papers on human factors in the design and use of control systems*. New York: Dover, 1961.

Maisto, A. A., & Baumeister, A. A. (1975). A developmental study of choice reaction time: The effects of two forms of stimulus degradation on encoding. *Journal of Experimental Child Psychology, 20*, 456–464.

Malone, M. A., Kershner, J. R., & Siegel, L. (1988). The effects of methylphenidate on levels of processing and laternality in children with attention deficit disorder. *Journal of Abnormal Child Psychology, 16*, 379–396.

Margalit, M. (1983). Diagnostic application of the Conners Abbreviated Symptom Questionnaire. *Journal of Clinical Child Psychology, 12*, 355–357.

Mattison, R. E., Bagnato, S. J., & Strickler, E. (1987). Diagnostic importance of combined parent and teacher ratings on the Revised Behavior Problem Checklist. *Journal of Abnormal Child Psychology, 15*, 617–628.

McGee, R., & Share, D. (1988). Attention-deficit disorder-hyperactivity and academic failure: Which comes first and what should be treated? *Journal of American Academy Child and Adolescent Psychiatry, 27*, 318–325.

Milich, R., Loney, J., & Landau, S. (1982). Independent dimensions of hyperactivity and aggression: A validation with playroom observation data. *Journal of Abnormal Psychology, 91*, 183–198.

Milich, R., & Fitzgerald, G. (1985). Validation of inattention/overactivity and aggression ratings with classroom observations. *Journal of Consulting and Clinical Psychology, 53*, 139–140.

Nuechterlein, K. (1983). Signal detection in vigilance tasks and behavioral attributes among offspring of schizophrenic mothers and among hyperactive children. *Journal of Abnormal Psychology, 92*, 4–28.

Nuechterlein, K., Parasuraman, R., & Jiang, Q. (1983). Visual and sustained attention: Image degradation produces rapid sensitivity decrement over time. *Science, 220,* 327–329.

O'Dougherty, M., Nuechterlein, K. H., & Drew, B. (1984). Hyperactive and hypoxic children: Signal detection, sustained attention, and behavior. *Journal of Abnormal Psychology, 93,* 178–191.

Ounsted, C. (1955). The hyperkinetic syndrome in epileptic children. *Lancet, 2,* 303–311.

Peeke, S. Halliday, R., Callaway, E., Prael, R., & Reks, V. (1984). Effects of two doses of methylphenidate on verbal information processing in hyperactive children. *Journal of Clinical Psychopharmacology, 4,* 82–88.

Peloquin, L. J., & Klorman, R. (1986). Effects of methylphenidate on normal children's mood, event-related potentials, and performance in memory scanning and vigilance. *Journal of Abnormal Psychology, 95,* 88–98.

Quay, H. C. (1986). Classification. In H. C. Quay & J. S. Werry (Eds.), *Psychopathological disorders in childhood* (3rd ed., pp 1–34). New York: Wiley.

Quay, H. C. (1988). Attention deficit disorder and the behavioural inhibition system: The relevance of the neuropsychological theory of Jeffrey A. Gray. In L. M. Bloomingdale & J. Sergeant (Eds.), *Attention Deficit Disorder V: Criteria, cognition, intervention* (pp. 117–126). Oxford: Pergamon Press.

Rabbitt, P. M. A., & Rogers, B. (1977). What does a man do after he makes an error: An analysis of response programming. *Quarterly Journal of Experimental Psychology, 29,* 727–743.

Rapoport, J. L., & Benoit, M. (1975). The relation of direct home observations to the clinic evaluation of school age boys. *Journal of Child Psychology and Psychiatry, 16,* 141–147.

Reitman, J. S. (1970). Computer simulation of an information-processing model of short-term memory. In D. E. Norman (Ed.), *Models of human memory* (pp. 117–148). London: Academic Press.

Rodnick, E. H., & Shakow, D. (1940). Set in the schizophrenic as measured by a composite reaction time index. *American Journal of Psychiatry, 97,* 214–225.

Rose, S. (1976). *The conscious brain.* London: Penguin.

Rosvold, H. E., Mirsky, A. F., Sarason, I., Bransome, E. D., & Beck, L. H. (1956). A continuous performance test of brain damage. *Journal of Consulting Psychology, 20,* 343–350.

Routh, D. K., & Schroeder, C. S. (1976). Standardized playroom measures as indices of hyperactivity. *Journal Abnormal Child Psychology, 4,* 199–207.

Rutter, M. (1989). Isle of Wight revisited: Twenty five years of child psychiatric epidemiology. *Journal of American Academy Child and Adolescent Psychiatry, 28,* 633–653.

Sanders, A. F. (1983). Towards a model of stress and performance. *Acta Psychologica, 53,* 61–97.

Sanders, A. F. (1990). Issues and trends in the debate on discrete versus continuous processing of information. *Acta Psychologica, 74,* 123–167.

Sandberg, S. T., Rutter, M., & Taylor, E. (1978). Hyperkinetic disorder in psychiatric clinic attenders. *Developmental Medicine and Child Neurology, 20,* 279–299.

Satterfield, J. H., & Dawson, M. E. (1971). Electrodermal correlates of hyperactivity in children. *Psychophysiology, 8,* 191–197.

Schachar, R., Rutter, M., & Smith A. (1981). The characteristics of situationally and pervasively hyperactive children: Implications for syndrome definition. *Journal of Child Psychology & Psychiatry, 22,* 375–392.

Schachar, R. (1991). Childhood hyperactivity. *Journal of Child Psychology & Psychiatry, 32,* 155–192.

Schachar, R., & Logan, G. D. (1990). Impulsivity and inhibitory control in normal development and childhood psychopathology. *Developmental Psychology, 26,* 710–720.

Schneider, W., & Shiffrin, R. M. (1977). Controlled and automatic human information processing: I. *Psychological Review, 84,* 1–66.

Schonfeld, J. S., Shaffer, D., O'Connor, P., & Portnoy, S. (1988). Conduct disorder and cognitive functioning: Testing three causal hypotheses. *Child Development, 59,* 993–1007.

Seidel, W. T., & Joschko, M. (1989). Evidence of difficulties in sustained attention in children with ADDH, *Journal of Abnormal Child Psychology, 18,* 217–229.

Sergeant, J. A. (1981). *Attentional studies in hyperactivity.* Groningen: Veenstra.

Sergeant, J. A. (1988). RDC for hyperactivity. In L. M. Bloomingdale & J. Sergeant (Eds.), *Attention Deficit Disorder V* (pp. 1–7). Oxford: Pergamon.

Sergeant, J. A., & Scholten, C. A. (1983). A stages-of-information processing approach to hyperactivity. *Journal of Child Psychology and Psychiatry, 22,* 49–60.

Sergeant, J. A., & Scholten, C. A. (1985a). On data limitations in hyperactivity. *Journal of Child Psychology and Psychiatry, 26,* 111–124.

Sergeant, J. A., & Scholten, C. A. (1985b). On resource strategy limitations in hyperactivity: Cognitive impulsivity reconsidered. *Journal of Child Psychology and Psychiatry, 26,* 97–109.

Sergeant, J. A., & van der Meere, J. J. (1988). What happens after a hyperactive commits an error? *Psychiatry Research, 28,* 157–164.

Sergeant, J. A., & van der Meere, J. J. (1990a). Convergence of approaches in localizing the hyperactivity deficit. In B. B. Lahey & A. E. Kazdin (Eds.), *Advances in clinical child psychology,* (Vol. 13, pp. 207–245).

Sergeant, J. A., & van der Meere, J. J. (1990b). Additive factor methodology applied to psychopathology with special reference to hyperactivity. *Acta Psychologica, 74,* 277–295.

Sergeant, J. A., & van der Meere, J. J. (1991). Ritalin effects and information processing in hyperactivity. In L. L. Greenhill & B. B. Osman (Eds.), *Ritalin: Theory and patient management,* (pp. 1–14). New York: Mat Ann Liebert, Inc.

Sergeant, J. A., van Winsum, W., & Geuze, R. (1987). Event-related desynchronization and P300. *Psychophysiology, 24,* 272–277.

Shiffrin, R. M., & Schneider, W. (1977). Controlled and automatic human information processing: II. Perceptual learning, automatic attending, and a general theory. *Psychological Review, 84,* 127–190.

Solanto, M. (1990). The effects of reinforcement and response-cost on a delayed response task in children with attention deficit hyperactivity disorder: A research note. *Journal of Child Psychology & Psychiatry, 31,* 803–808.

Sonuga-Barke, E. J. S., Taylor, E., & Heptinstall, E. (1992). Hyperactivity and delay aversion—I. The effect of delay choice. *Journal of Child Psychology & Psychiatry, 33,* 387–398.

Sonuga-Barke, E. J. S., Taylor, E., Sembi, S., & Smith, J. (1992). *Journal of Child Psychology & Psychiatry, 33,* 399–410.

Sprague, R. L., Barnes, K. R., & Werry, J. (1970). Methylphenidate and thioridazine: Learning, reaction time, activity and classroom behavior in disturbed children. *American Journal of Orthopsychiatry, 40,* 615–628.

Sternberg, S. (1969). Discovery of processing stages: Extensions of Donders' method. In

W. G. Koster (Ed.), *Attention and performance* II (pp. 276–315). Amsterdam: North-Holland.

Sutton, S., Hakarem, G., Zubin, J., & Portnoy, M. (1961). The effect of shift of sensory modality on serial reaction time: A comparison of schizophrenics and normals. *American Journal of Psychology, 74,* 224–232.

Sykes, D. H., Douglas, V. I., Weiss, G., & Minde, K. K. (1971). Attention in hyperactive children and the effect of methylphenidate (Ritalin). *Journal of Child Psychology and Psychiatry, 12,* 129–139.

Sykes, D. H., Douglas, V. I., & Morgenstern, G. (1973). *Journal of Child Psychology and Psychiatry, 14,* 213–220.

Szatmari, P., Offord, D. R., Siegel, L. S., Finlayson, M. A. J., & Tuff, L. (1990). The clinical significance of neurocognitive impairments among children with psychiatric disorders: Diagnosis and situational specificity. *Journal of Child Psychology and Psychiatry, 31,* 287–299.

Tannock, R., Schachar, R., Carr, R. P., Chajczyk, D., & Logan, G. D. (1989). Effects of methylphenidate on hibitory control in hyperactive children. *Journal Abnormal Child Psychology, 17,* 473–491.

Taylor, E. A., Sandberg, S., & Thorley, G. (1991). *The epidemiology of childhood hyperactivity.* Oxford: Oxford University Press.

Vaessen, W. (1988). *Ecological validity of hyperactivity studies.* Thesis, University of Groningen: University Press.

van Geert, P. (1991). A dynamic systems model of cognitive and language growth. *Psychological Review, 98,* 3–53.

van der Meere, J. J. (1988). *Attention deficit disorder with hyperactivity: A misconception.* Groningen: University Press.

van der Meere, J. J., & Sergeant, J. A. (1987). A divided attention experiment in pervasively hyperactive children. *Journal of Abnormal Child Psychology, 16,* 379–391.

van der Meere, J. J., & Sergeant, J. A. (1988a). Controlled processing and vigilance in hyperactivity: Time will tell. *Journal Abnormal Child Psychology, 16,* 641–655.

van der Meere, J. J., & Sergeant, J. A. (1988b). A focused attention experiment in pervasively hyperactive children. *Journal of Abnormal Child Psychology, 16,* 627–639.

van der Meere, J. J., & Sergeant, J. A. (1988c). Acquisition of attentional skill in pervasively hyperactive children. *Journal of Child Psychology and Psychiatry, 29,* 301–310.

van der Meere, J. J., van Baal, M., & Sergeant, J. A. (1989). The additive factor method: A differential diagnostic tool in hyperactivity and learning disablement. *Journal of Abnormal Child Psychology, 17,* 409–422.

van der Meere, J. J., Wekking, E., & Sergeant, J. A. (1990). Sustained attention and pervasive hyperactivity. *Journal of Child Psychology and Psychiatry, 32,* 275–284.

van der Meere, J. J., Vreeling, H. J., & Sergeant, J. A. (1992). A motor presetting study in hyperactives, learning disabled and control children. *Journal of Child Psychology and Psychiatry, 34,* 1347–1354.

van der Meere, J. J., Gunning, B., & Stemerding, N. (1991). Two impulsivity studies in ADHD children with and without ticks. Paper presented to the Society for Research in Child and Adolescent Psychopathology, Zandvoort, The Netherlands, June.

van der Meere, J. J., Hughes, K. A., Broekhaar, G., & Salee, R. (1992). The effect of payment on sustained attention in ADHD children with and without conduct disorder. Paper presented to the Society for Research in Child and Adolescent Psychopathology, Santa Fe, NM, February.

van Winsum, W., Sergeant, J. A., & Geuze, R. (1984). The functional significance of event related desynchronization of alpha rhythm in attentional and activating tasks. *Electro-encephalography & Clinical Neurophysiology, 58,* 519–524.

Venables, P. H., & Tizard, J. (1958). The effect of auditory stimulus intensity on the reaction time of schizophrenics. *Journal of Mental Science, 104,* 1160–1164.

Weiss, G., Hechtman, L., Perlman, T., Hopkins, J., & Wener, A. (1979). Hyperactives as young adults: A controlled prospective follow-up of 75 children. *Archives of General Psychiatry, 36,* 675–681.

Wickens, C. D. (1984). *Engineering psychology and human performance* Columbus: Merril.

Wiener, A. L. (1987). Application of vigilance research: Rare, medium, well-done? *Human Factors, 29,* 725–736.

Zahn, T., Kruesi, M. J. P., & Rapoport, J. L. (1991). Reaction time indices of attention deficits in boys with disruptive behavior disorders. *Journal of Abnormal Child Psychology, 19,* 233–252.

# Combining Visual and Auditory Tasks in the Assessment of Attention-Deficit Hyperactivity Disorder

## STEVEN K. SHAPIRO and LEAH A. HEROD

### Introduction

Attention-deficit hyperactivity disorder (ADHD) is the diagnostic label in the *Diagnostic and Statistical Manual of Mental Disorders* (3rd ed., revised) (DSM-III-R) (American Psychiatric Association, 1987) that is characterized by developmentally inappropriate hyperactivity, impulsivity, and inattention. Although empirical research has provided various suggestions regarding possible etiology, appropriate assessment practices, and relatively effective intervention strategies, considerable controversy still exists. Changes in diagnostic labels and conceptualization of core symptoms, as well as the use of inconsistent criteria to select subjects, have impinged on establishing the validity of various aspects of ADHD. According to Rutter (1989, p. 20), "we are not yet at a stage where there can be consensus on precisely how this concept should be operationalized, nor do we adequately understand the mechanisms in-

STEVEN K. SHAPIRO and LEAH A. HEROD • Department of Psychology, Auburn University, Auburn, Alabama 36849-5214.

*Disruptive Behavior Disorders in Childhood*, edited by Donald K. Routh. Plenum Press, New York, 1994.

volved." The development of reliable and valid assessment techniques has been of particular interest to clinical researchers in an attempt to go beyond the criteria established in DSM-III-R and to utilize a multi-method psychometric approach. Thus, research has continued to delineate laboratory-based assessment strategies that possess concurrent, predictive, and ecological validity, the latter referring to the degree to which the test results are representative of "real-world" behavior (Barkley, 1991). The purpose of this chapter is to summarize recent lines of research focusing on ADHD and its relationship with Central Auditory Processing Disorder (CAPD) and to provide preliminary information on the utility of several standardized clinic-based visual and auditory tasks.

## Primary Features of ADHD

Symptoms that now characterize ADHD are many of the same symptoms that represented previous related diagnostic categories such as Minimal Brain Dysfunction, Hyperkinesis, and Attention Deficit Disorder with or without Hyperactivity (Barkley, 1990b; Pelham, 1986; Ross & Ross, 1982; Silver, 1990). Work conducted by Douglas (1972) and her colleagues was instrumental in the criteria set forth in DSM-III (APA, 1980), which distinguished between two subtypes of attention deficits (ADD) based on the presence of absence of hyperactivity (ADDH or ADDWO, respectively). DSM-III-R (APA, 1987) does not formally recognize this distinction but includes two disorders referred to as ADHD and undifferentiated attention-deficit disorder (UADD). Reviews of the literature, however, provide support for the ADDH versus ADDWO distinction (Cantwell & Baker, 1992; Goodyear & Hynd, 1992; Lahey & Carlson, 1991).

The symptoms that are repeatedly used to describe and diagnose ADHD are inattention, impulsivity, and hyperactivity. The latter two descriptors appear to best distinguish ADHD and other psychiatric disorders in children (Barkley, 1990a,b), although a diagnosis of ADHD can result without the presence of all three symptoms. *Inattention* may involve difficulty in perceiving, processing, and acting on information in an organized manner (Dienske & Sanders-Woodstra, 1985). Work by Posner and his colleagues have attempted to provide more specific information regarding components of attention and related neural systems (Posner, 1988; Posner & Peterson, 1990). *Impulsivity* refers to a failure to inhibit responses according to situational demands, particularly when the rapidity or suddenness of the behavior is inappropriate for the given context (Barkley, 1990b; Milich & Kramer, 1985; Sergeant & van der

Meere, 1989). *Hyperactivity* is viewed as excessive motor activity that is not situation dependent, is deemed inappropriate in certain situations, and is presumably due to physiological composition rather than anxiety (Ross & Ross, 1982; Silver, 1990). The evaluation of ADHD has employed various standardized behavior rating scales, direct observational procedures, monitoring devices, clinical interviews, psychological and laboratory tests, and medical examinations. Reviews of available procedures and instruments are provided by Barkley (1990b) and Schachar (1991).

## Selected Associated Characteristics of ADHD

### Processing Speed

Results from various studies suggest that compared to non-ADHD subjects, ADHD children perform differently on tasks involving speed. ADDWO children have demonstrated slower perceptual motor speed compared to ADDH and control children (Barkley, DuPaul, & McMurray, 1990). Both ADDWO and ADDH children have shown poorer performance on visual and auditory sequential memory tasks (Frank & Ben-Nun, 1988) and slower performance on high-speed visual-search tasks (Sergeant & Scholten, 1983). Hyperactivity has been associated with slower and more variable task performance involving visual classification (Hynd, Nieves, Connor, Stone, Town, Becker, Lahey, & Lorys, 1989), memory recognition (van der Meere & Sergeant, 1988a), auditory memory search (Sergeant & Scholten, 1983) and reaction time to auditory stimuli (Prior, Sanson, Freethy, & Geffen, 1985). However, on tasks measuring speed of writing and naming, the performance of ADDH children has not significantly differed from control children (Ackerman, Anhalt, Holcomb, & Dykman, 1986). Taken together, these results suggest that ADHD children may exhibit a deficit in their speed of cognitive information processing.

### Speech and Language

Children with ADHD appear prone to speech and language problems. For example, Baker and Cantwell (1987a,b) reported that in a sample of 600 children with identified speech–language impairment, 19% were diagnosed as ADDH, whereas 7% were diagnosed as learning disabled (LD). Of 300 children who were followed up 4 to 5 years, 30% were LD; of these LD children, over half met criteria for ADHD (Cantwell & Baker, 1991). Other studies investigating the incidence of LD in

ADHD samples have found concurrence rates ranging from 10% to 92% (see Riccio, González, & Hynd, in press; Riccio & Hynd, 1994b), although methodological differences can partially account for the variability reflected in these findings.

## Introduction to Central Auditory Processing Disorder

An area that is related to speech and language is that of central auditory processing, which refers to the process by which auditory signals are translated into meaningful stimuli by the brain and central nervous system (Lasky & Katz, 1983). Certain auditory abilities are presumed to be necessary for auditory comprehension and subsequent language learning. Individuals who are unable to receive and process information will have comprehension difficulties and thus, integration with expressive abilities is unlikely (Matkin & Hook, 1983). The American Speech-Language-Hearing Association (ASHA, 1992) has defined Central Auditory Processing Disorder (CAPD) as a processing deficit of audible signals that cannot be attributed to impaired peripheral hearing sensitivity or intellectual impairment in which there are "limitations in the ongoing transmission, analysis, organization, transformation, elaboration, storage, retrieval, and use of information contained in audible signals" (p. 2).

Disputes exist regarding whether CAPD reflects primarily a perceptual or language deficit. Audiologists generally view CAPD as a perceptual disorder, in which auditory information becomes "scrambled" as it moves higher in the neural pathway (Johnson, 1991). This "bottom-up" perceptual deficit results in receptive difficulty in which there is an essential problem in attending to, analyzing, and comprehending relevant stimuli (Young & Protti-Patterson, 1984).

Speech–language pathologists view CAPD as a language deficit. This "top-down" perspective suggests that cognitive functions are primary, and perception of the auditory signal is a component that cannot be separated from the language processes (Young & Protti-Patterson, 1984). Analysis of the auditory signal is deemphasized because individual phenomes are not easy to identify, and listening depends on the context as well as a knowledge of the language. A language disorder may result "because of insufficient or inefficient linguistic, semantic, and cognitive processing skills that prevent the child from developing strategies for dealing with auditory perceptual tasks" (Keith, 1984, p. 49).

More recently, it has been suggested that these two theoretical views can be combined to understand children's difficulties in language and learning (Young & Protti-Patterson, 1984). With the growing acceptance that CAPD is partly a function of both views, the controversy surrounding which one is primary is diminishing (Keith, 1988).

## Evaluation of Central Auditory Processing Disorder

Both behavioral and electrophysiological tests are currently employed in the measurement of CAPD (Hall, 1991; Stach, 1992). Requiring an overt response, behavioral tests frequently involve altering the auditory signal to cause "stress" on the central auditory nervous system. This is done with the assumption that "normal" listeners can compensate for some disruption in the auditory signal and still perceive it accurately (Lasky, 1983).

Auditory behavioral tests can be classified as monaural, dichotic, or binaural. Monaural tests include those employing filtered speech, time-altered speech, pattern recognition, or ipsilateral signals. Filtered speech involves electronically removing certain frequencies of the auditory signal. Time-altered speech involves either compressing or expanding the auditory signal. Pattern recognition refers to indicating the sequence of low or high tones following their presentation. An ipsilateral competing message test typically requires the listener to identify synthetic sentences that are presented concurrently with a competing message (often a story) in the same ear.

Dichotic tests present stimuli to both ears and include tasks such as dichotic digits, the Staggered Spondaic Words test (SSW; Arnst, 1982), and contralateral competing messages. Dichotic digits tests require repeating a 2 to 3 digit sequence for each ear or adding the digits presented at the end of each sequence. The frequently used SSW test requires repeating a series of word pairs, with each pair presented in a staggered fashion. Contralateral competing message tests present the target message to one ear, and the competing message to the other.

Binaural tests include tests of binaural synthesis and masking-level differences. In the former, a word is presented to both ears, with one ear presented with the lower-frequency components and the other with upper-frequency components in a simultaneous fashion. Tests of masking-level differences present words to both ears with concurrent in- and out-of-phase delivery of a masking noise (Baran & Musiek, 1991).

Tests of filtered speech, compressed speech, pattern recognition, and the SSW technique have been recommended for identifying CAPD in children (Willeford & Burleigh, 1985). Ipsilateral competing messages that use sentences as stimuli are recommended only for those children who can read. Even then, "easier, more practical, and less time consuming" tasks preclude its general utility (Willeford & Burleigh, 1985, p. 109).

Electrophysiological tests have included auditory-evoked response techniques, which record neural activity following tonal stimulation through peripheral channels. Responses are measured in terms of wave form, amplitude, and latency of characteristic components, which reflect brain stem and cortical activity. Response patterns may be deviant in children with auditory processing difficulties (Jirsa & Clontz, 1990; Northern & Downs, 1991; Protti, 1983). Although evoked-response techniques may be useful in pinpointing lesion sites in individuals with brain insult, they may neglect to detect more subtle CAPDs in children (Willeford & Burleigh, 1985).

## Relationship between ADHD and CAPD

Manifestations of CAPD and ADHD overlap to a large extent. Children with CAPD have been described as inattentive/distractible, hyperactive, restless, impulsive, and disruptive (Butler, 1983; Hoffman, 1983; Keith, 1984; Young, 1985). Similarly, hyperactive children and children meeting criteria for various forms of ADD have demonstrated poor performance on tests designed to measure CAPD (Gascon, Johnson, & Burd, 1986; Keith & Engineer, 1991; Keith, Rudy, Donahue, & Katbamna, 1989; Ludlow, Cudahy, Bassich, & Brown, 1983). Confounding any attempt to establish discriminant validity for either disorder are observations that the two disorders share a host of other behavioral, psychoeducational, and socioemotional sequelae (Riccio, 1992; Riccio & Hynd, 1993a). Preliminary research (Riccio, 1992) has estimated a 45% rate of comorbidity between CAPD and ADHD, using several measures with established sensitivity to each.

Interested in clarifying whether tests of central auditory processing also measure aspects of attention, Gascon et al. (1986) administered a series of neurodevelopmental attention and central auditory processing tests to children diagnosed as having attention-deficit disorders. Thirty-two percent of the children performed below expected age levels on the attentional tasks, whereas all of the children performed poorly on the tests of central auditory processing. Auditory tests appeared to be more sensitive to the effects of stimulant medication compared to neurodevelopmental testing. The authors concluded that "the clinical picture of 'central auditory processing disorder' is indistinguishable from that of attention deficit disorder" (p. 31).

A handful of studies have focused on auditory attention in hyperactive children. Davidson and Prior (1978) reported that children with extreme behavioral ratings of hyperactivity were no different from normal children in hemispheric specialization for verbal stimuli, as assessed by a dichotic listening task using word pairs. More recent studies have reported a "developmentally immature" level of auditory attention in ADDH and ADDWO subjects (comorbid for several other diagnoses), using more complex tasks requiring divided auditory attention (Prior et al., 1985) and attentional reorientation or switching (Pearson, Lane, & Swanson, 1991).

Using the Screening Test of Auditory Processing Disorders (SCAN; Keith, 1986), Keith et al. (1989) evaluated a group of children who had been referred for possible auditory- or language-processing disorders, some of whose histories were consistent with ADHD. ADHD children obtained significantly lower scores on the SCAN composite score. In addition, 64% of the ADHD children were accurately classified by using only the Auditory Figure Ground subtest of the SCAN.

Keith and Engineer (1991) provided further evidence for positive changes in auditory attention with methylphenidate in a group of ADHD children. In the context of a pretest–posttest design, an auditory continuous performance task (ACPT), the SCAN, and the Token Test (de Renzi & Vignolo, 1962) were employed to measure aspects of auditory vigilance, auditory processing, and receptive language, respectively. Statistically significant improvements while on methylphenidate were noted on the ACPT and two subtests of the SCAN (Filtered Word and Competing Word). These results contrast those reported by Hiscock, Kinsbourne, Caplan, and Swanson (1979) who failed to document methylphenidate effects on a dichotic-digit listening task.

Results from auditory-evoked response testing have suggested differences between normal children and those with CAPD or ADHD. Jirsa and Clontz (1990) demonstrated that, compared to normal children, CAPD subjects had greater P300 latency and reduced amplitude. Similarly, children with ADHD have been shown to produce a decreased P300 amplitude, although P300 response increased with age, and no significant differences were found with younger children (Satterfield, Schell, Nicholas, Satterfield, & Freese, 1990).

## Combining Visual and Auditory Tasks

Few investigators have compared the relative efficacy of standardized visual tasks in conjunction with standardized auditory tasks. Sutter, Bishop, and Battin (1987) administered a screening battery of visual and auditory attention tasks to 54 ADDH or ADDWO and control subjects. Discriminant analyses indicated that the auditory tests differentiated most significantly between the two groups. Of the five tests *not* meeting criteria for entry, four supposedly tapped visual rather than auditory attention.

Continuous performance tests (CPTs) that present stimuli visually have been considered to be most reliable for discriminating ADHD from normal children (Barkley, 1990b). ADHD children have slower reaction times on CPTs compared to normal children (Chee, Logan, Schachar, Lindsay, & Wachsmuth, 1989). Information-processing issues may help to explain such performance patterns (van der Meere & Sergeant, 1988b). However, studies investigating the ecological validity of CPTs and other widely used measures (e.g., Matching Familiar Figures Test; MFFT; Kagan, 1966) have yielded disappointing findings. Such results raise questions about the utility of these measures in assessing individual children (DuPaul, Anastopoulos, Shelton, Guevremont, & Metevia, 1992), rather than simply discriminating between ADHD and non-ADHD children. For example, DuPaul et al. (1992) found that scores from the MFFT and the vigilance task of the Gordon Diagnostic System (GDS; Gordon, 1983), either alone or in combination, resulted in classifications decisions that were counter to those based on parent interview and behavior ratings. Although the false-positive rate of the GDS vigilance task is quite low, false-negative rates can vary from 50% to 85% (Gordon, DiNiro, & Mettelman, 1988). Fischer, Newby, and Gordon (1993) have provided information on what factors are related to this high false-negative rate. Nonetheless, the field is still in desperate need for instruments, that when used alone or in combination, are both sensitive and specific to the core features of ADHD.

The purpose of the research described in this chapter was to compare the relative efficacy of several objective and standardized visual and auditory tests, most of which are commonly used to assess for ADHD or CAPD, and some of which show promise as diagnostic measures. Five instruments were employed—an auditory and visual CPT, a screening battery for CAPD, a speed of mental-processing test, and a color-naming test. Such a comparison could yield a diagnostically sensitive and specific battery that could be implemented by audiologists, school personnel, and clinical diagnosticians when evaluating for the presence of ADHD.

## Outline of Procedures

The results described in this chapter are taken from an ongoing investigation of measures appropriate for ADHD evaluation and the differential diagnosis of ADHD and CAPD. The sample was drawn from small city and rural areas of eastern and southeastern counties in Alabama and were predominantly middle class and Caucasian. Twenty-seven ADHD children and 27 controls were matched on the basis of gender and age. Nineteen males and 8 females, ranging in age from 7 to 12 ($M$ = 9.4) comprised each group. Subjects were drawn from local school systems, pediatricians, and psychologists.

All participants had to meet the following criteria: (1) IQ estimate of 85 or above on a standardized IQ test given within the past year or on the WISC-R (Wechsler, 1974) Vocabulary and Block Design short form administered just prior to the laboratory measures; (2) no evidence of deafness, blindness, severe language delay, cerebral palsy, autism, or psychosis; (3) normal hearing sensitivity as measured by an audiogram; and (4) no ear infections in the past 2 months or a normal tympanogram.

ADHD subjects met the following criteria: (1) a DSM-III-R diagnosis of ADHD based on a previous, independent psychological evaluation; (2) endorsement of 8 or more symptoms rated 2 or 3 on the ADHD Rating Scale (DuPaul, 1991) completed by the child's parent or teacher; (3) $T$-scores at or above 65 on the ADHD-related scales on the Conners Parent Rating Scale (Conners, 1989) or Conners Teacher Rating Scale (Conners, 1989); and (4) stimulant medication-free (if currently prescribed) for at least 48 hours prior to administration of the laboratory measures.

Control children had to meet the following criteria: (1) no history of psychiatric diagnosis or academic problems; (2) scores on the above measures below the established clinical cutoff ($T < 65$).

## Description of Dependent Measures

### SCAN: A Screening Test for Auditory Processing Disorders

The SCAN (Keith, 1986) consists of three auditory tests that purportedly deemphasize cognitive abilities or memory strategies and provide information about the integrity of the auditory nervous system.

FILTERED WORDS. This auditory closure task presents a series of words in which a portion of the word is missing. Poor performance may be indicative of a receptive language disorder or word comprehension difficulties (Keith, 1984).

AUDITORY FIGURE GROUND. This discrimination task presents words accompanied by various levels of background noise (e.g., fan or busy cafeteria). Poor performance is assumed to reflect auditory figure–ground perception and/or attentional problems (Keith, 1984).

COMPETING WORDS.   This dichotic listening task presents two different words simultaneously to both ears. Performance on this subtest can indicate auditory maturation (Keith, 1986).

Adequate criterion-related validity of the SCAN has been reported (Keith et al., 1989; Sanger & Deshayes, 1986). Evidence also exists for moderate test–retest reliability (except for Filtered Words) and adequate internal consistency for subtest and composite scores (Keith, 1986).

## Gordon Diagnostic System (GDS)

The GDS is an electronic device that is designed to measure attention and impulsivity in children suspected of having an attention deficit (Gordon, 1986; Gordon & Mettelman, 1988). The GDS has gained popularity due to its standardized administration procedures, available normative data, and ability to discriminate between ADHD and non-ADHD children (Barkley, 1990b; Gordon & Mettelman, 1988). Although GDS scoring provides information about response patterns in terms of "blocks" within each task, total scores were analyzed in the present investigation.

DELAY TASK.   Following a differential reinforcement of low-rate responding paradigm, the child is instructed to press a button and then pause before pressing again. A six-second interval is set as the minimum latency between responses in order to receive reinforcement in the form of an illuminated light and accumulating points. Total responses, total correct, and the ratio of the two ("efficiency ratio") serve as the dependent variables. McClure and Gordon (1984) provided evidence for this task to differentiate between hyperactive and nonhyperactive children and to largely agree with criterion measures of hyperactivity.

VIGILANCE TASK.   In this task, the child is instructed to respond only after a 1 to 9 sequence appears on the screen in the context of other numbers appearing at the same fixed interval of one per second. Total number of correct responses ("hits") and responses to nontarget stimuli ("commissions") are generated. Adequate test–retest reliability has been reported (Gordon & Mettelman, 1987). Omission errors have corresponded to criterion measures of inattention (Halperin, Wolf, Pascualvaca, Newcorn, Healey, O'Brien, Morganstein, & Young, 1988). Commission errors have correlated with measures of impulsivity (Halperin et al., 1988), although only a 50% classification (normal versus abnormal) agreement between task performance and teacher ratings of

ADHD or examiner observations of test behavior has been found (Gordon, DiNiro, Mettelman, & Tallmadge, 1989).

DISTRACTIBILITY TASK. This task is analogous to the vigilance task with the added presentation of other numbers appearing on either side of the center portion of the display screen, thus serving as potential distractors.

Overall, the GDS has adequate mean test–retest reliability, has been shown to not significantly correlate with IQ, and has distinguished between ADD and reading disabled, overanxious, and normal children (Gordon & Mettelman, 1987, 1988).

## Speed of Information Processing (SIP) Test

The SIP is one subtest of the Differential Ability Scales (Elliott, 1990) and requires a child to visually scan rows of numbers on a series of pages and mark the largest one in each row. Elliott (1990) has shown the SIP to possess a low $g$-loading and high test–retest reliability. The SIP may provide information about the ability to perform simple cognitive operations quickly and efficiently (Buckhalt & Jensen, 1989). Evidence for discriminant validity has been provided by Byrd and Buckhalt (1991). In addition, SIP scores have been shown to negatively correlate with teacher behavior ratings of conduct and attention problems (Buckhalt, Shapiro, Elliott, & McCallum, 1991).

## Stroop Color and Word Test

The Stroop (1935; Golden, 1978) task consists of three pages, each containing evenly arranged stimuli. The first page consists of a series of color words printed in black. The second page consists of a series of four Xs ("XXXX") printed in one of three colors. The third page presents the color word printed in an incongruent color. Subjects are given 45 seconds to read as many stimuli as possible. Raw scores are converted to yield a *T*-score on each subtest.

The Stroop has been used to differentiate between brain-injured and normal or non-brain-injured individuals (Golden, 1976). More recently, it has demonstrated the ability to discriminate between ADHD and normal children (Grodzinsky, 1990) and between ADDH and ADD-WO children (Barkley, Grodzinsky, & DuPaul, 1992). The utility of the Stroop in ADHD assessment may lie in its sensitivity to impulsivity (Barkley, 1990b).

*Auditory Continuous Performance Test*

Currently being standardized by Robert Keith and his associates, the ACPT consists of a series of words presented via a tape recorder, to which the subject must raise his or her thumb when the target word ("dog") is presented. Dependent variables include correct responses ("hits"), missed targets (i.e., commissions or "false alarms"), and late responses ("delays"—a response following the onset of a stimulus word presented immediately after the target word).

Normative data and other information regarding psychometric characteristics are not yet available. However, although group differences were not statistically significant, LD children have shown greater variability in omissions and commissions across trials, compared to normal children (Katbamna, Keith, & Johnson, 1990). In addition, the ACPT appears sensitive to effects of stimulant medication in ADHD children (Keith & Engineer, 1991).

## Results

Analyses showed the ADHD and control groups to be statistically equivalent in terms of demographic characteristics and hearing sensitivity. Behavior ratings suggested concurrent clinically significant learning and behavioral problems (except anxiety) in the ADHD group, compared to control group averages below a $T$ of 50 (all group comparisons were statistically significant). Reflecting known occurrences of comorbidity, half of the ADHD group were receiving services for a learning disability; one-third of the control children were classified as "gifted." Prorated IQ differences were found between the ADHD children ($M = 98.33$) and controls ($M = 110.70$), $t = -4.06$, $p < .001$. Subsequent analyses used IQ as a covariate.

Space precludes the presentation of partial correlation matrices. However, the most consistent finding was the positive relationship between ACPT commission errors and behavior ratings (parent and teacher) of inattention, hyperactivity, and impulsivity. In addition, although several patterns of dependent measure intercorrelations emerged, few relationships involving the GDS did.

The focus of the analyses was placed on determining group differences; estimates of sensitivity, specificity, and diagnostic power; and the strength of the dependent measures to discriminate between ADHD and control subjects. Table 1 presents group descriptive statistics and ANCOVA results. Group differences emerged on the SIP, all three Stroop subtests, the Competing Word score and Composite score on the

**Table 1. ADHD and Control Group Comparisons on Dependent Measures**

| Variable | ADHD ($n = 27$) | | Control ($n = 27$) | | | |
| | M | SD | M | SD | F | P |
| --- | --- | --- | --- | --- | --- | --- |
| SIP (T-scores) | 43.19 | 10.52 | 55.78 | 8.50 | 12.50 | .001 |
| Stroop (T-scores) | | | | | | |
| Word | 40.30 | 6.03 | 49.00 | 6.76 | 13.13 | .001 |
| Color | 42.00 | 6.45 | 47.15 | 4.48 | 5.08 | .05 |
| Color-Word | 44.37 | 8.65 | 50.96 | 5.52 | 4.93 | .05 |
| Scan | | | | | | |
| Filtered words | 11.74 | 2.43 | 11.33 | 2.95 | 0.95 | NS |
| Figure ground | 9.48 | 2.03 | 10.56 | 2.41 | 1.24 | NS |
| Competing words | 7.63 | 2.20 | 10.89 | 2.29 | 13.94 | .001 |
| Composite score | 92.89 | 11.50 | 105.93 | 12.17 | 6.81 | .05 |
| GDS | | | | | | |
| Delay | | | | | | |
| Efficiency ratio | 0.80 | 0.14 | 0.80 | 0.12 | 0.30 | NS |
| Total correct | 42.00 | 7.68 | 45.19 | 12.59 | 0.00 | NS |
| Total responses | 53.33 | 14.16 | 57.11 | 18.96 | 0.29 | NS |
| Vigilance | | | | | | |
| Total correct | 38.27 | 6.02 | 41.62 | 3.13 | 2.34 | NS |
| Commissions | 8.65 | 8.68 | 3.96 | 5.02 | 4.45 | .05 |
| Distractibility | | | | | | |
| Total correct | 18.08 | 11.16 | 26.63 | 13.01 | 1.80 | NS |
| Commissions | 21.00 | 20.71 | 9.18 | 11.33 | 2.35 | NS |
| ACPT | | | | | | |
| Correct | 93.81 | 16.27 | 103.85 | 11.62 | 2.73 | NS |
| False alarms | 13.42 | 6.73 | 6.56 | 3.10 | 20.17 | .001 |
| Delays | 8.96 | 4.70 | 6.48 | 3.85 | 0.56 | NS |

Note. IQ served as a covariate.

SCAN, GDS Vigilance task commission error score, and ACPT false alarm scores.

Exploratory analyses dividing subjects into four groups did not yield any further distinction that was not already reflected in the two-group analyses (i.e., ADHD, ADHD + LD ≠ Control, Gifted Control). However, it is worthwhile noting that for those variables showing an overall group difference, the ADHD + LD group performed the worst compared to the other three groups, although not significantly so.

Dependent measures, alone and in combination, were subjected to computation of sensitivity (true positive rate), specificity (true negative rate), and diagnostic power (overall "hit" or true result rate). These analyses were conducted to "reflect typical clinical practice of attempting to integrate test data to reach diagnostic decisions" (DuPaul et al., 1992).

Each child's score was classified as being in the "abnormal" (at or beyond the 93rd percentile) or "normal" (less than the 86th percentile) range, based on normative data available for all measures except the ACPT. To complement these procedures and to include IQ and ACPT results, a series of discriminant function analyses were performed. Discriminant analyses would address the relative strength of the dependent measures to predict group membership.

Table 2 depicts the rates of sensitivity, specificity, and diagnostic power associated with each variable on which normative data are available. Overall, the SIP test of the DAS, the Competing Word subtest of the SCAN, and the Word subtest of the Stroop yielded the highest sensitivity and specificity.

All variables yielding significant group differences were entered into a stepwise discriminant-function analysis. Summarized in Table 3, the analyses identified seven significant discriminators—three predomi-

Table 2. Sensitivity, Specificity, and Diagnostic Power
of Norm-Based Dependent Measures

| | Abnormal versus normal | | |
| Variable | Sensitivity | Specificity | Diagnostic power |
| --- | --- | --- | --- |
| SIP | 30 | 96 | 68 |
| Stroop | | | |
|   Word | 25 | 100 | 68 |
|   Color | 18 | 100 | 65 |
|   Color-Word | 15 | 100 | 64 |
| SCAN | | | |
|   Filtered words | 0 | 96 | 47 |
|   Figure ground | 0 | 100 | 53 |
|   Competing words | 29 | 100 | 71 |
|   Composite score | 20 | 100 | 61 |
| GDS | | | |
|   Delay | | | |
|     Efficiency ratio | 9 | 92 | 54 |
|     Total correct | 8 | 92 | 49 |
|     Total responses | 7 | 91 | 45 |
|   Vigilance | | | |
|     Total correct | 25 | 96 | 63 |
|     Commissions | 23 | 92 | 59 |
|   Distractibility | | | |
|     Total correct | 57 | 77 | 66 |
|     Commissions | 52 | 86 | 69 |

Table 3. Discriminant Function Analysis for ADHD
and Control Groups

| Discriminating variable | F to enter | Wilks's lambda | p |
|---|---|---|---|
| SIP | 24.32 | .50 | .001 |
| Stroop-Word | 18.41 | .46 | .001 |
| SCAN-Competing Words | 14.73 | .44 | .001 |
| ACPT-False alarms | 12.27 | .42 | .001 |
| GDS-Vigilance Commissions | 12.86 | .41 | .001 |
| SCAN-Composite Score | 11.11 | .40 | .001 |
| IQ | 9.91 | .38 | .001 |

nantly visual tasks, three auditory tasks, and IQ. These discriminators defined distinctly different groups, illustrated by a canonical correlation of .79 for the discriminant function (Wilks's Lambda = .38, $p < .001$). The function correctly classified all but three ADHD subjects (88%), and all but one control subject (96%), resulting in a 92% accuracy of predicted group membership.

Emphasizing a more practical approach similar to the procedures depicted in Table 2, discriminating variables were combined based on an abnormal versus normal distinction. The three variables showing the strongest unique discriminating power resulted in a sensitivity rate of 72 and a specificity rate of 95, if "abnormal" was defined as a deviant score on at least one of the measures. More stringent criteria (e.g., deviant scores on more than one measure) dramatically decreased sensitivity estimates, suggesting that different ADHD subjects are identified by different measures.

## Conclusions

Based on review of the literature and preliminary results of the investigation described in this chapter, there is strong evidence to support the use of several measures in the assessment of ADHD. Specifically, tasks of auditory vigilance, auditory processing (dichotic listening), and cognitive visual processing speed contributed unique discriminating power to the distinction between a heterogeneous group of ADHD and control children, seemingly over and above the discrimination offered by a widely used visual vigilance task (i.e., GDS).

Previous research has documented the sensitivity of the Stroop task to ADHD and LD. Barkley et al. (1992) found that these children performed significantly worse on the Word and Interference (Color-Word) portion of the Stroop. Golden (1978) suggested that the word task, relative to the other Stroop components, may be particularly sensitive to dyslexia. Trends in the data presented in this chapter supported similar suggestions. In conjunction with Stroop results, the present findings related to the SIP task lead to similar conclusions made by Barkley et al. (1992)—that ADHD and LD share similar deficits in rapid scanning, rapid naming, general reading fluency, and slower processing speed.

Previous studies have obtained conflicting results when using the SCAN in samples of variously defined ADHD children, in terms of which subtest reflects significantly different group performance (Keith et al., 1989; Keith & Engineer, 1991). Results presented herein suggest the utility of clarifying what components of ADHD are reflected in SCAN performance. It would appear that the SCAN Competing Words subtest, as suggested by Keith and Engineer (1991), reflects susceptibility to the effects of attention.

Few published studies with ADHD children have employed the ACPT, which could be considered an auditory counterpart to the GDS. Additional work to establish the psychometric properties of the ACPT will be essential, as well as developing a more automated means of responding and recording. Nonetheless, the ACPT appears to warrant further consideration as a tool for ADHD evaluation. Intuitively, the task structure and demands of auditory measures appear more similar than visual measures to what an ADHD child may encounter in the classroom. Correlation patterns between behavior ratings and both the ACPT and the SCAN support this preliminary contention of potentially stronger ecological validity.

There has been a recent interest in combining ADHD-sensitive measures to delineate the additive diagnostic power of the "battery" approach. Clearly, this approach recognizes the limitations inherent in any one measure, the heterogeneous nature of ADHD, and the probable existence of numerous subtypes. Grodzinsky (1990) correctly classified 81% of ADHD and control subjects using the Stroop Color-Word subtest and the GDS Vigilance scores. Sutter et al. (1987) provided some evidence for auditory tests, compared to visual tasks, to differentiate most significantly between ADD and non-ADD subjects. DuPaul et al. (1992) established a 62% agreement between criterion measures and a combination of the GDS Vigilance score and MFFT. Results presented in this chapter clearly support the superiority of combining measures over the unitary measure approach.

Information presented in this chapter suggests the need for several methodological improvements. For example, subject selection needs to be based on a standardized, formal, empirically supported diagnostic evaluation completed just prior to study participation. Criteria need to be established so that distinct subgroups of ADHD (ADDH, ADDWO; comorbid LD, conduct disorders, and/or anxiety disorders) and CAPD (alone and in combination) can be delineated. This would allow for clarification of comorbidity rates. It would also provide an opportunity to investigate the relative sensitivity and specificity of various visual and auditory measures in identifying subgroups of ADHD and CAPD children. Eventually, subtype profiles might be developed. Ultimately, the utility of any measure and associated subtypes rests on the ability to assist in effective intervention planning.

# References

Ackerman, P. T., Anhalt, J. M., Holcomb, P. J., & Dykman, R. A. (1986). Presumably innate and acquired automatic processes in children with attention and/or reading disorders. *Journal of Child Psychology and Psychiatry, 27*, 513–529.

American Psychiatric Association. (1987). *Diagnostic and statistical manual of mental disorders* (3rd ed., rev.). Washington, DC: Author.

American Psychiatric Association. (1980). *Diagnostic and statistical manual of mental disorders* (3rd ed.). Washington, DC: Author.

American Speech-Language-Hearing Association (ASHA). (1992). Issues in central auditory processing disorders: A report from the ASHA Ad Hoc Committee on central auditory processing. Washington, DC: Author.

Arnst, D. (1982). Overview of the Staggered Spondaic Word test and the Competing Environmental Sounds test. In D. Arnst & J. Katz (Eds.), *Central Auditory Assessment: The SSW Test* (pp. 1–41). San Diego: College-Hill Press.

Baker, L., & Cantwell, D. P. (1987a). A prospective psychiatric follow-up of children with speech/language disorders. *Journal of the American Academy of Child and Adolescent Psychiatry, 26*, 546–553.

Baker, L., & Cantwell, D. P. (1987b). Comparison of well, emotionally disordered, and behaviorally disordered children with linguistic problems. *Journal of the American Academy of Child and Adolescent Psychiatry, 26*, 193–196.

Baran, J. A., & Musiek, F. E. (1991). Behavioral assessment of the central auditory nervous system. In W. F. Rintelmann (Eds.), *Hearing Assessment* (2nd ed, pp. 549–602). Austin, TX: PRO-ED, Inc.

Barkley, R. A. (1990a). A critique of current diagnostic criteria for attention deficit hyperactivity disorder: Clinical and research implications. *Developmental and Behavioral Pediatrics, 11*, 343–352.

Barkley, R. A. (1990b). *Attention deficit hyperactivity disorder: A handbook for diagnosis and treatment.* New York: Guilford Press.

Barkley, R. A. (1991). The ecological validity of laboratory and analogue assessment methods of ADHD symptoms. *Journal of Abnormal Child Psychology, 19*, 149–178.

Barkley, R. A., DuPaul, G. J., & McMurray, M. B. (1990). Comprehensive evaluation of attention deficit disorder with and without hyperactivity as defined by research criteria. *Journal of Consulting and Clinical Psychology, 58*, 775–789.

Barkley, R. A., Grodzinsky, G., & DuPaul, G. J. (1992). Frontal lobe functions in attention deficit disorder with and without hyperactivity: A review and research report. *Journal of Abnormal Child Psychology, 20,* 163–188.

Buckhalt, J. A., & Jensen, A. R. (1989). The British Ability Scales Speed of Information Processing subtest: What does it measure? *British Journal of Educational Psychology, 59,* 100–107.

Buckhalt, J. A., Shapiro, S. K., Elliott, C. D., & McCallum, R. S. (August, 1991). *Evaluation of learning disabled students with the Differential Ability Scales.* Poster presented at the annual meeting of the American Psychological Association, San Francisco, CA.

Butler, K. G.. (1983). Language processing: Selective attention and mnemonic strategies. In E. Z. Lasky & J. Katz (Eds.), *Central auditory processing disorders* (pp. 297–315). Baltimore: University Park Press.

Byrd, P. D., & Buckhalt, J. A. (1991). A multitrait-multimethod construct validity study of the Differential Ability Scales. *Journal of Psychoeducational Assessment, 9,* 121–129.

Cantwell, D. P., & Baker, L. (1991). Association between attention deficit hyperactivity disorder and learning disorders. *Journal of Learning Disabilities, 24,* 88–95.

Cantwell, D. P., & Baker, L. (1992). Attention deficit disorder with and without hyperactivity: A review and comparison of matched groups. *Journal of the American Academy of Child and Adolescent Psychiatry, 31,* 432–438.

Chee, P., Logan, G., Schachar, R., Lindsay, P., & Wachsmuth, R. (1989). Effects of event rate and display time on sustained attention in hyperactive, normal, and control children. *Journal of Abnormal Child Psychology, 17,* 371–391.

Conners, C. K. (1989). *Conners' Rating Scale Manual.* North Tonawanda, NY: Multi-Health Systems, Inc.

Davidson, E. M., & Prior, M. R. (1978). Laterality and selective attention in hyperactive children. *Journal of Abnormal Child Psychology, 6,* 475–481.

de Renzi, E., & Vignolo, L. A. (1962). The Token Test: A sensitive test to detect receptive language disturbances in aphasics. *Brain, 85,* 665–678.

Dienske, H., & Sanders-Woudstra, J. A. R. (1985). A critical and conceptual consideration of attention deficit and hyperactivity from an ethological point of view. In L. M. Bloomingdale & J. A. Sergeant (Eds.), *Attention deficit disorder: Criteria, cognition, intervention* (pp. 43–63). Elmsford, NY: Pergamon Press.

Douglas, V. I. (1972). Stop, look, and listen: The problem of sustained attention and impulse control in hyperactive and normal children. *Canadian Journal of Behavioral Science, 4,* 258–282.

DuPaul, G. J. (1991). Parent and teacher ratings of ADHD symptoms: Psychometric properties in a community-based sample. *Journal of Clinical Child Psychology, 20,* 245–253.

DuPaul, G. J., Anastopoulos, Shelton, T. L., Guevremont, D. C., & Metevia, L. (1992). Multimethod assessment of attention-deficit hyperactivity disorder: The diagnostic utility of clinic-based tests. *Journal of Clinical Child Psychology, 21,* 394–402.

Elliott, C. D. (1990). *The Differential Ability Scales: Introductory and technical handbook.* San Antonio, TX: The Psychological Corporation.

Fischer, M., Newby, R. F., & Gordon, M. (1993). Who are the false negatives? *ADHD/Hyperactivity Newsletter,* #19, 5–7. DeWitt, NY: Gordon Systems.

Frank, Y., & Ben-Nun, Y. (1988). Toward a clinical sub-grouping of hyperactive and nonhyperactive attention deficit disorder: Results of a comprehensive neurological and neuropsychological assessment. *American Journal of Diseases in Children, 142,* 153–155.

Gascon, G. G., Johnson, R., & Burd, L. (1986). Central auditory processing and attention deficit disorder. *Journal of Child Neurology, 1,* 27–33.

Golden, C. J. (1976). The diagnosis of brain damage by the Stroop test. *Journal of Clinical Psychology, 32,* 654–658.

Golden, C. J. (1978). *The Stroop Color and Word Test: A manual for clinical and experimental uses.* Wood Dale, IL: Stoelting.

Goodyear, P., & Hynd, G. W. (1992). Attention deficit disorder with (ADD/H) and without (ADD/WO) hyperactivity: Behavioral and neuropsychological differentiation. *Journal of Clinical Child Psychology, 21,* 273–305.

Gordon, M. (1983). *The Gordon Diagnostic System.* DeWitt, NY: Gordon Systems.

Gordon, M. (1986). How is a computerized attention test used in the diagnosis of attention deficit disorders? *Journal of Children in Contemporary Society, 19,* 53–64.

Gordon, M., & Mettelman, B. B. (1987). *Technical guide to the Gordon Diagnostic System.* DeWitt, NY: Gordon Systems.

Gordon, M., & Mettelman, B. B. (1988). The assessment of attention: I. Standardization and reliability of a behavior-based measure. *Journal of Clinical Psychology, 44,* 682–690.

Gordon, M., DiNiro, D., & Mettelman, B. B. (1988). Effect upon outcome of nuances in selection criteria for ADHD/hyperactivity. *Psychological Reports, 62,* 539–544.

Gordon, M., DiNiro, D., Mettelman, B. B., & Tallmadge, J. (1989). Observations of test behavior, quantitative scores, and teacher ratings. *Journal of Psychoeducational Assessment, 7,* 141–147.

Grodzinsky, G. M. (1990). Assessing frontal lobe functioning in boys with attention-deficit hyperactivity disorder. *ADHD/Hyperactivity Newsletter,* #14, 4–6. DeWitt, NY: Gordon Systems.

Hall, J. W. (1992). *Handbook of auditory evoked responses.* Boston, MA: Allyn & Bacon.

Halperin, J. M., Wolf, L. E., Pascualvaca, D. M., Newcorn, J. H., Healey, J. M., O'Brien, J. D., Morganstein, A., & Young, J. G. (1988). Differential assessment of attention and impulsivity in children. *Journal of the American Academy of Child and Adolescent Psychiatry, 27,* 326–329.

Hiscock, M., Kinsbourne, M., Caplan, B., & Swanson, J. M. (1979). Auditory attention in hyperactive children: Effects of stimulant medication on dichotic listening performance. *Journal of Abnormal Psychology, 88,* 27–32.

Hoffman, M. (1983). Psychological interventions for the child with central auditory processing disorder. In E. Z. Lasky & J. Katz (Eds.), *Central auditory processing disorders* (pp. 319–330). Baltimore: University Park Press.

Hynd, G. W., Nieves, N., Connor, R. T., Stone, P., Town, P., Becker, M. G., Lahey, B. B., & Lorys, A. R. (1989). Attention deficit disorder with and without hyperactivity: Reaction time and speed of cognitive processing. *Journal of Learning Disabilities, 22,* 573–580.

Jirsa, R. E., & Clontz, K. B. (1990). Long latency auditory event-related potentials from children with auditory processing disorders. *Ear and Hearing, 11,* 222–232.

Johnson, J. (1991, November). *Auditory processing disorders: A developmental and medical perspective.* Workshop conducted at the annual meeting of ASHA, Atlanta, GA.

Kagan, J. (1966). Reflection-impulsivity: The generality and dynamics of conceptual tempo. *Journal of Abnormal Psychology, 71,* 17–24.

Katabamna, B., Keith, R. W., & Johnson, J. L. (1990). Auditory-processing abilities in children with learning disabilities: A pilot study. *Hearsay,* Fall/Winter, 125–131.

Keith, R. W. (1984). Central auditory dysfunction: A language disorder? *Topics in Language Disorders, 4,* 48–56.

Keith, R. W. (1986). *SCAN, A screening test for auditory processing disorders.* San Antonio, TX: The Psychological Corp.

Keith, R. W. (1988). Tests of central auditory function. In R. J. Roeser & M. P. Downs (Eds.),

*Auditory disorders in school children* (2nd ed., pp. 83–96). New York: Thieme Medical Publishers.

Keith, R. W., & Engineer, P. (1991). Effects of methylphenidate on the auditory processing abilities of children with attention-deficit hyperactivity disorder. *Journal of Learning Disabilities, 24*, 630–636.

Keith, R. W., Rudy, J., Donahue, P. A., & Katbamna, B. (1989). Comparison of SCAN results with other auditory language measures in a clinical population. *Ear and Hearing, 10*, 382–386.

Lahey, B. B., & Carlson, C. L. (1991). Validity of the diagnostic category of attention deficit disorder without hyperactivity: A review of the literature. *Journal of Learning Disabilities, 24*, 110–120.

Lasky, E. Z. (1983). Parameters affecting auditory processing. In E. Z. Lasky & J. Katz (Eds.), *Central auditory processing disorders* (pp. 11–29). Baltimore: University Park Press.

Lasky, E. Z., & Katz, J. (1983). Perspectives on central auditory processing. In E. Z. Lasky & J. Katz (Eds.), *Central auditory processing disorders* (pp. 3–10). Baltimore: University Park Press.

Ludlow, C. L., Cudahy, E. A., Bassich, C., & Brown, G. L. (1983). Auditory processing skills of hyperactive, language-impaired, and reading disabled boys. In E. Z. Lasky & J. Katz (Eds.), *Central auditory processing disorders* (pp. 163–184). Baltimore: University Park Press.

Matkin, N. D., & Hook, P. E. (1983). A multidisciplinary approach to central auditory processing evaluations. In E. Z. Lasky & J. Katz (Eds.), *Central auditory processing disorders* (pp. 223–242). Baltimore: University Park Press.

McClure, F. D., & Gordon, M. (1984). Performance of disturbed hyperactive and non-hyperactive children on an objective measure of hyperactivity. *Journal of Abnormal Child Psychology, 12*, 561–572.

Milich, R., & Kramer, J. (1985). Reflections on impulsivity: An empirical investigation of impulsivity as a construct. In K. D. Gadow & I. Bialer (Eds.), *Advances in learning and behavioral disabilities* (Vol. 3). Greenwich, CT: JAI Press.

Northern, J. L., & Downs, M. P. (1991). *Hearing in children* (4th ed.). Baltimore: Williams & Wilkins.

Pearson, D. A., Lane, D. M., & Swanson, J. M. (1991). Auditory attention switching in hyperactive children. *Journal of Abnormal Child Psychology, 19*, 479–492.

Pelham, W. E. (1986). What is attention deficit disorder: In E. K. Sleator & W. E. Pelham (Eds.), *Attention deficit disorder* (pp. 43–78). Norwalk, CT: Appleton-Century-Crofts.

Posner, M. I. (1988). Structures and functions of selective attention. In T. Boll & D. K. Bryant (Eds.), *Clinical neuropsychology and brain function: Research, assessment, and practice* (pp. 173–202). Washington, DC: American Psychological Association.

Posner, M. I., & Petersen, S. E. (1990). The attention system of the brain. *Annual Review of Neuroscience, 13*, 25–42.

Prior, M., Sanson, A., Freethy, C., & Geffen, G. (1985). Auditory attentional abilities in hyperactive children. *Journal of Child Psychology and Psychiatry, 26*, 289–304.

Protti, E. (1983). Brainstem auditory pathways and auditory processing disorders: Diagnostic implications of subjective and objective tests. In E. Z. Lasky & J. Katz (Eds.), *Central auditory processing disorders* (pp. 117–140). Baltimore: University Park Press.

Riccio, C. A. (1992, November). *Central auditory processing disturbances and the relationship to ADHD*. Paper presented as part of a double-miniseminar at ASHA, San Antonio, TX.

Riccio, C. A., & Hynd, G. W. (1993a). *Attention-deficit hyperactivity disorder: Relationship to central auditory processing disorder*. Manuscript submitted for publication.

Riccio, C. A., & Hynd, G. W. (1993b). Developmental language disorders in children: Relationship with learning disability and attention deficit hyperactivity disorder. *School Psychology Review, 22,* 693–706.

Riccio, C. A., Gonzalez, J. J., & Hynd, G. W. (in press). Attention-deficit hyperactivity disorder (ADHD) and learning disabilities. *Learning Disabilities Quarterly.*

Ross, D. M., & Ross, S. A. (1982). *Hyperactivity: Current issues, research, and theory* (2nd ed.). New York: Wiley-Interscience.

Rutter, M. (1989). Attention deficit disorder/Hyperkinetic Syndrome: Conceptual and research issues regarding diagnosis and classification. In T. Sagvolden & T. Archer (Eds.), *Attention deficit disorder: Clinical and basic research* (pp. 1-24). Hillsdale, NJ: Lawrence Erlbaum Associates.

Sanger, D., & Deshayes, I. (1986). Criterion-related validity. In R. W. Keith (Ed.), *SCAN, A screening test for auditory processing disorders* (pp. 67–70). San Antonio, TX: The Psychological Corporation.

Satterfield, J. H., Schell, A. M., Nicholas, T. W., Satterfield, B. T., & Freese, T. E. (1990). Ontogeny of selective attention effects on event-related potentials in attention-deficit hyperactivity disorder and normal boys. *Biological Psychiatry, 28,* 879–903.

Schachar, R. (1991). Childhood hyperactivity. *Journal of Child Psychology and Psychiatry, 32,* 155–191.

Sergeant, J. A., & Scholten, C. A. (1983). A stages-of-information processing approach to hyperactivity. *Journal of Child Psychology and Psychiatry, 24,* 40–60.

Sergeant, J., & van der Meere, J. J. (1989). The diagnostic significance of attentional processing: Its significance for ADDH classification—A future DSM. In T. Sagvolden & T. Archer (Eds.), *Attention deficit disorder: Clinical and basic research* (pp. 151–166). Hillsdale, NJ: Lawrence Erlbaum Associates.

Silver, L. B. (1990). Attention-deficit hyperactivity disorder: Is it a learning disability or a related disorder? *Journal of Learning Disabilities, 23,* 394–397.

Sutter, E., Bishop, P., & Battin, R. R. (1987). Psychometric screening for attention deficit disorder in a clinical setting. *Journal of Psychoeducational Assessment, 5,* 227–235.

Stach, B. A. (1992). Controversies in the screening of central auditory processing disorders. In F. H. Bess & J. W. Hall, III (Eds.), *Screening children for auditory dysfunction* (pp. 43–72). New York: Grune & Stratton.

van der Meere, J. J., & Sergeant, J. A. (1988a). Acquisition of attention skill in pervasively hyperactive children. *Journal of Child Psychology and Psychiatry, 29,* 301–310.

van der Meere, J. J., & Sergeant, J. A. (1988b). Controlled processing and vigilance in hyperactivity: Time will tell. *Journal of Abnormal Child Psychology, 16,* 641–655.

Wechsler, D. (1974). *Wechsler Intelligence Scale for Children—Revised.* New York: Psychological Corporation.

Willeford, J. A., & Burleigh, J. M. (1985). *Handbook of central auditory processing disorders in children.* Orlando, FL: Grune & Stratton.

Young, L. (1985). Central auditory processing through the looking glass: A critical look at diagnosis and management. *Journal of Childhood Communication Disorders, 9,* 31–42.

Young, M. L., & Protti-Patterson, E. (1984). Management perspectives of central auditory problems in children: Top-down and bottom-up considerations. *Seminars in Hearing, 5,* 251–261.

# Behavioral Disinhibition and Underlying Processes in Adolescents with Disruptive Behavior Disorders

RICHARD MILICH, CYNTHIA M. HARTUNG,
CATHERINE A. MARTIN,
and EDWARD D. HAIGLER

A decade ago, we offered some reflections on the research underlying the construct of impulsivity (Milich & Kramer, 1984). We noted that there was widespread agreement that problems in disinhibition played a crucial role in the major externalizing disorders of childhood, especially attention-deficit hyperactivity disorder (ADHD) and conduct disorder (CD). In addition, many secondary problems of childhood, including peer and academic difficulties, were at least in part attributed to poor impulse control. Nevertheless, despite the recognized role that impulsivity played in explaining these difficulties, the research investigating this construct was quite discouraging. Numerous problems were identified that would preclude making meaningful advances in our under-

RICHARD MILICH, CYNTHIA M. HARTUNG, and EDWARD D. HAIGLER • Department of Psychology, University of Kentucky, Lexington, Kentucky 40506.     CATHERINE A. MARTIN • Department of Psychiatry, University of Kentucky, Lexington, Kentucky 40506.
*Disruptive Behavior Disorders in Childhood,* edited by Donald K. Routh. Plenum Press, New York, 1994.

standing of the role of impulsivity in accounting for childhood behavior problems.

The goal of the present chapter is to review the progress we have made in our thinking and research concerning impulsivity over the last decade and then to offer the results of a study that attempts to advance recent theorizing and findings in this area. However, before we start with where current research and thinking on impulsivity is, it may be helpful to see where we were 10 years ago. The following section offers a brief review of earlier conceptual and empirical problems relating to the construct of impulsivity (see Milich & Kramer, 1984).

## Initial Conceptual and Empirical Problems

The first issue noted by Milich and Kramer (1984) was the lack of a clear consensus as to what constitutes impulsive behavior. Perhaps the clearest evidence for these definitional problems was the impulsivity symptoms offered by DSM-III (American Psychiatric Association, 1980) for the diagnosis of attention-deficit disorder (ADD). It was unclear how the six symptoms were identified as reflecting impulsive behavior, and several of them (e.g., has difficulty organizing work, needs a lot of supervision) appeared to have little direct relationship with impulsivity. In fact, factor analyses of the DSM-III symptoms of ADD often split the impulsivity items in two, with some of them loading with the inattention symptoms and some with the hyperactivity items (Lahey et al., 1988).

Given the lack of a widely agreed upon definition of impulsivity, a plethora of tests were created, designed to measure impulsivity, which tapped into a variety of different psychological and behavioral processes. There are at least three essential problems with this test-specific approach to defining and understanding the construct of impulsivity. First, as Milich and Kramer (1984) note, many of these early tasks exhibited very high correlations with traditional demographic measures, such as age, IQ, and SES. Although it is quite understandable that a measure of impulsivity would correlate to some degree with variables such as age or IQ, the question arose as to whether these impulsivity measures showed any incremental validity, that is, were they measuring anything beyond age or IQ. If the construct of impulsivity is to have any utility, then it must offer valid information regarding an individual's behavior, beyond that which can be predicted by age or IQ. As noted by Milich and Kramer (1984), many of the most commonly employed measures of impulsivity failed this essential test.

Second, most commonly employed measures of impulsivity showed little if any empirical convergence, especially when one controlled for common variance due to age, IQ, and SES. This may reflect the fact that the construct is quite complex and the different measures are tapping into different aspects of disinhibitory behavior. Alternatively, the lack of convergence may mean that some if not all of these measures are failing to capture any aspect of the construct of impulsivity.

Perhaps the major shortcoming to the earlier work on impulsivity was the dearth of theory-driven research. Instead, as noted, impulsivity was defined by the task used to operationalize it. This tended to produce a circular sort of reasoning in which the task defined the construct and the construct then validated the task. For example, the widely used Matching Familiar Figures Test was identified as a measure of impulsivity, and its validity was derived from the fact that it successfully differentiated samples (e.g., ADHD children) known to have problems in impulse control from those who did not. However, there are many other psychological processes (e.g., attentional or motivational difficulties) that could account for this differentiation.

This atheoretical approach to understanding the construct of impulsivity adversely affected progress in this area. First, no guidelines were available to help generate predictions about the performance of various diagnostic groups under differing situational or motivational conditions. Thus, there was little theorizing about the specific environmental conditions that would increase or decrease the likelihood that a given population would exhibit impulsive behavior. Second, there was little attempt to link observed behavioral performance with underlying psychological or biological models. The conceptual and empirical work never got beyond descriptions of the overt behaviors manifested. Finally, given this atheoretical approach, it was difficult to develop a logical sequence of research questions in the study of impulsivity; earlier findings did not automatically produce a logical series of subsequent studies. Thus, there was a variety of piecemeal research, with investigators going off in different directions, but studies were not clearly building on previous findings.

Milich and Kramer (1984), having reviewed the state of impulsivity research, offered the following, somewhat disappointing conclusions:

> Undertaking this review, however, has also been discouraging, in that it highlights the relatively primitive state of impulsivity research. After years of study and hundreds of articles, we still do not have an acceptable and valid definition of impulsive behavior. We also do not know whether one is likely to find an underlying unitary

construct of impulsivity or whether one should concentrate instead on different domains of impulsivity to identify different aspects of this behavior. Unfortunately, researchers have too often avoided these issues by adopting one widely accepted measure (i.e., the MFF) whose relationship to impulsivity is questionable. Everyone seems to agree on the importance of impulsivity in childhood behavior problems, but getting everyone to agree on what is meant by the term seems to be more difficult. (p. 89)

Although the state of theory and research regarding impulsivity was discouraging in 1984, as we shall presently see, a decade later things look much more promising.

## Current Conceptualizations of Impulsivity

As noted above, a major problem with previous work in the area of impulsivity was the lack of theory-driven research. With few exceptions (e.g., Eysenck, 1969; Gray, 1975), models were not being offered to account for this behavior, and there was little attempt to integrate diverse aspects of functioning into a comprehensive picture. Fortunately, within the last decade, major advances in our thinking about impulsivity have been made, and several comprehensive models have been offered. Researchers including Cloninger (1986), Newman (1987), Quay (1988a,b, 1993), and Zuckerman (1983) have all attempted to offer systematic theories to increase our understanding of impulsive or disinhibited behavior (see McBurnett, 1992, for a comprehensive review of this recent work).

There are several important factors that differentiate these theoretical approaches from the earlier work in impulsivity. First, these investigators have attempted to integrate different theories of behaviors to arrive at a clearer picture of impulsivity. Thus, research reflecting the different fields of psychobiology, personality theory, psychopathology, information processing, psychopharmacology, and social psychology all have been incorporated to some degree in each of the emerging theories of disinhibitory behavior (Newman & Wallace, 1993).

Consistent with this cross-disciplinary approach to understanding impulsivity, testable hypotheses have been generated that tap into different areas of functioning. Thus, as Quay (1993) notes, these emerging theories allow for the examination of overt behavioral differences among individuals, differences in psychophysiological responses to varying stimulus conditions, and the effects of diverse psychopharmacological agents on performance.

Finally, these new theoretical perspectives allow for specific predictions about individual differences in performance under varying stimulus and motivational conditions. These theories attempt to relate differences in individuals' temperament, biological functioning, and behavioral history to their subsequent performance on a variety of disinhibitory tasks that vary along a number of important dimensions. Thus, the same overt impulsive behavior may reflect diverse underlying causal mechanisms, or conversely, the same underlying process may produce different disinhibitory behaviors among subgroups of individuals (Newman & Wallace, 1993). Stated differently, disinhibition may be the final common pathway for different covert processes (e.g., overactive activation system, dysfunctional inhibitory system, a combination of activation and inhibitory difficulties, deficiency in response modulation). Recent theorizing allows for the identification of these covert processes, and for predictions that capture these behavioral and biological differences. Of the more recent theories, two of the most fruitful avenues of investigation have been the theoretical and empirical work of Newman and Quay, who have adapted the neuropsychological model developed by Gray.

## Newman's Theoretical and Empirical Work

In 1980, Gorenstein and Newman proposed a "septal model" as a useful framework for explaining the role of disinhibition in the behavior of adult psychopaths. This model was based on disinhibited behavior in rats that resulted from lesions in the septohippocampal region of the brain. Since that time, Newman's research has been aimed at the "elucidation of the psychological processes underlying disinhibition" (Newman, 1987, p. 466). His work has been closely associated with Gray's (1975) neuropsychological model, which is also derived from the "septal model."

In 1975, Gray proposed a model that consists of three interacting systems of arousal: the Behavioral Activation System (BAS), the Behavioral Inhibition System (BIS), and the Nonspecific Arousal System (NAS). The BAS is sensitive to reinforcing stimuli and is responsible for behavioral activation. Quay (1993) points out that this behavioral activation may involve not only approach behavior but also behaviors involved in escape and active avoidance. Ultimately, the BAS is responsible for behavior directed toward attainment of a goal whether that goal involves acquisition or avoidance.

In contrast to the BAS, BIS activation results in the interruption of ongoing BAS activity in response to threatening environmental cues. The BIS is sensitive to threatening stimuli and is responsible for interrupting behaviors so the individual can focus attention on potentially aversive stimuli in the environment (McBurnett, 1992). Both the BAS and the BIS are increasingly activated by exposure to rewarding and punishing stimuli, respectively. Increased activity in either behavioral system results in heightened activity in a third system, the Nonspecific Arousal System (NAS). The speed of behavioral responses—action and inhibition—is mediated by the NAS, in addition to the respective behavioral systems. Therefore, activation of the NAS also results in increased speed and force of responses. It is important to note, as Newman and Wallace (1993) do, that the NAS is not responsible for activation or inhibition per se, but rather the degree of strength and quickness of activation or inhibition as medicated by the BAS and BIS.

Newman has conducted a series of studies investigating the effects of various motivational conditions on these hypothetical behavioral systems in psychopaths and other disinhibited individuals (i.e., extraverts and juvenile delinquents). In 1980, Gorenstein and Newman suggested an oversensitivity to reward, as opposed to an insensitivity to punishment, as an explanation for psychopaths' inability to learn from punishment. That is, they proposed that the problem was in the BAS rather than the BIS. Since that time, Newman has consistently found that disinhibited individuals, when faced with competing reward and punishment contingencies, exhibit response perseveration (Newman, Patterson, & Kosson, 1987) and are deficient in passive avoidance learning (Newman & Kosson, 1986; Newman, Widom, & Nathan, 1985). This information alone appears to support the overactive BAS theory. However, a closer look at these studies reveals that the mechanism of disinhibition in these individuals may not be this simple.

Newman et al. (1987) used a card-playing task to measure response perseveration in male psychopaths who were prison inmates. Subjects were divided into psychopathic and control groups based on their scores on Hare's (1980) psychopathy checklist. While playing the card task, subjects had the opportunity to win money for each card they played. The task was administered on a computer, and the deck of cards consisted of 100 playing cards. Face cards were arbitrarily designated as winning cards (S+), and number cards were arbitrarily designated as losing cards (S−). The cards were presented in a preprogrammed order, and the probability of winning decreased by 10% (i.e., from 90% in the first 10 cards to 0% in the final 10 cards) for each 10 consecutive cards. Before playing each card, the subjects were asked if they wanted to play another card, and they could quit at any time. In order to win an optimal amount of money, subjects needed to quit before the sixth set of cards was played because at this point the probability of losing exceeded the probability of winning. The dependent variable was the number of cards played.

Results indicated that, as expected, psychopaths exhibited greater response perseveration than controls by playing more cards and winning less money. These results support the overactive BAS theory; psychopaths were unable to inhibit responding in reaction to the potent reinforcers they were receiving, even though the reinforcement payoff was no longer in their favor. This result may be due to the overactivation of the BAS in the presence of cues for reward. However, it is also possible that psychopaths have an inhibitory deficit; that is, the BIS is not responding adequately even in the presence of cues for punishment (i.e., loss of reward). Additional studies were run that addressed these competing hypotheses, both with juvenile delinquents (Newman et al., 1985) and with adult psychopaths (Newman & Kosson, 1986).

Newman et al. (1985) used a go/no-go discrimination task to study passive avoidance in 14- to 18-year-old adolescents from a correctional school in Indiana. Subjects were divided into psychopathic and non-psychopathic groups based on their scores on Scale 4 (psychopathic deviate, Pd) and the Welsh Anxiety Scale of the MMPI. Primary psychopaths ($n = 11$) were those adolescents who had high Pd and low anxiety scores; nonpsychopaths ($n = 31$) had low-Pd and low anxiety scores.

In the go/no-go task, subjects had the opportunity to win tokens for responding to positive stimuli (S+) and lose tokens for responding to negative stimuli (S−). The stimuli consisted of 64 index cards with two-digit numbers on them. Within the deck, there were eight sets of eight identical numbers. Of these eight numbers, four were arbitrarily designated as S+, and the other four were S−. The cards were turned over, one at a time, in front of the subject, and the subject was given 2 seconds to respond (i.e., go) by tapping the card with his finger, or to withhold from responding (i.e., no-go). Their task was to learn, by trial and error, when to respond and when to withhold from responding (i.e., passive avoidance). Subjects were run in one of two conditions, a combined reward plus punishment (R + P) condition and a reward-alone (R) condition. In condition R + P, subjects were rewarded for responding to S+ but punished for responding to S−. In reward-alone, subjects were rewarded for responding to S+ and rewarded for withholding a response to S−.

Newman et al. (1985) predicted that disinhibited subjects (i.e., psychopathic adolescents) would respond significantly more often and demonstrate a deficit in passive avoidance learning when both cues for reward and punishment were present. Results were consistent with this hypothesis, as subjects in the primary psychopathic group made significantly more passive avoidance errors (i.e., errors of commission) than subjects in the nonpsychopathic group in the (R + P) condition; they responded to significantly more S— stimuli. Thus, it appears that the increased focus on reward interfered with the processing of punishment cues for these characteristically impulsive individuals; they seemed to attend to reward cues at the expense of punishment cues (Newman et al., 1985). However, the group difference was absent in the reward-alone condition when subjects were rewarded for responding to S+ and also rewarded for appropriately inhibiting responses to S—. This latter result suggests that disinhibited individuals do not overrespond in all situations involving reward. Further, this finding challenges the overactive BAS theory because the disinhibited group did not demonstrate BAS overactivity relative to the control group when they were rewarded for appropriately inhibiting a response. This may suggest that the problem this group experiences is instead a dysfunctional BIS, but the Newman and Kosson (1986) results that follow appear to undermine this alternative hypothesis.

In 1986, Newman and Kosson used a computerized version of the go/no-go discrimination task in an attempt to replicate the Newman et al. (1985) findings with adult psychopaths. Subjects were 60 adult males from a minimum security prison in Wisconsin who were divided into psychopathic experimental and nonpsychopathic control groups based on their responses to Hare's (1980) Psychopathy Checklist. In addition, subjects were divided into two incentive conditions: One condition involved both reward and punishment, similar to the R + P condition described earlier. The other condition involved punishment alone, in which subjects lost money for responding to S— and also for failing to respond to S+. Consistent with other results, they found psychopaths to perform more poorly than controls in the R + P condition; they made more passive avoidance errors and won less money. However, Newman and Kosson (1986) did not find significant group differences in the punishment-alone condition. Under these circumstances, the psychopathic individuals were as successful as control subjects at inhibiting their behaviors. For this reason, disinhibition in these individuals cannot be attributed solely to a weak inhibitory system (i.e., BIS).

Based on the findings in punishment-alone and reward-alone conditions of the go/no-go task, Newman (1987) concluded that the passive-avoidance deficit found in disinhibited individuals does not reflect solely an oversensitivity to reward or a lack of concern for punishment. However, the unequivocal findings regarding disinhibited behavior in conditions involving competing reward and punishment contingencies have led him to argue for a unique deficit in response modulation in these individuals. That is, disinhibited individuals demonstrate less than optimal performance in these experimental conditions because they establish a dominant response set for reward early in the task and then have difficulty switching their focus to punishment cues later on. Essentially, the BAS dominates over the BIS when both are activated in these individuals. This theory of a response-modulation deficit is more complex than the overactive BAS theory because it involves the relative responsiveness of the two systems. When both systems are activated, this deficit results in the BIS being unable to interrupt the ongoing activity of the BAS (see Newman & Wallace, 1993, for an extended discussion of this theory).

## Implications for Childhood Psychopathology

When the term *syndromes of disinhibition* is applied to childhood, two major externalizing disorders come to mind: conduct disorder (CD) and attention-deficit hyperactivity disorder (ADHD). For many years, these were thought of as subgroups of the same disorder. Indeed, they are currently grouped together in DSM-III-R (1987) under the rubric of Disruptive Behavior Disorders. These childhood phenomena have a common link in that both involve problems in disinhibition (Milich & Kramer, 1984). Although the current literature suggests that ADHD and CD are two different but overlapping disorders (Hinshaw, 1987), it is not clear whether they reflect different problems in reward activation and response inhibition.

Quay (1988a,b, 1993) has adapted the work of both Newman and Gray to argue that CD and ADHD reflect different problems in BAS and BIS functioning. According to Quay (1993), both conduct disorder (specifically, undersocialized aggressive conduct disorder) and antisocial personality disorder can be characterized by BAS dominance. When rewards and punishments are present, these individuals perform poorly on tasks measuring impulsivity because they focus on reward at the expense of punishment, and the BAS dominates over the BIS (Daugherty & Quay, 1991; Newman et al., 1985; Shapiro, Quay, Hogan, & Schwartz, 1988).

Due to the assumed similarities between disinhibited behavior in children with ADHD and those with CD, it might be assumed that ADHD is also characterized by BAS dominance. Instead, Quay has recently suggested that a dysfunctional BIS is responsible for impulsive behavior in children with ADHD (Daugherty & Quay, 1991; Quay, 1988a,b). Whereas CD and antisocial personality disorder may be associated with a dominant BAS that is particularly sensitive to reward cues in situations involving both reward and punishment, ADHD may reflect a deficient inhibitory system resulting in impulsive behavior regardless of the presence of reward cues. Furthermore, Daugherty and Quay (1991) have suggested that the relatively greater impairment in functioning of children comorbid with ADHD and CD symptoms, as opposed to either disorder alone, may be due to an overactive BAS in combination with a dysfunctional BIS.

There are several lines of evidence supporting Quay's hypotheses. Shapiro et al. (1988) used the Newman et al. (1987) computerized card-playing task to test differences in response perseveration between conduct-disordered children and a control sample. As in the Newman et al. study, the probability of winning systematically decreased over the course of the task, and the subjects had the opportunity to quit before every trial.

The CD group consisted of 9 children (5 male, 4 female) with a mean age of 13.7 years. The comparison group consisted of 10 children who were of similar age ($M$ = 14.6 years), IQ, and SES. As predicted, the CD group played significantly more cards, and won less money, than the comparison group. These results are consistent with the Newman et al. findings for psychopaths and provide support for the BAS-dominance theory in CD.

In a second study, Daugherty and Quay (1991) attempted to provide further support for Quay's hypotheses regarding the relative strengths and weaknesses of the behavioral activation and inhibition systems in CD, ADHD, and children with both ADHD and CD. Similar to the card-playing task previously described (Newman et al., 1987; Shapiro et al., 1988), Daugherty and Quay employed a computer-administered perseveration task. However, this involved a door-opening task, with 100 doors presented in a preprogrammed order with the probability of winning systematically decreasing from 90% to 0%. Subjects were public-school children in grades 3 through 6 matched by age, gender, and ethnicity. The CD group ($n$ = 10), ADHD group ($n$ = 9), and ADHD/CD group ($n$ = 10) were identified based on the Revised Problem Behavior Checklist (RPBC; Quay & Peterson, 1987) scores that were at least one SD above the mean on the respective scales of interest, with no other significantly elevated scales. Children in the control group had scores at or below the mean on all RPBC scales and were matched on all other variables (i.e., age, gender, ethnicity).

As predicted, the CD and ADHD/CD groups demonstrated greater response perseveration by opening significantly more doors, and winning less money, than the control group. Although the ADHD group opened more doors than controls, this difference was not significant. In summarizing their results, Daugherty and Quay suggest that a task that activates the BIS and not the BAS is necessary to adequately test Quay's hypothesis regarding ADHD. A recent study by Schachar and Logan (1990) fulfills this requirement.

Schachar and Logan (1990) used a stop-signal task that required inhibition following continuous activation, similar to the go/no-go task employed by Newman et al. (1985) and Newman & Kosson (1986). Specifically, in this paradigm, subjects are engaged in a primary task (e.g., discrimination learning), and a signal (e.g., a tone) appears periodically indicating they must inhibit their ongoing response. However, in contrast to the tasks employed by Newman and Quay, the Schachar and Logan stop/signal task did not involve the use of reward or punishment as an incentive.

Schachar and Logan (1990) found boys with CD to perform similarly to a control group, whereas boys with ADHD were unable to inhibit their responding. These results are consistent with the idea that CD is characterized by an overactive activation system (i.e., BAS) and, consequently, an oversensitivity to reward. Thus, in a situation where inhibitory behavior was required but reward was not a factor, CD subjects performed as well as controls. It appears that the inhibitory system in CD is quite functional given the appropriate circumstances. These results are also consistent with Quay's hypothesis that a maladaptive inhibitory system is responsible for the inhibitory deficit observed in ADHD. Even though reward cues were not present, the ADHD subjects still had difficulty inhibiting their responses. (See Schachar, Tannock, & Logan, 1993, for a further elaboration of this line of research.)

These theories of disinhibition based on responses to reward are very compelling; however, the role of punishment in the process of disinhibition in these groups must also be considered. One of the most effective interventions for ADHD is the punishment paradigm (O'Leary, 1985; Pelham & Hinshaw, 1992). It is known to be more effective than positive reinforcement alone and comparable to reinforcement and punishment combined. It may be that punishment activates an otherwise weak inhibitory system (i.e., BIS) in children with ADHD. O'Leary (1985) notes that punishment contingencies (e.g., reprimands and response cost) effectively reduce off-task behavior with ADHD children. In fact, Abramowitz, O'Leary, and Rosen (1987) found children with ADHD to be more responsive to response cost than praise. It appears that merely rewarding appropriate behavior is not sufficient in helping ADHD children to suppress inappropriate behavior (O'Leary, 1985; Pfiffner & Barkley, 1990). Response cost appears to be not only effective but necessary for controlling disinhibition in these children (O'Leary, 1985).

These findings can be conceptualized as being consistent with Quay's (1988a) hypothesis regarding the process of disinhibition in the ADHD group. If the underlying mechanism is a dysfunctional inhibitory system (BIS), then the presence or absence of reward, which is thought to affect the activation system (BAS), would not be expected to result in appropriate inhibition. However, punishment contingencies would be expected to affect the inhibition system by increasing the activation of the BIS, and the aforementioned findings regarding the effectiveness of response cost with ADHD children support this expectation.

Further indirect support for the dysfunctional BIS hypothesis in ADHD is found in the study of the pharmacological treatment of ADHD (Quay, 1988b). Currently, stimulants are the treatment of choice for ADHD, and it has been suggested that methylphenidate (MPH) may act on the inhibitory system (Quay, 1993). This would help explain why giving stimulants to overly active children has a beneficial effect. If the medication stimulates the inhibitory system, this would increase the likelihood of inhibitory behavior in the presence of cues for punishment. If this is the case, we would expect ADHD subjects taking MPH to exhibit less impulsivity in situations requiring inhibitory control than those not medicated.

For example, Tannock, Schachar, Carr, Chajczyk, and Logan (1989) investigated the effects of MPH in ADHD children using their stop-signal task and found MPH to improve inhibitory control. Similarly, Trommer, Hoeppner, and Zecker (1991) also found MPH to be effective in controlling impulsivity in children with ADHD. They used a go/no-go task and found that ADHD children made fewer errors of commission when taking MPH than when unmedicated. These pharmacological studies are consistent with the theory that a weak BIS is responsible for disinhibition problems in children with ADHD.

## The Current Study

We recently completed a study designed to further the line of investigation started by Quay. Specifically, as Daugherty and Quay (1991) proposed, we were interested in determining whether differences in overt behavioral manifestations of disinhibition, under varying motivational conditions, would differentiate the two primary disruptive behavior disorders of childhood (i.e., ADHD and CD). This project was intended to disentangle the underlying processes of disinhibition in ADHD and CD and to determine if these two disorders reflect different aspects of the construct of disinhibition. The guiding hypotheses of this investigation were that CD primarily reflects a BAS that dominates over the BIS, whereas ADHD reflects a dysfunctional BIS (Daugherty & Quay, 1991; Quay, 1988a,b).

There were several aspects of this study that were unique to this type of research with nonadult samples. First, two different tasks, one with varying motivational conditions, were employed in an attempt to tease apart the role that BAS and BIS functioning may play in accounting for disinhibited behavior. Newman's card-playing task, shown to be sensitive to psychopathy, was designed to measure response perseveration characteristic of BAS-dominant individuals. Newman's go/no-go discrimination task, designed to measure response inhibition, or passive avoidance, was run under two different conditions (i.e., reward plus punishment and reward alone) to tap into different problems in BAS and BIS functioning. Although Daugherty and Quay (1991) used the card perseveration task with both ADHD and CD children, the present study is apparently the first to include the go/no-go task with these two diagnostic groups.

A second feature of this study was the use of a dimensional rather than a categorical approach to examine ADHD and CD symptomatology. Such a dimensional approach has been used previously to successfully differentiate hyperactive and aggressive symptomatology (Milich, Loney, & Landau, 1982) and is being recommended with greater frequency (Newman & Wallace, 1993). Although DSM-III-R uses a categorical approach to the diagnosis of mental disorders, the dimensional approach has been advocated by adult theorists and has recently been found to be preferable in the diagnosis of borderline personality disorder (Trull, Widiger, & Guthrie, 1990).

There are several reasons why a dimensional approach is preferable. First, it more accurately reflects the nature of reality, in that it does not require the arbitrary dichotomization of individuals into categories. In other words, in real life these symptom patterns may reflect quantitative differences among individuals rather than discrete, qualitative differences. Second, this approach offers a more powerful statistical test of the hypotheses because dichotomizing continuous measures results in the loss of potentially useful information.

A third unique feature of this investigation was the inclusion of both male and female subjects, so that gender differences in the relationship between the externalizing disorders and disinhibitory behavior could be examined. Routinely, girls are not included in studies of CD and ADHD, so that little is known about potential gender differences in the manifestations of these disorders. Those few studies of sex differences in ADHD tend to find that boys exhibit greater behavioral difficulties than girls (Berry, Shaywitz, & Shaywitz, 1985; Breen & Altepeter, 1990; deHaas, 1986). Although not as compelling, there is some evidence to suggest that girls with ADHD experience greater academic and cognitive difficulties than boys with ADHD (Berry et al., 1985; Brown, Madan-Swain, & Baldwin, 1991; James & Taylor, 1990). Thus, one of the purposes of the present study was to determine whether ADHD and CD symptomatology was similarly associated with performance on the two tasks for both males and females.

Based on Quay's (1988a,b) theorizing, several specific hypotheses were investigated. In the combined reward and punishment condition of the go/no-go task, subjects were rewarded for responding to positive stimuli and were punished for responding to negative stimuli. Because reward activates the BAS and subjects who are BAS dominant were expected to establish a dominant response set for responding, it was expected that ADHD and CD symptomatologies would be positively and significantly correlated with errors of commission and negatively and significantly correlated with the amount of money won.

In the reward-only condition of the go/no-go task, subjects were rewarded for responding to positive stimuli and for withholding response to negative stimuli. In this condition, it was expected that ADHD symptomatology would correlate significantly with errors of commission (i.e., responding to a negative stimulus). The CD subjects, like Newman's juvenile delinquents, were not expected to demonstrate an overactive BAS when punishment cues were not competing and, thus, CD symptomatology was not expected to be correlated with errors of commission or amount of money won.

The card-perseveration task involves monetary rewards and, beyond an optimum point, subjects begin to lose more money than they win. For this task, it was expected that ADHD and CD symptomatologies would be positively and significantly correlated with number of cards played and negatively and significantly correlated with amount of money won.

## Subjects

Subjects in the study were 90 adolescents with a history of various psychiatric or behavioral disorders. The adolescents were recruited from three sources: (1) 34 of the adolescents were seen approximately 2 years earlier at an adolescent clinic in an outpatient psychiatry department; (2) 40 of the adolescents were new patients at the same clinic; and (3) 16 were recruited from an alternative school and had been identified as having severe disciplinary problems. Of the 90 subjects, 60 were males

(67%), and 30 were females (33%). Subjects ranged in age from 13.1 to 21.7 years ($M$ = 16.3, $SD$ = 2.1): Females ($M$ = 17.1, $SD$ = 2.1) were older than the males ($M$ = 15.9, $SD$ = 2.1) on average, $t$ (88) = 2.51, $p$ < .05.

The diagnostic status of the subjects was established through the use of a diagnostic interview with the adolescents. The interview included the DSM-III-R criteria for both ADHD and CD. For the ADHD criteria, adolescents were asked if the symptom was problematic when they were younger. If the symptom was endorsed by history, then the interviewee was asked if it was currently problematic. This procedure was intended to provide data regarding ADHD symptomatology in both childhood and adolescence. Because the DSM-III-R criteria for CD are appropriate for adolescents, this procedure was not employed for the CD criteria. Adolescents were asked to give examples to clarify their endorsement of ADHD and CD criteria when necessary.

By the adolescents' self-reports, males ($M$ = 7.6 symptoms) showed significantly more ADHD symptomatology by history than females ($M$ = 5.6), $t$ (88) = 2.4, $p$ < .05. However, in terms of current ADHD symptomatology, males ($M$ = 3.8) and females ($M$ = 4.0) did not differ significantly, $t$ < 1. There was also no significant difference in the number of CD symptoms reported by males ($M$ = 2.4) and females ($M$ = 1.9), $t$ < 1.

To test the reliability of the diagnostic information obtained, identical interviews with the mothers of the adolescents were undertaken. These were then correlated with the adolescent interview data. The results of these correlations are presented in Table 1. For both males and females, the number of self-reported ADHD and CD symptoms was significantly correlated with maternal reports of ADHD and CD symptoms, respectively. These correlational data provide evidence for good convergent validity as well as some evidence for discriminant validity between ADHD and CD symptomatologies; in most cases the correlations between CD and ADHD symptomatologies were nonsignificant. Issues of convergent and discriminant validity are particularly relevant given the acknowledged overlap of these two disorders (Hinshaw, 1987).

A comparison of the level of symptomatology reported by mothers and the adolescents revealed no significant differences between the absolute levels of ADHD and CD symptomatologies as reported by the female adolescents and their mothers. However, the mothers reported significantly greater levels of current ADHD, and significantly less CD symptomatology, than did their adolescent sons, although the two sources did not differ in their reports of the degree of ADHD symptomatology by history exhibited by the sons.

**Table 1. Correlations of Mother and Adolescent Interviews**

| | Adolescent interview | | |
| --- | --- | --- | --- |
| | ADHD history | ADHD current | CD current |
| Females ($n = 28$) | | | |
| Mother | | | |
| ADHD-history | .56*** | .53** | −.11 |
| ADHD-current | .42* | .38* | −.22 |
| CD | .03 | .02 | .49** |
| Males ($n = 58$) | | | |
| Mother | | | |
| ADHD-history | .28* | .25* | −.10 |
| ADHD-current | .27* | .36** | −.04 |
| CD | .12 | .27* | .52*** |
| Total sample ($N = 86$) | | | |
| Mother | | | |
| ADHD-history | .43*** | .33*** | −.05 |
| ADHD-current | .35*** | .36*** | −.04 |
| CD | .09 | .18* | .49*** |

*Note.* The interviews for four mothers were missing.
*$p < .05$, **$p < .01$, ***$p < .001$.

## Procedure

The design of the study consisted of administering two laboratory measures of disinhibition to subjects in a counterbalanced order. One measure was the go/no-go discrimination task employed by Newman et al. (1985) to measure the passive-avoidance deficit in disinhibited individuals. The other measure was the card-playing task originally designed by Siegel (1978) to measure response perseveration in psychopaths. The version modified by Newman et al. (1987) was employed in this study.

GO/NO-GO DISCRIMINATION TASK.    The go/no-go discrimination task was identical to that described earlier and consisted of eight sets of eight index cards. On each of the eight cards in a set was a different two-digit number. Four of the eight numbers were arbitrarily designated as positive stimuli, and the remaining four were designated as negative stimuli.

The subjects' task was to learn, by trial and error, to respond to the positive stimuli and withhold response to the negative stimuli. The deck of cards was placed face down in front of the subject, and the cards were turned over one at a time. The subject was given 2 seconds to respond, or withhold responding, to each card before the next one was presented.

Correct responses included responding to a positive stimulus and with-holding a response to a negative stimulus. Incorrect responses included responding to a negative stimulus (i.e., an error of commission) and withholding a response to a positive stimulus (i.e., an error of omission).

Subjects were randomly assigned to one of two experimental conditions that differed only in reinforcement schedules. These conditions were identical to those used by Newman, Widom, and Nathan (1985). Condition R + P involved reinforcement and punishment (i.e., response cost). In this condition, subjects earned 25 cents for responding to a positive stimulus and lost 25 cents for responding to a negative stimulus. There was no consequence for withholding a response.

The second condition, Condition R, involved reinforcement only, as subjects earned 25 cents for any correct response. That is, they earned 25 cents if they responded to a positive stimulus or inhibited a response to a negative stimulus. However, subjects did not lose money for incorrect responses. That is, they did not lose money for responding to a negative stimulus (i.e., error of commission), nor did they lose money for with-holding a response to a positive stimulus (i.e., error of omission).

CARD-PERSEVERATION TASK. The materials consisted of 100 standard playing cards, including number and face cards. The cards were presented in a prearranged random order, and the frequency of each type of card could not be predicted from knowledge of a standard deck. Face cards were designated as winning cards, and number cards were designated as losing cards. The probability of winning (i.e., face card) decreased by 10% with each successive block of 10 cards, from 90% in the first block of 10 cards to 0% in the final block. Within each block of cards the winning and losing cards were presented in a prearranged random order.

Subjects earned 25 cents each time a winning card was played, and they lost 25 cents each time a losing card was played. Before every trial, subjects were asked if they wanted to continue playing. If the subject chose to continue, a card was turned over, and the subject was told if he/she won or lost 25 cents. Subjects could play as many cards as they wished, and they had the opportunity to quit before every trial. The dependent measures were the number of cards played before quitting and the amount of money won.

## Results

Initial analyses of the data revealed no relationship between any of the dependent variables and either age or sex. Thus, these demographic variables were ignored in subsequent analyses. Because the primary analyses involved using a dimensional approach to quantify ADHD and CD symptomatologies, analyses were conducted by correlating the ADHD and CD dimensions, as reported by the adolescents, with performance on each of the two tasks. These analyses were undertaken separately for males and females.

The results for condition R + P of the go/no-go discrimination task are presented in Table 2. It was expected that both ADHD and CD symptomatologies would be positively correlated with errors of commission and negatively correlated with amount of money won. As predicted, ADHD symptomatology in males was significantly and positively correlated with commission errors and significantly and negatively correlated with amount of money won. There were no significant correlations with CD symptomatology for males.

For females in Condition R + P, there were no significant correlations between task performance and ADHD or CD symptomatology, although for the ADHD measure these correlations were in the predicted directions. It appears that the weaker results are due to the decrease in power resulting from the smaller sample size when analyses were conducted separately for males and females.

Contrary to initial hypotheses, there were no significant correlations between adolescent self-reported CD symptoms and commission

**Table 2. Correlations of DBD Symptoms and Go/No-Go Task Performance Reward and Punishment Condition**

|  | Adolescent interview | | |
|  | ADHD history | ADHD current | CD current |
|---|---|---|---|
| Females ($n = 17$) | | | |
| Commission | .39 | .32 | .32 |
| Omission | −.12 | −.37 | .08 |
| Money won | −.20 | −.04 | −.34 |
| Males ($n = 28$) | | | |
| Commission | .47** | .33* | −.23 |
| Omission | .00 | .22 | .07 |
| Money won | −.36* | −.40* | .12 |
| Combined ($n = 45$) | | | |
| Commission | .41** | .33* | .00 |
| Omission | −.02 | .00 | .09 |
| Money won | −.27* | −.20 | −.09 |

*Note.* DBD = Disruptive Behavior Disorders.
*$p < .05$, **$p < .01$.

Table 3. Correlations of DBD Symptoms and Go/No-Go
Task Performance Reward-Alone Condition

| | Adolescent interview | | |
| --- | --- | --- | --- |
| | ADHD history | ADHD current | CD current |
| Females (n = 13) | | | |
| Commission | .45 | .53* | .08 |
| Omission | −.09 | −.15 | −.10 |
| Money won | −.33 | −.36 | −.02 |
| Males (n = 32) | | | |
| Commission | .00 | .06 | −.26 |
| Omission | −.23 | −.03 | −.24 |
| Money won | .15 | .00 | .34* |
| Combined (n = 45) | | | |
| Commission | .17 | .17 | −.17 |
| Omission | −.12 | −.04 | −.19 |
| Money won | −.05 | −.08 | .24 |

Note. DBD = Disruptive Behavior Disorders.
*p < .05.

errors or amount of money won. There were no significant correlations between either ADHD or CD symptomatology and errors of omission.

Table 3 presents the results of the analyses for Condition R. Here the initial predictions were somewhat different. Because the characteristic inhibitory deficit of psychopaths and juvenile delinquents has only been found in situations involving both reward and punishment, it was expected that there would not be a significant correlation between CD symptomatology and number of commission errors or amount of money won. However, it was expected that ADHD symptomatology would continue to be significantly and positively correlated with commission errors and significantly and negatively correlated with amount of money won as it was in the combined reward-and-punishment condition. This hypothesis was based on findings that suggest punishment is necessary to help ADHD subjects control their inhibitory deficit.

Contrary to predictions, ADHD symptoms in males were not predictive of commission errors or winning less money. However, for the females there was a significant, positive correlation between self-reported, current ADHD symptomatology and errors of commission. Interestingly, CD symptomatology, as reported by adolescent males, was significantly and positively correlated with amount of money won and showed a trend ($p < .10$) for being negatively correlated with both errors of commission and omission. That is, CD symptoms were predictive of making fewer errors and winning more money. However, it was only for the males that these findings were significant. In fact, for the females, there was no relationship between CD symptomatology and performance.

The results for the card-playing task are presented in Table 4. This task was designed to elicit problems in an overactive BAS and is hypothesized to be associated with CD. It was expected that ADHD and CD symptomatologies would be significantly and positively correlated with number of cards played and significantly and negatively correlated with amount of money won.

For males, ADHD symptomatology by history was significantly and negatively correlated with amount of money won. In addition, ADHD symptomatology, both current and by history, showed a trend for being ($p < .10$) positively correlated with number of cards played. That is, ADHD symptoms were predictive of winning less money and tended to be associated with playing more cards. For females, ADHD symptomatology, both current and by history, was significantly and negatively correlated with amount of money won. However, there were no significant correlations between number of cards played and ADHD symptomatology for females. CD symptomatology was not significantly correlated with the number of cards played or the amount of money won.

**Table 4. Correlations of DBD Symptoms and Card Perseveration Task Performance**

|  | Adolescent interview | | |
| --- | --- | --- | --- |
|  | ADHD history | ADHD current | CD current |
| Females ($n = 30$) |  |  |  |
| Cards played | .01 | .16 | .20 |
| Money won | −.31* | −.39* | −.05 |
| Males ($n = 60$) |  |  |  |
| Cards played | .19 | .17 | .00 |
| Money won | −.22* | −.16 | −.03 |
| Total sample ($N = 90$) |  |  |  |
| Cards played | .10 | .17 | .05 |
| Money won | −.23* | −.24* | −.03 |

Note. DBD = Disruptive Behavior Disorders.
*$p < .05$.

## Discussion

The purpose of this study was to examine the underlying processes of disinhibition in male and female adolescents with ADHD and CD. Two measures of response inhibition and perseveration were used to study disinhibition under varying motivational conditions. The results provide some interesting differences between the performance of males and females and between adolescents with ADHD and CD symptomatologies.

Performance associated with ADHD symptomatology was similar to that of Newman's psychopaths (Newman et al., 1985; Newman & Kosson, 1986; Newman et al., 1987). This is particularly evident in the card-perseveration task and Condition R + P of the go/no-go discrimination task and was especially true for males. Specifically, in the combined reward-and-punishment condition of the go/no-go discrimination task, ADHD symptomatology for males was associated with making more errors of commission and winning less money. Although results were in a similar direction for females, they were not significant. The lack of significant results for females is difficult to interpret due to the low power in this condition ($n = 17$). On the card-perseveration task, for both males and females, ADHD symptomatology was associated with winning less money, and for males there was a trend toward playing more cards.

The results suggest that in many ways adolescents with ADHD are performing like adults with antisocial personality disorder; when cues for both reward and punishment are in conflict, the ADHD adolescents are unable to inhibit inappropriate responses. Why might it be that adolescents with ADHD are exhibiting a pattern similar to that found for adult psychopaths? One possible explanation is that adolescents with ADHD are at risk for developing antisocial personality disorder in adulthood, and the obtained results may suggest that these boys are exhibiting early signs of psychopathy or antisocial behavior, at least as measured by laboratory tasks. In a follow-up study by Gittelman, Mannuzza, Shenker, and Bonagura (1985), 25% of the boys with ADHD in the sample were found to exhibit persistent antisocial behavior in adulthood. For ADHD children whose symptoms persisted, their rate of antisocial personality disorder reached 48% (Klein & Mannuzza, 1991). Thus, a significant number of ADHD adolescents are at risk for antisocial personality disorder, and this subgroup may be accounting for the pattern of results similar to that exhibited by Newman's psychopaths.

However, one factor mitigating against this argument is that a similar pattern of results was obtained for females in the current study. Because antisocial personality disorder in adult females is relatively uncommon, this suggests that this particular pattern of task performance may not be automatically associated with antisocial personality disorder.

Another possible explanation for these findings is that both adolescents with ADHD and adult males with antisocial personality disorder may have a similar response-modulation deficit when faced with motivational situations involving competing reward-and-punishment contingencies. That is, in the presence of competing reward-and-punishment cues, they may have difficulty switching their focus from rewards to punishments and may have problems with inhibiting their behavior in order to perform adaptively. Thus, both adolescents with ADHD and adult psychopaths may have similar problems with response modulation, but the behavioral outcomes of this underlying disorder may differ for the two groups (see also, Newman & Wallace, 1993).

The hypothesis that ADHD youngsters may have difficulty with response modulation is consistent with theorizing by Douglas (1983) and with empirical results offered by Whalen, Henker, Collins, McAuliffe, and Vaux (1979) and Landau and Milich (1988). Whalen et al. found that ADHD children, performing in a "space flight" task, were less likely than control children to adjust their social-communication behaviors as the role requirements shifted. Similarly, Landau and Milich found that ADHD children playing a "TV Talk Show" game were less willing or able than control children to shift their communicative behaviors between the roles of host and guest. Thus, Newman and Wallace's (1993) conclusion that ADHD children may also exhibit a response-modulation deficit is consistent with both the present findings and previous research, reflecting both laboratory and social-interaction tasks.

We undertook this study to test Quay's (1988a) hypothesis that the primary deficit of ADHD children is a dysfunctional BIS. On the surface, the present results appear to be more consistent with the response-modulation deficit proposed by Newman and Wallace (1993) than with a dysfunctional BIS. However, it is still possible that the performance of the adolescents with ADHD symptomatology is a result of a weak BIS. Newman was able to rule out this possibility with male psychopaths by using a punishment-alone condition in the go/no-go discrimination task (Newman & Kosson, 1986). He found no significant differences between the psychopaths and normals in this condition and, thus, concluded that the deficit was associated with activation of both the BAS and BIS rather than either system alone. The results of the present study cannot make this distinction for adolescents with ADHD because a punishment-alone condition was not run.

Another possible explanation for the performance of the adolescents with ADHD relates to Douglas's (1985) work on partial reinforcement. She proposes that children with ADHD experience considerable frustration when an expected reward is not obtained. Consistent with this hypothesis, she has found children with ADHD to perform poorly under conditions of partial reinforcement and extinction (Douglas & Parry, 1983), and she attributes this poor performance to frustration. This type of frustration is one possible explanation for the poorer performance associated with ADHD symptomatology on the tasks in this study. In Condition R + P of the go/no-go task, the same behavior (i.e., tapping the card) could result in either reward or punishment depending on the stimulus number presented. When the subjects responded to a card, they expected that this behavior would result in reward, and thus they may have become frustrated if punishment occurred instead. Douglas and Parry (1983) argue that the performance of children with ADHD may deteriorate in response to rewards that are inconsistent or do not appear when anticipated (e.g., partial reinforcement). Although the rewards and punishments in Condition R + P of the go/no-go task were systematic, it is possible that the subjects viewed them as inconsistent. This may have been particularly true at the beginning of the task before learning had occurred. Thus, this condition may have evoked frustration similar to that described by Douglas (Douglas, 1985; Douglas & Parry, 1983), thereby producing the high rates of passive avoidance errors.

The poor performance associated with ADHD in males on the reward-and-punishment condition of the go/no-go discrimination task may also have some implications for treating impulsivity in boys with ADHD. Although it has been found that response cost is effective with ADHD (O'Leary, 1985), the motivational condition in this task may be somewhat different than typically studied. In the task, the subjects were rewarded for responding to positive stimuli and punished for responding to negative stimuli. However, in each case, the response was the same (i.e., tapping a card). Therefore, the children were rewarded and punished for displaying the same behavior under different stimulus conditions. In typical behavior modification systems, reinforcement is used when the child exhibits an appropriate behavior (e.g., complimenting a peer), and response cost is used when the child exhibits an inappropriate behavior (e.g., teasing a peer). These behaviors are considered mutually exclusive, and it is hoped that the appropriate behavior will begin to replace the inappropriate behavior.

The behaviors described above (i.e., complimenting and teasing) are two different behaviors. Consider the situation where a child who often makes jokes on the playground is reinforced by peers' laughter. Yet when this child makes a joke in the classroom, he or she is reprimanded by the teacher. Alternatively, a child who is cheered for aggression on the football field is punished for aggression on the playground. In these cases, the child is being reinforced and punished for exhibiting the same behavior under different circumstances, and he or she must learn to discriminate between appropriate and inappropriate situational cues for that behavior. This discrimination may be of particular difficulty for children with ADHD, and it is this type of discrimination that was required on the go/no-go task. The poorer performance associated with ADHD may not be surprising given previous findings that children with ADHD have difficulty adapting behavior to situational demands (Landau & Milich, 1988), and it suggests that future research should investigate the circumstances under which disinhibition occurs.

ADHD symptomatology was associated with impulsive responding on the tasks in both males and females under particular circumstances. This is one of a few studies to find clear evidence of problems with impulsivity among females with ADHD. Although the patterns of disinhibition on the tasks varied somewhat for males and females with ADHD symptomatology, ADHD was associated with impulsive responding for both sexes. This may suggest that the underlying mechanisms of disinhibition are different in males and females with ADHD but that both groups have problems with impulsivity.

Both males and females exhibited problems with disinhibition on the card-perseveration task. However, in males, ADHD symptomatology was clearly associated with problems in the combined reward-and-punishment condition relative to the reward-alone condition. In contrast, ADHD symptomatology in females was significantly associated with difficulty in the reward-alone condition, whereas the results regarding the R + P condition were more equivocal. The results regarding the reward-alone condition are especially intriguing because this means that the females were unable to inhibit their responding, even when they could earn reward for such inhibition. This may suggest that the female adolescents with ADHD symptomatology have an unusually weak inhibitory system, or an overreactive BAS, or some combination of the two. Whatever the explanation, these findings suggest that females whose ADHD symptomatology persists into adolescence are prone to problems of disinhibition. In some ways, this problem is an especially pervasive one because it was evident under several different motivational conditions.

One potentially perplexing finding concerns the results for the card-perseveration task. For both males and females, ADHD symptomatology was associated with winning less money. However, for neither sex was there a significant correlation between ADHD and cards played, although there was a trend for males. On the surface, these results may appear counterintuitive, especially because Newman and Quay have consistently found both cards played and money won to be significantly associated with psychopathy or conduct disorder, respectively. However, the present results are consistent with those obtained in an earlier study (Hartung, Milich, & Pelham, 1992), in which ADHD was associated with winning less money on the card-perseveration task, but it was unrelated to the number of cards played. An analysis of the individual data in the Hartung et al. (1992) study revealed that there were two subgroups of ADHD children who had difficulty with this task. One group, consistent with Newman's psychopaths, clearly won less money as a result of playing too many cards. The other group won less money because they gave up too early. Given the nature of the task, either strategy results in low levels of money earned.

There are two possible explanations for the performance of the ADHD children in the Hartung et al. (1992) study who gave up too quickly. One possibility is that those subjects who quit too early are a subgroup of the subjects with ADHD experiencing comorbid anxiety. Walker et al. (1992) discuss comorbid anxiety in the presence of CD. They suggest that children with CD and comorbid anxiety disorder are impulsive, but they are less likely to develop behaviors that are blatantly antisocial. The issue of externalizing disorders and comorbid anxiety, and how anxiety may affect disinhibition deserves further exploration. The second possible explanation for the findings in Hartung et al. (1992) is that ADHD children are notorious for getting frustrated easily and failing to persevere (Douglas, 1985). Thus, the subgroup who quit early may reflect this response style instead.

Contrary to initial expectations, there was only one significant association between conduct-disorder symptomatology and performance on the tasks, and this was in an unpredicted direction. Thus, conduct-disorder symptomatology among males was unrelated to performance on the combined reward-and-punishment condition of the go/no-go discrimination task. This finding is contrary to the hypothesis based on Newman's results with psychopaths and juvenile delinquents. It is interesting, however, that CD symptomatology in males was related to improved performance on the reward-alone condition. That is, CD symptoms were associated with winning significantly more money and with a trend ($p < .10$) toward fewer commission errors.

There are at least two possible explanations for this finding. First, it must be kept in mind that the sample consisted entirely of psychiatrically referred adolescents, so that those with high levels of conduct-disorder symptoms were being contrasted with adolescents with other psychiatric problems (e.g., ADHD, depression, etc.). Thus, the improved performance of the CD adolescents on the reward-alone condition is only relative to adolescents with other psychiatric problems, and it is not clear how they would compare to a normal control group.

The second possible explanation for this finding relates to the notion of socialized delinquency (Quay, 1987). This subgroup of conduct disorder is described as a relatively high-functioning group with fewer problems in disinhibition, self-control, and peer relations than the other subgroups. The socialized group is not noted to suffer from psychopathology per se, but instead their problems are assumed to reflect environmental or situational factors (Quay, 1987). Thus, for example, Henn, Bardwell, and Jenkins (1980) found that, among institutionalized delinquents, the socialized group had fewer problems during their stay and clearly had the best outcome. Given that the subjects with CD in this study did not demonstrate impulsive behavior and responded well to positive incentives, they may represent the socialized type of delinquency.

## Future Directions

The present results offer some interesting leads for future directions in this field. First, the results regarding sex differences suggest that problems of disinhibition among adolescent females may be greater than the results of the limited childhood data would suggest. In addition, the present results offer the possibility that there are differential patterns of disinhibition among males and females. Although these findings must be interpreted cautiously, especially given the relatively small number of females in the study, they clearly warrant further investigation.

The present sample consisted entirely of psychiatrically referred adolescents. Thus, the lack of a normal control group in the study limits conclusions regarding the relationship of the behavior of the disinhibited subjects to normal adolescents. Although significant correlations indicate a relationship between symptomatology and task behavior, this is relative to a psychiatric control group. This fact must be considered when interpreting the results of this study, and in future studies it would be advantageous to use both normal and psychiatric controls.

The results of the present study raise interesting questions regarding the role of the BIS in ADHD. Future investigators may want to further address this issue by examining the performance of adolescents with ADHD in a condition involving punishment alone in order to rule out BIS functioning as problematic in this population. If the performance of subjects with ADHD were again found to be associated with poorer performance in a combined reward-and-punishment condition, but not in a condition involving punishment alone, this would eliminate the BIS as solely responsible for the poorer performance associated with ADHD in the present study. Such a finding would implicate a response-modulation deficit in the presence of both reward-and-punishment cues as has been suggested with male psychopaths (Newman & Kosson, 1986).

A final avenue for further investigation involves the relationship between performance on these laboratory tasks and disinhibitory behavior in the real world. Some have argued that laboratory tasks such as the card-perseveration and go/no-go discrimination tasks have limited relevance to behavior outside of the laboratory. Although these tasks have repeatedly differentiated adult males with psychopathy from normal controls, we cannot determine whether the underlying processes of disinhibited behavior in the laboratory are consistent with the underlying processes of disinhibited behavior in naturalistic settings.

## Summary

We began this chapter by summarizing the difficulties that Milich and Kramer (1984) had noted regarding previous research in the area of impulsivity. Especially salient was the lack of theory-driven research to further our understanding of this clinically important problem. We then noted that over the last decade considerable progress has been made in theoretically based, programmatic research in this area. The work of both Newman and Quay has demonstrated that it is possible to elucidate the conditions under which both children and adults, with a variety of behavioral disorders, may exhibit disinhibitory behavior. The research presented in this chapter was designed to further contribute to this line of work, by examining conditions under which male and female adolescents, who exhibit either ADHD or CD symptomatology, may display disinhibitory behavior. The results revealed that both gender and psychiatric status interact with motivational conditions to determine a given individual's level of impulsivity. Future lines of investigation were identified that would further our understanding of the roles that personality and situational factors may play in the manifestation of disinhibition.

Whereas Milich and Kramer (1984) ended their review on a somewhat discouraging note, we feel much more optimistic that the next decade will continue to see important advances in theory and research underlying the construct of impulsivity.

Acknowledgments. This research was supported by a grant from the Department of Psychiatry to C. A. Martin. The authors wish to acknowledge their valuable discussions with Joe Newman in conceptualizing the study and interpreting the results. Monica Harris and Steven Landau offered very valuable suggestions on an early version of this chapter.

## References

Abramowitz, A. J., O'Leary, S. G., & Rosen, L. A. (1987). Reducing off-task behavior in the classroom: A comparison of encouragement and reprimands. *Journal of Abnormal Child Psychology, 15,* 153–163.

American Psychiatric Association (1980). *Diagnostic and Statistical Manual of Mental Disorders* (3rd ed.). Washington, DC: Author.

American Psychiatric Association (1987). *Diagnostic and statistical manual of mental disorders* (3rd ed. rev.). Washington, DC: Author.

Berry, C. A., Shaywitz, S. E., & Shaywitz, B. A. (1985). Girls with attention deficit disorder: A silent minority? A report on behavioral and cognitive characteristics. *Pediatrics, 76,* 801–809.

Breen, M. J. (1989). Cognitive and behavioral differences in ADHD boys and girls. *Journal of Child Psychology and Psychiatry, 30,* 711–716.

Breen, M. J., & Altepeter, T. S. (1990). Situational variability in boys and girls identified as ADHD. *Journal of Clinical Psychology, 46,* 486–490.

Brown, R. T., Madan-Swain, A., & Baldwin, K. (1991). Gender differences in a clinic-referred sample of attention-deficit-disordered children. *Child Psychiatry and Human Development, 22,* 111–128.

Cloninger, C. R. (1986). A unified biosocial theory of personality and its role in the development of anxiety states. *Psychiatric Developments, 3,* 167–226.

deHaas, P. A. (1986). Attention styles and peer relationships of hyperactive and normal boys and girls. *Journal of Abnormal Child Psychology, 14,* 457–467.

Daugherty, T. K., & Quay, H. C. (1991). Response perseveration and delayed responding in childhood behavior disorders. *Journal of Child Psychology and Psychiatry, 32,* 453–461.

Douglas, V. I. (1985). The response of ADD children to reinforcement: Theoretical and clinical implications. In L. M. Bloomingdale (Ed.), *Attention deficit disorder: Identification, course, and treatment rationale* (pp. 49–66). New York: Spectrum.

Douglas, V. I., & Parry, P. A. (1983). Effects of reward on delayed reaction time task performance of hyperactive children. *Journal of Abnormal Child Psychology, 11,* 313–326.

Eysenck, H. J. (1969). Nature and history of human typology. In H. J. Eysenck & S. B. G. Eysenck (Eds.), *Personality structure and measurement* (pp. 3–140). London: Routledge & Kegan Paul.

Gorenstein, E. E., & Newman, J. P. (1980). Disinhibitory psychopathology: A new perspective and model for research. *Psychological Review, 87*, 301–315.

Gittelman, R., Mannuzza, S., Shenker, R., & Bonagura, N. (1985). Hyperactive boys almost grown up. *Archives of General Psychiatry, 42*, 937–947.

Gray, J. A. (1975). *Elements of a two-process theory of learning.* London: Academic Press.

Hare, R. D.. (1980). A research scale for the assessment of psychopathy in criminal populations. *Personality and Individual Differences, 1*, 111–119.

Hartung, C. M., Milich, R., & Pelham, W. E. (1992, October). *Response perseveration in ADHD boys.* Paper presented at the Inaugural Kentucky Conference on Advanced Studies in Psychopathology, Lexington, KY.

Henn, F. A., Bardwell, R., & Jenkins, R. L. (1980). Juvenile delinquents revisited. *Archives of General Psychiatry, 37*, 1160–1163.

Hinshaw, S. P. (1987). On the distinction between attention deficits/hyperactivity and conduct problems/aggression in child psychopathology. *Psychological Bulletin, 101*, 443–463.

James, A., & Taylor, E. (1990). Sex differences in the hyperkinetic syndrome of childhood. *Journal of Child Psychology and Psychiatry, 31*, 437–446.

Klein, R. G., & Mannuzza, S. (1991). Long-term outcome of hyperactive children: A review. *Journal of American Academy of Child and Adolescent Psychiatry, 30*, 383–387.

Lahey, B. B., Pelham, W. E., Schaughency, E. A., Atkins, M. S., Murphy, H. A., Hynd, G., Russo, M., Hartdagen, S., & Lorys-Vernon, A. (1988). *Journal of the American Academy of Child and Adolescent Psychiatry, 27*, 330–335.

Landau, S., & Milich, R. (1988). Social communication patterns of attention deficit-disordered boys. *Journal of Abnormal Child Psychology, 16*, 69–81.

McBurnett, K. (1992). Psychobiological approaches to personality and their applications to child psychopathology. In B. B. Lahey & A. E. Kazdin (Eds.), *Advances in clinical child psychology* (Vol. 14, pp. 107–164). New York: Plenum Press.

Milich, R., & Kramer, J. (1984). Reflections on impulsivity: An empirical investigation of impulsivity as a construct. In K. D. Gadow (Ed.), *Advances in learning and behavioral disabilities* (Vol. 3, pp. 57–94). Greenwich, CT: JAI Press.

Milich, R., & Loney, J. (1979). The role of hyperactive and aggressive symptomatology in predicting adolescent outcome in hyperactive children. *Journal of Pediatric Psychology, 12*, 93–112.

Milich, R., Loney, J., & Landau, S. (1982). Independent dimensions of hyperactivity and aggression: Validation with playroom observation data. *Journal of Abnormal Psychology, 91*, 183–198.

Newman, J. P. (1987). Reaction to punishment in extroverts and psychopaths: Implications for the impulsive behavior of disinhibited individuals. *Journal of Research in Personality, 21*, 464–480.

Newman, J. P., & Kosson, D. S. (1986). Passive avoidance learning in psychopathic and nonpsychopathic offenders. *Journal of Abnormal Psychology, 95*, 252–256.

Newman, J. P., Patterson, C. M., & Kosson, D. S. (1987). Response perseveration in psychopaths. *Journal of Abnormal Psychology, 96*, 145–148.

Newman, J. P., & Wallace, J. F. (1993). Diverse pathways to deficient self-regulation: Implications for disinhibitory psychopathology in children. *Clinical Psychology Review, 13*, 699–720.

Newman, J. P., Widom, C. S., & Nathan, S. (1985). Passive avoidance in syndromes of disinhibition: Psychopathy and extraversion. *Journal of Personality and Social Psychology, 43*, 1316–1327.

O'Leary, S. G. (1985, November). *It's time to stop avoiding punishment.* Invited Address, Association for the Advancement of Behavior Therapy Convention, Houston, TX.

Pelham, W. E., & Hinshaw, S. (1992). Behavioral intervention for attention deficit disorder. In S. M. Turner, K. S. Calhoun, & H. E. Adams (Eds.), *Handbook of clinical behavior therapy* (Vol. 2). New York: Wiley & Sons.

Pfiffner, L. J., & Barkley, R. A. (1990). Educational placement and classroom management. In R. Barkley (Ed.), *Attention deficit hyperactivity disorder: A handbook for diagnosis and treatment.* New York: Guilford Press.

Quay, H. C. (1987). Patterns of delinquent behavior. In H. C. Quay (Ed.), *Handbook of juvenile delinquency* (pp. 118–138). New York: Wiley.

Quay, H. C. (1988a). Attention deficit disorder and the behavioral inhibition system: The relevance of the neuropsychological theory of Jeffrey A. Gray. In L. M. Bloomingdale & J. Sergeant (Eds.), *Attention deficit disorder; Criteria, cognition, intervention* (pp. 117–125). Oxford: Pergamon.

Quay, H. C. (1988b). The behavioral reward and inhibition systems in childhood behavior disorders. In L. M. Bloomingdale (Ed.), *Attention deficit disorder* (Vol. 3, pp. 176–186). Oxford: Pergamon.

Quay, H. C. (1993). The psychobiology of undersocialized aggressive conduct disorder. *Development and Psychopathology, 5,* 165–180.

Quay, H. C., & Peterson, D. R. (1987). *Manual for the Revised Problem Behavior Checklist.* Coral Gables, FL: University of Miami.

Robins, L. N. (1966). *Deviant children grown up.* Baltimore: Williams & Wilkins.

Schachar, R., & Logan, G. D. (1990). Impulsivity and inhibitory control in normal development and childhood psychopathology. *Developmental Psychology, 26,* 710–720.

Schachar, R. J., Tannock, R., & Logan, G. D. (1993). Inhibitory control, impulsiveness and attention deficit hyperactivity disorder. *Clinical Psychology Review, 13,* 721–739.

Shapiro, S. K., Quay, H. C., Hogan, A. E., & Schwartz, K. P. (1988). Response perseveration and delayed responding in undersocialized aggressive conduct disorder. *Journal of Abnormal Child Psychiatry, 97,* 371–373.

Siegel, R. A. (1978). Probability of punishment and suppression of behavior in psychopathic and nonpsychopathic offenders. *Journal of Abnormal Psychology, 87,* 514–522.

Tannock, R., Schachar, R. J., Carr, R. P., Chajczyk, D., & Logan, G. D. (1989). Effects of methylphenidate on inhibitory control in hyperactive children. *Journal of Abnormal Child Psychology, 17,* 473–491.

Trommer, B. L., Hoeppner, J. B., & Zecker, S. G. (1991). The go-no go test in attention deficit disorder is sensitive to methylphenidate. *Journal of Child Neurology, 6,* S128–S131.

Trull, T. J., Widiger, T. A., & Guthrie, P. (1990). Categorical versus dimensional status of borderline personality disorder. *Journal of Abnormal Psychology, 99,* 40–48.

Walker, J. L., Lahey, B. B., Russo, M. F., Frick, P. J., Christ, M. A., McBurnett, K., Loeber, R., Stouthamer-Loeber, M., & Green, S. M. (1991). Anxiety, inhibition, and conduct disorder in children: I. Relations to social impairment. *Journal of the American Academy of Child and Adolescent Psychiatry, 30,* 187–191.

Whalen, C. K., Henker, B., Collins, B. E., McAuliffe, S., & Vaux, A. (1979). Peer interaction in a structured communication task: Comparisons of normal and hyperactive boys and of methylphenidate (Ritalin) and placebo effects. *Child Development, 50,* 388–401.

Zuckerman, M. (Ed.). (1983). *Biological bases of sensation seeking, impulsivity and anxiety.* Hillsdale, NJ: Lawrence Erlbaum.

—————— 6 ——————

# Framework for a Developmental Model of Oppositional Defiant Disorder and Conduct Disorder

## BENJAMIN B. LAHEY and ROLF LOEBER

It is a heartfelt honor to have been asked to contribute to this volume honoring Herbert C. Quay for his contributions to the field of developmental psychopathology. We have long benefitted personally in our teaching and research from his voluminous and seminal work and have valued his friendship and mentoring immensely over the years. In choosing a topic for this chapter, we selected one that we have discussed many times with Herb, a model of the *development* of serious conduct problems. We chose this topic because it reflects, and indeed incorporates, many of Herb's contributions to the classification and development of conduct problems. Because the scope of Herb's work and impact is broad, however, we could just as easily have chosen to write on our views on the environmental and biological correlates of conduct disorder, as his work has stimulated our interest in that field as well.

It is a truism that one cannot understand any maladaptive pattern of

BENJAMIN B. LAHEY • Department of Psychiatry, University of Chicago, Chicago, Illinois 60637-1470.    ROLF LOEBER • Western Psychiatric Institute and Clinic, University of Pittsburgh, 3811 O'Hara Street, Pittsburgh, Pennsylvania 15213.
*Disruptive Behavior Disorders in Childhood,* edited by Donald K. Routh. Plenum Press, New York, 1994.

behavior in children and adolescents without understanding how that syndrome changes during the course of development. We change throughout our lives, but at no time more rapidly than in childhood and adolescence, and the psychological disorders that afflict us change as well. In spite of this truism, we have typically studied disorders in cross-sectional samples that provide no more than static "snapshots" of the disorder. This strategy has been costly, as a definitive understanding of phenomenology, prognosis, immature precursors to later serious maladaptive behaviors, and factors that cause and maintain psychological disorders can only come from longitudinal research.

Gradually, however, progress has been made in the longitudinal study of conduct problems, beginning with the pioneering longitudinal studies of delinquency and antisocial behavior of Robins (1966; Robins & Ratcliff, 1979), Glueck and Glueck (1968), West and Farrington (1977), Henn, Bardwell, and Jenkins (1980), MacFarlane, Allen, and Honzik (1962), and Greene et al. (1973). More recently, important longitudinal studies have been conducted by Anderson, Williams, McGee, and Silva (1987), Harrington, Fudge, Rutter, Pickles, and Hill (1991), Offord et al. (1992), Stanger, McConaughy, and Achenbach (1992), Stattin and Magnusson (1989), and Verhulst and van der Ende (1992). We will draw on these studies and our own ongoing prospective and cross-sectional studies as sources for the developmental model presented in this chapter. Our focus will be on the maladaptive patterns of behavior known as oppositional defiant disorder (ODD) and conduct disorder (CD).

## Framework for a Developmental Model

In this chapter, we will sketch the broad outline of a developmental model of ODD and CD. In doing so, we will be elaborating ideas laid down in earlier papers (Lahey, Loeber, Quay, Frick, & Grimm, 1992; Loeber, 1988; Loeber, Lahey, & Thomas, 1991). The sketchiness of this outline reflects the relative paucity of relevant literature, but enough is now known to begin to describe the development of child problem behavior in broad terms. At the end of this chapter, we will point to several areas for future elaboration of this model. We will not discuss factors that give rise to and maintain conduct problems, but we will discuss some ways in which viewing ODD and CD from a developmental perspective may facilitate studies of such factors.

The essential postulates of this model are summarized in Figure 1. The developmental relationships among the maladaptive behaviors referred to as ODD and CD are assumed to be predominantly nonrandom.

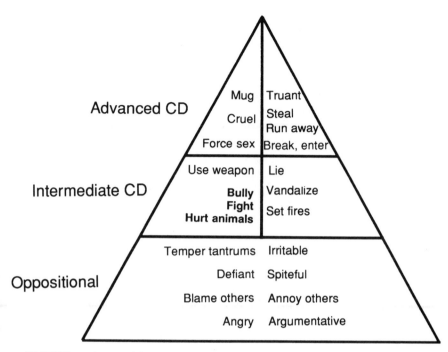

**FIGURE 1.** A visual heuristic describing the developmental levels model.

That is, some behaviors regularly tend to emerge earlier in the course of development and to proceed other behaviors. These relationships can be described in the visual heuristic of a "developmental pyramid," with ODD behaviors at the base and CD behaviors above them.

The horizontal dimension of the pyramid represents prevalence, and the vertical dimension represents age of the first occurrence (age of onset) of the maladaptive behaviors. The CD behaviors are arranged on top of the ODD behaviors not only because they are less prevalent and tend to onset at later ages but because we believe that ODD and CD are related developmentally. We hypothesize that relatively large numbers of young children develop ODD behaviors, with some of them exhibiting enough ODD behaviors to meet DSM criteria for the diagnosis of ODD. With increasing age, some boys with ODD will cease to engage in significant numbers of these problematic behaviors, whereas others will continue to exhibit ODD for long periods of time. As the children who persistently display high numbers of ODD behaviors grow older, some of them add enough CD behaviors to their repertoire to meet diagnostic criteria for that disorder. The fact that the pyramid is less wide at the level of CD behaviors reflects both the fact that each CD behavior is less prevalent than each ODD behavior and the fact that not all children with ODD will develop CD (i.e., will remain at the level of ODD or will improve).

A distinction also is drawn in this model between *two developmental levels of CD* behaviors. We hypothesize that many children who develop enough behaviors to meet diagnostic criteria for CD will not progress beyond the most prevalent CD behaviors with the earliest ages of onset (fighting, bullying, lying, etc.). Some of these youths will improve over time, whereas others will not progress beyond this early stage of CD (termed *intermediate* CD in this model). Some youths who reach the intermediate level of CD, however, will develop enough serious CD behaviors that they will penetrate to the *advanced* level of CD. Again, the narrowness of the pyramid at the top reflects the low prevalence of these severe behaviors and the relatively small number of youths who reach this level.

The developmental progression from one level to the next is hypothesized to be mostly a process of *accretion,* with new behaviors being added to the existing repertoire with little loss of existing behaviors. As we will discuss later in this chapter, there is evidence that the prevalence of the milder behaviors that onset earliest decreases over the course of development in the general population, but we posit that this average decrease in prevalence is mostly due to improvement in those youths who drop below the diagnostic threshold for ODD or CD over time, rather than a process of deletion of milder behaviors and replacement with more severe behaviors over time in youths with persistent CD. Youths with the most persistent and severe cases of CD appear to retain behaviors from their previous level, even after they have progressed to the next developmental level, with little deletion of milder behaviors.

It should be emphasized that we are not hypothesizing that the distinctions between ODD and the levels of CD are qualitative, or even clear-cut quantitative distinctions. We have knowingly drawn lines of demarcation at points along a continuum. Although the points of demarcation are not arbitrary, the fact that we have divided a developmental continuum into discrete "levels" must be recognized. The distinctiveness of each will surely prove to be no greater than any other developmental "stages" in physical or cognitive domains. To borrow a good analogy, the difference between levels will resemble the muted difference between colors in a rainbow. This does not mean, however, that we believe that the distinction among development levels of conduct problems will not prove to be useful.

It should be admitted, and even emphasized, that at this point in the development of the model, it is not yet fully clear at which level each behavior should be placed. There is little doubt about the placement of some behaviors, for example, defiance of caretaker requests and temper tantrums are undoubtedly at the base of the pyramid. Similarly, bullying, fighting, and lying are clearly the earliest CD behaviors to emerge (and are prime examples of the "intermediate" level of CD), and there is little doubt that breaking and entering, theft with confrontation of the victim, and forced sex are serious behaviors that emerge late in the development of CD and exemplify the "advanced" level.

However, there is some doubt at this point about the placement of a few behaviors in the developmental model. This lack of certainty is due to three factors. First, the several studies that we have conducted to distinguish among levels of conduct problems have used different strategies, methods, and different samples, and consequently have yield somewhat different conclusions. Second, behaviors are classified at the different developmental levels based on multiple criteria (statistical covariation, age of onset, developmental course, and severity). In many cases, these indices converge to indicate clearly at which level a symptom should be placed, but in the case of other symptoms, there is some disagreement among the indices.

What is most important is that some behaviors present inherent obstacles to classification in this developmental framework because these conduct problems *themselves* change over the course of development. The behaviors "stealing without confrontation" and "use of a weapon" provide good examples of this point. Both of these problem behaviors first emerge at early ages in immature forms. Young children with conduct problems often steal toys, school supplies, and small items from stores, but later, more serious and developmentally advanced forms of stealing expensive items, automobiles, and the like emerge in youths that have penetrated to "advanced" CD. Similarly, it is not uncommon for young aggressive children to use weapons such as rocks and sticks in fights, but the use of knives, guns, and more harmful weapons does not emerge until later ages. Therefore, some behaviors could legitimately be considered to be both "intermediate" and "advanced" CD behaviors, depending on their seriousness. This issue is of such importance that it may account for much of the differences between the different studies and indices reviewed below. For all of these reasons, the developmental model presented in this chapter should be considered to be a "first approximation" to a model that will be clarified and refined through further study.

It also should be noted that we believe that the developmental levels model described in this chapter only applies to children who first meet criteria for CD before puberty. We will have more to say on this topic later in the chapter when we discuss developmental subtypes of CD.

In the following sections of this chapter, we will review the evidence that led to the induction of the developmental levels model and the type of empirical tests that will support, modify, or refute the model in the future. The organization of the remainder of this chapter will reflect the fact that the three putative developmental levels of ODD and CD can be distinguished on the following grounds:

1. Statistical covariation among the behaviors at each level.
2. Age of onset of the behaviors at each level.
3. Developmental course of the behaviors at each level.
4. Seriousness ratings of the behaviors at each level and severity of impairment.
5. Developmental sequencing of the levels.
6. Different correlates of the levels.
7. Different stability and prognosis of conduct problems at different levels.

## Distinction between ODD and CD

In the DSM framework, the diagnostic categories of ODD and CD distinguish between patterns of disruptive behavior that differ in severity (DSM-III-R, p. 56). As defined in both DSM-III and DSM-III-R, ODD is an enduring pattern of oppositional, irritable, and defiant behavior, whereas CD is a persistent pattern of more serious violations of the rights of others and social norms. Since the introduction of separate diagnoses of ODD and CD in DSM-III (APA, 1980), clinicians and researchers have debated the utility of such a distinction, with some favoring one diagnostic entity instead of two (Anderson et al., 1987; Rey et al. 1988; Reeves, Werry, Elkind, & Zametkin, 1987; Werry, Reeves, and Elkind, 1987). Indeed, the distinction between ODD and CD in DSM-III and DSM-III-R has been honored by researchers far more by its nonobservance than its observance. ODD and CD have been combined in a single category in nearly all published studies since the publication of DSM-III (e.g., Anderson et al., 1987; Bird et al., 1988; Offord, Boyle et al., 1987; Werry et al., 1987), except for a few studies that have specifically addressed the validity of the diagnosis of ODD that are reviewed in this chapter. This decision clearly reflects an assumption that ODD and CD are similar enough to combine and still draw meaningful conclusions about the combined ODD/CD group.

We take the position that the maladaptive behaviors that define ODD and CD can and should be distinguished, particularly in DSM diagnostic terms, but that they are intimately related in both taxonomic and developmental terms. We will first summarize the principal reasons for distinguishing between ODD and CD, then provide our view of their developmental relationship. In doing so, we will follow Quay's (1986a) strategy for the empirical induction of dimensions and categories of maladaptive behavior. We will first describe and operationally define "those features said to constitute the category or the continuum" (p. 2), demonstrate that the features of ODD and CD each "exist as a cluster of covarying characteristics" (p. 2), then validate the distinction against external criteria. We will review evidence on patterns of behavioral covariation, age of onset, developmental course and stability, severity, developmental sequencing, and correlates. Finally, on the basis of the available evidence, we will present a developmental model of ODD and CD that can be tested for its utility in future studies.

## Patterns of Statistical Covariation

### Factor Analysis

The fundamental question concerning any putative syndrome of maladaptive behavior is whether the defining behaviors covary. The first clear picture of the patterns of statistical covariation among the symptoms of ODD and CD was provided by Quay (1986a), who reviewed over 60 factor analyses of parent and teacher ratings of disruptive child behaviors. He judged whether factors of misbehaviors extracted in each study were substantially similar and tallied the number of times that each behavior loaded on each factor. He concluded that there were two patterns of statistical covariation (factors) underlying child conduct problems. One factor consisted of such behaviors as disobedience, temper tantrums, defiance of adult requests, physical fighting, destructiveness, and bullying. The second factor included theft, truancy from school, staying out late at night, running away from home, and loyalty to delinquent friends. Interestingly, lying loaded on both factors. Notice that the first dimension was composed of DSM-III and DSM-III-R symptoms of ODD but also included the CD behaviors that we have assigned to the first, or "intermediate," level of CD behaviors (fighting, bullying, vandalism, and lying). The second factor consisted mostly of those behaviors that we have assigned to the "advanced" CD level.

Strong support for the patterns of behavioral covariation noted by

Quay (1986a) has come from a large-scale factor-analytic study of 8,694 clinic-referred American and Dutch youths, aged 6 to 16 (Achenbach, Conners, Quay, Verhulst, & Howell, 1989). The authors factor-analyzed all nonoverlapping items from three widely used parent rating scales of child behavior and extracted two factors of conduct problem behaviors for boys. Consistent with Quay's (1986a) previous review, one factor included ODD behaviors plus lying, bullying, and fighting, and the second factor was composed of more serious CD behaviors plus substance use and having delinquent companions.

Similar results were reported by Frick et al. (1990) who factor-analyzed ODD and CD behaviors from structured diagnostic interviews of clinic-referred boys ages 7 to 12 years. Because both parents and teachers were interviewed separately, behaviors from these two informants were factor-analyzed separately, yielding nearly identical results. Two factors were extracted, with one factor consisting almost exclusively of ODD behaviors and the second consisting of aggressive and nonaggressive CD behaviors. Unlike previous studies that did not use the full DSM-III and DSM-III-R lists of symptoms, fighting, lying, and bullying did not load clearly on the ODD factor, but rather showed weak loadings on both factors. Interestingly, a factor analysis of 1,285 elementary-school children produced three factors: a cluster of ODD behaviors, a cluster of mostly "intermediate" CD behaviors, and a cluster of mostly "advanced" CD behaviors (Lindgren et al., 1990). However, like Frick et al. (1990), the "intermediate" aggressive behaviors tended to have joint loadings with the ODD factor.

Although factor-analytic studies of conduct problems in separate samples of girls have consistently found two factors similar to those described for boys, a third factor has been extracted in two studies composed of physical aggression against persons, property, and animals (Achenbach et al., 1989; Achenbach & Edelbrock, 1979). Because many of these items actually loaded more strongly on the oppositional–aggression factor, it is unclear whether this reflects a unique dimension of disruptive behavior for girls, but it is certainly an issue worthy of future study.

## Quantitative Meta-Analyses of Factor-Analytic Studies

A meta-analysis was conducted by Loeber and Schmaling (1985) to integrate the findings of 28 factor-analytic studies quantitatively. They cross-tabulated the frequency with which each pair of behaviors loaded significantly on the same factor, irrespective of factor labels. This matrix was then subjected to multidimensional scaling. Loeber and Schmaling

(1985) extracted a single bipolar scale of disruptive child behavior, with ODD behaviors and aggression at one pole, disobedience in the middle, and all other CD behaviors, substance use, and having delinquent companions at the other pole. Because each pole is equivalent to a different factor, the results of this quantitative meta-analysis are quite consistent with Quay's (1986a) conclusions.

More recently, Frick et al. (1993) conducted an extended multidimensional scaling meta-analysis using a larger set of 64 well-conducted factor-analytic studies available in 1990 (based on 23,401 children and adolescents, including the 28 factor analyses covered by Loeber and Schmaling, 1985). The item pool consisted of symptoms of CD and ODD (from both DSM-III and DSM-III-R), plus substance use. When one bipolar dimension of statistical covariation was extracted, the ODD behaviors and aggressive CD behaviors clustered at one pole, whereas the remaining nonaggressive CD behaviors clustered at the other pole. Thus, the first bipolar dimension almost perfectly replicated the earlier findings of Loeber and Schmaling (1985).

However, the extraction of two dimensions was more justifiable on statistical grounds in the meta-analysis of the extended sample conducted by Frick et al. (1993). As shown in Figure 2, when the second bipolar dimension of statistical covariation was extracted, the aggressive CD behaviors (Quadrant B) separated from the ODD behaviors (Quadrant D). Importantly, physical aggression grouped together with the nonaggressive CD behaviors that we have labeled *intermediate* CD behaviors (Quadrant A) on the same pole of the second dimension of statistical covariation. Thus, although physical aggression (particularly fighting and bullying) are related to ODD behaviors in terms of the *first* dimension of statistical covariation, physical aggression is also related to the milder nonaggressive CD behaviors that appear earliest in the developmental sequence in terms of the *second* dimension of statistical covariation. In addition, the extraction of the second dimension resulted in the separation of the "intermediate" nonaggressive CD behaviors (Quadrant A) from those nonaggressive CD behaviors than tend to appear at older ages (Quadrant C).

Frick et al. (1993) used the results of the two-dimensional solution of the multidimensional scaling as the basis for a cluster analysis to extend and validate the meta-analysis using an independent sample. The subjects in the cross-validation sample were the 177 clinic-referred boys of the first year of the Developmental Trends Study for whom the numbers of ODD and CD were assessed using multiinformant structured diagnostic interviews. The number of behaviors in the four quadrants of Figure 2 was used to create four scores that were analyzed to identify

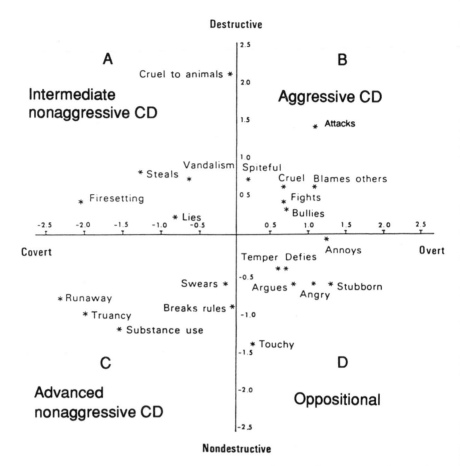

FIGURE 2. Results of the two-dimension solution of a meta-analysis of 68 factor-analytic studies using multidimensional scaling. The behaviors are arrayed along two dimensions of statistical covariation, displayed horizontally and vertically.

homogeneous patterns of elevations on these scores using k-means cluster analysis.

The results of the cluster analysis suggested a four-cluster solution. As shown in Figure 3, the first cluster, termed *not deviant*, was not elevated on any of the four groupings of ODD and CD behaviors. The *ODD* cluster showed a marked elevation on ODD behaviors (Quadrant D) and a moderate elevation on aggressive CD behaviors. The third cluster was termed the *younger CD* cluster because of its pattern of eleva-

Mean Quadrant Scores

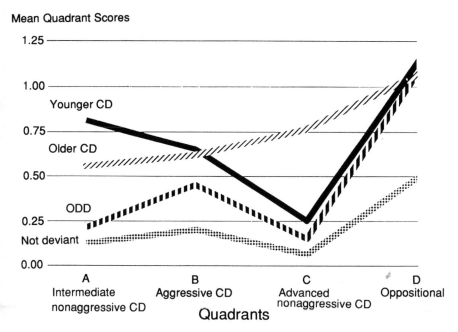

**FIGURE 3.** K-means cluster analysis of a sample of clinic-referred boys identified four homogeneous profiles of elevations on the behaviors in the four quadrants of Figure 2.

tions on the four groupings of conduct problems and because the boys in this cluster were significantly younger than the boys in the other cluster with elevations on CD behaviors. The *younger* CD cluster showed marked deviance in property violations, aggression, and oppositional behavior but was not significantly more deviant on "advanced" nonaggressive behaviors than the *ODD* cluster. In contrast, a small cluster of older boys with CD (*older CD* cluster) showed significant elevations on all four groupings of behaviors. As will be discussed below when we integrate findings on statistical covariation, these results are generally consistent with the developmental levels model.

## A Priori Tests of the Developmental Levels Model Based on Statistical Covariation

Loeber, Keenan, Lahey, Green, and Thomas (1993) and Russo, Loeber, Lahey, and Keenan (1992) have conducted tests of the developmental levels model using data from the Developmental Trends Study (clinic-referred boys) and the Pittsburgh Youth Study (a large school-based community sample selected to oversample boys with conduct problems). These two studies tested the placement of behaviors at each level of the developmental pyramid using statistical covariation as the criterion, by comparing groups created using tentative a priori definitions of the three developmental levels.

## Behaviors That Discriminate ODD from "Normal"

First, boys who met DSM-III-R criteria for ODD, CD, or both were combined in a single group and compared to boys who met criteria for neither disorder on the frequency of each ODD and CD behavior to determine if these behaviors discriminated boys who had entered at least the lowest level of the developmental pyramid from boys without conduct problems. In order to avoid biasing the comparison in favor the symptom, the boys were classified as exhibiting the disorder *without including* the symptom in question in the symptom list for the disorder. It should be noted that this conservative strategy provides a stringent test of the association of each symptom with its hypothesized developmental level. This is particularly true of "strong" symptoms of a given level, as the omission of a key behavior from the symptom list would result in the underclassification of youths at that developmental level.

In the Pittsburgh Youth Study (Russo et al., 1992), every ODD symptom and nearly every CD symptom were significantly more prevalent among boys who met criteria for either ODD or CD than among boys without these disorders. The exceptions were fighting, physical cruelty, and forced sex. The lack of significant difference for the latter two behaviors was probably due their low prevalence, but as will be seen in the next set of analyses, the lack of statistical significance for fighting reflects the fact that it was prevalent in this sample only among boys with CD and was quite infrequent among boys with ODD. Thus, when boys with ODD and CD were combined in one group, the resulting comparison did not reach customary levels of statistical significance.

In the Developmental Trends Study (Loeber et al., 1993), every symptom of ODD and CD was significantly more common among boys who met criteria for ODD or CD, except for truancy, breaking and entering, theft with confrontation of the victim, running away from home, and forced sex. Again, the lack of statistical significance for these behaviors reflected the fact that they were uncommon in this sample. In addition, some of these behaviors (truancy, breaking and entering, and theft with confrontation of the victim) were so highly concentrated in the CD group and infrequent in the ODD group that the comparison was not significant when ODD and CD were combined.

## Behaviors That Discriminate CD from ODD

In these comparisons, boys who met DSM-III-R criteria for CD were compared to those who met criteria for ODD to identify behaviors that discriminate the two CD levels from the ODD level. Again, boys were classified as exhibiting CD *without including* the symptom in question in the symptom list for the disorder to avoid biasing the comparison in favor of CD behaviors. In the Developmental Trends Study (Loeber et al., 1993), lying, fighting, bullying, theft without confrontation of the victim, truancy, vandalism, use of a weapon, cruelty to animals, breaking and entering, theft with confrontation with the victim, and physical cruelty were significantly more common among boys who met criteria for CD than boys who met criteria for ODD. Only the uncommon behaviors of forced sex and running away from home were not significantly more common among boys with CD. Similarly, in the Pittsburgh Youth Study (Russo et al., 1992), nearly every CD symptom was significantly more prevalent among boys who met criteria for CD than ODD, except for lying, truancy, physical cruelty, and forced sex. Thus, all CD behaviors were found to discriminate between the ODD level and the two CD levels in at least one of the two samples, except for the very low-rate symptom of forced sex.

## Behaviors That Discriminate "Intermediate" CD from "Advanced" CD

In these comparisons, boys who met a priori criteria for "advanced" CD were compared to boys who met criteria for "intermediate" CD to identify behaviors that discriminate between the two levels of CD levels. Again, boys were classified as exhibiting "intermediate" or "advanced" CD *without including* the symptom in question in the symptom list for the disorder to avoid biasing the comparisons. These comparisons were the most problematic to design as there is no tradition of diagnostic criteria for these two levels of CD as there are for ODD and CD. In addition, a number of symptoms that are not part of DSM criteria were included in order to study their diagnostic utility, but their inclusion broadened the definitions of ODD and CD in ways that may have influenced the results.

The presence of at least three symptoms of CD was required to meet criteria for either level of CD, with at least two symptoms of theft with confrontation, threatening, physical cruelty, use of a weapon, forced sex, vandalism, firesetting, breaking and entering, and running away from home being required to meet criteria for "advanced" rather than "intermediate" CD. Again, a symptom was not used to define the level in the analysis of the association of that symptoms with the level to avoid bias. In the Developmental Trends Study, theft without confrontation, vandalism, use of a weapon, and physical cruelty were more prevalent in the "advanced" CD group than the "intermediate" CD group in the first year of the study, and the less-prevalent behaviors of theft with confrontation, breaking and entering, and firesetting were more common in the "advanced" CD group when the prevalence of each symptom across the first three annual assessments of this longitudinal study was combined in the comparisons. In contrast, the Pittsburgh Youth Study, which had smaller numbers of boys who met criteria for the two levels of CD because the sample was not clinic-referred, only use of a weapon and vandalism were significantly more common in the "advanced" CD group than the "intermediate" CD group.

Thus, these two studies that tested the association of symptoms to a priori definitions of the levels were more consistent in identifying behaviors that discriminate between "normality" and the ODD level, and between ODD and "intermediate" CD, than between "intermediate" and "advanced" CD. The fact that these studies were conducted in advance of the availability of much of the information contained in this chapter suggests that such analyses may be more successful in distinguishing between "intermediate" and "advanced" CD behaviors in the future when more information converges to define the levels. However, these two studies were consistent in identifying the existence of three levels of intercorrelated conduct problems and were in agreement on their implications for the placement of the great majority of the ODD and CD behaviors at the three developmental levels.

## Implications of Studies of Statistical Covariation

In summary, factor-analytic studies consistently indicate that there are at least two dimensions of child conduct problems. When factor analysis was used, or when one multidimensional scale was extracted, a factor of both ODD behaviors and "intermediate" CD behaviors consistently has been found to be distinct from of a second factor composed of the "advanced" CD behaviors. One could conclude, therefore, that these studies of statistical covariation support the distinction between the "advanced" CD behaviors in the developmental pyramid, on the one hand, and the two lower levels of the pyramid (ODD behaviors and "intermediate" CD behaviors), on the other hand, but do not support the distinction between the two lower levels of the developmental model.

Indeed, Achenbach and his colleagues (Achenbach et al., 1989) have strongly argued that the most justifiable distinction among conduct problems would be between what he labels *aggression* (essentially our ODD and "intermediate" CD levels) and *delinquency* (essentially our "advanced" CD level). Clearly, a great deal of empirical support can and has been marshalled in support of such a distinction. Our model is consistent with that of Achenbach and colleagues, except in our distinguishing two levels in what he terms *aggression* and in viewing these dimensions as being linked developmentally.

There is, however, evidence from three sources to support our hypothesis that the ODD and "intermediate" CD levels of CD are separable in terms of statistical covariation. First, when the DSM ODD and CD behaviors are factor-analyzed, the "intermediate" CD behaviors (particularly fighting, bullying, and lying) tend to load weakly on both of the two factors of conduct problems. Although ODD behaviors and "intermediate" CD behaviors rarely factor separately, the frequent finding of weak loadings of "intermediate" CD symptoms on both factors suggests that these behaviors are partially distinct from, but intimately related to both ODD and "advanced" CD behaviors. In this sense, our hypothesis that "intermediate" CD behaviors are developmentally based on ODD behaviors and form the developmental foundation for "advanced" CD behaviors is not inconsistent with the factor-analytic findings.

Second, the results of the meta-analytic summary of the factor-analysis literature conducted by Frick et al. (1993) provides support for the distinction between ODD and "intermediate" CD in terms of statistical covariation. When two bipolar dimensions were extracted in the meta-analysis, ODD behaviors were separated from all of the groupings of CD behaviors. This finding that ODD and aggressive CD behaviors are similar along the first dimension of statistical covariation but are distinct in terms of the second dimension of covariation (which is arguably a developmental dimension) is also quite consistent with the developmental model. In essence, we hypothesize that all of the ODD and CD behaviors are related, and that ODD behaviors are most closely related to "intermediate" CD behaviors, in the sense that all youths who exhibit "intermediate" CD behaviors will also exhibit ODD behaviors, but ODD and "intermediate" CD behaviors differ both in the sense that not all youths with ODD will exhibit "intermediate" CD behaviors and because the age of onset of the two groups of behaviors tends to differ.

The validation of the results of the two-dimension solution of the meta-analysis of Frick et al. (1993) using cluster analysis of the four groupings of ODD and CD behaviors in an independent sample was also consistent with the developmental levels model. This inductive statistical procedure identified a cluster of youths with only ODD behaviors, a cluster with both ODD and "intermediate" CD behaviors, and a cluster boys with ODD, "intermediate" CD, and "advanced" CD behaviors. Furthermore, the finding that boys who exhibited all three levels of ODD and CD behaviors were significantly older than the two other clusters is consistent with the hypothesis that the "advanced" CD behaviors were added to the earlier behaviors during the course of development.

However, the results of the meta-analysis (Frick et al., 1993) were not consistent with the hypothesis that "advanced" aggressive CD behaviors should be placed in the same developmental level with "advanced" nonaggressive behaviors. In the two-dimensional solution shown in Figure 2, the two behaviors reflecting serious physical aggression, "attacks" and "cruel," covaried with milder aggressive behaviors on both dimensions of statistical covariation, rather than with the "advanced" nonaggressive CD behaviors. There are two reasons why these findings may be artifactual, however. First, only two behaviors reflecting serious aggression were included in these factor analyses, and it is likely that these serious aggressive behaviors were rare in most of the non-referred samples of school-age children. Therefore, the clustering of serious aggressive behaviors could have been influenced by their small numbers and low prevalence. Second, the data used in the meta-analysis were based on parent and teacher rating scales rather than structured diagnostic interviews. It is easy to see how an adult rater might endorse items such as "attacks others" for a young child who was engaging in mild aggressive behaviors that another rater might also describe as "fighting." In addition, it is often the case that parents and teachers are unaware of the more severe forms of aggressive behaviors (forced sex, physical cruelty, and theft with confrontation of the victim) that are conducted out of the view of adults. More definitive assessments of the severity of aggression in future studies will help to clarify this issue, but other data to be considered in this section are also relevant.

The tests of the association of symptoms with levels of CD that were defined a priori (Loeber et al., 1993; Russo et al., 1992) provide the third and most informative source of evidence in differentiating between ODD behaviors and "intermediate" CD in terms of behavioral covariation. In both studies, all symptoms of "intermediate" CD were more common in boys at that level than at the ODD level. That is, boys who exhibited at least three symptoms of CD were more likely to exhibit every "intermediate" CD behavior, even when that behavior was not used to define CD. Thus, in this sense, there is clear statistical covariation among the "intermediate" CD behaviors that is at least partially distinct from ODD behaviors. In addition, these studies provided support for the hypothesis that serious aggressive behaviors with later ages of onset should be classified with serious nonaggressive behaviors at the "advanced" CD level. These analyses not only indicated that serious nonaggressive CD behaviors should be considered to be "advanced" behaviors, as did the meta-analysis of Frick et al. (1993), but the serious aggressive behaviors of use of a weapon, physical cruelty, and theft with confrontation also emerged as significantly more common in boys said to exhibit "advanced" CD.

Therefore, the several complementary methods of examining statistical covariation among ODD and CD behaviors are consistent with the developmental levels model *when considered together*. The large factor-analytic literature strongly supports the model at the level of the distinction between "advanced" and "intermediate" CD, and the two-dimensional solution of the meta-analysis of these studies by Frick et al. (1993) is also consistent with the distinction between the ODD and "intermediate" CD levels. The tests of statistical covariation based on a priori definitions of the three developmental levels are quite consistent with the distinction between the ODD and "intermediate" CD levels but also suggest that both serious aggressive and nonaggressive CD behaviors should be placed together at the "advanced" CD level.

It should be emphasized that the relative lack of crisp and consistent findings is not unexpected. Given the hypothesis that youths begin the developmental sequence with ODD behaviors and then add behaviors at higher levels during the process of development with little deletion of earlier behaviors (and, therefore, youths who reach the highest level of CD will exhibit substantial numbers of behaviors at all three levels), it is not surprising that the differentiation of the three hypothesized levels in terms of statistical covariation among behaviors is not entirely clear. Indeed, it is the degree of convergence among the several sources of information on statistical covariation, and the consistency of these findings with the data on age of onset, seriousness ratings, developmental sequencing, and stability that will be reviewed below, that is impressive.

A final important point should be made concerning statistical covariation among conduct problems and the developmental levels model. Factor-analytic studies of preschool children have consistently yielded a single factor composed of oppositional and mildly aggressive behaviors (Achenbach, Edelbrock, & Howell, 1987; Fowler & Parke,

1979; Kohn, 1977; McDermott, 1983; O'Donnell & Van Tuinan, 1979). These findings reflect the elimination of items on the more developmentally advanced CD behaviors because they were not endorsed sufficiently frequently to be included in factor analyses (or not including them in the item pool to begin with). These findings are fully consistent with the developmental levels model that asserts that there is a single oppositional-defiant dimension of conduct problems during the preschool years, but that some children advance to higher levels of CD soon thereafter.

## Age of Onset of ODD and CD Behaviors

Evidence exists on the age of onset of conduct problems that sheds important light on the distinction between the putative levels of ODD and CD. Loeber et al. (1991) reviewed findings that suggest that ODD behaviors are not uncommon by 4 to 5 years of age (Achenbach & Edelbrock, 1981; Campbell, 1990; MacFarlane et al., 1962). These same studies suggest that the earliest ages of onset of "intermediate" CD behaviors overlaps with the latest ages of onset of oppositional behaviors, with more serious CD behaviors appearing much later. Unfortunately, as with other aspects of ODD and CD, little is known about the age of onset of conduct problems in girls.

Lahey et al. (1992) addressed the issue of age of onset using retrospective parent reports of onset of ODD and CD behaviors the first year of the Developmental Trends Study of clinic-referred boys when they were 7 to 12 years of age. However, because the boys in the Developmental Trends Study were assessed annually for 4 years during the risk period for the onset of disruptive behaviors, the best estimate of age of onset is one that includes both the retrospective age of onset of symptoms present in Year 1 and the age of onset of behaviors that emerged for the first time in Years 2 to 4. Ages of onset calculated in this way for ODD and CD behaviors are shown in Table 1, rounded to the nearest half year. Except for swearing, which onsets much later than other ODD behaviors (and which will not be included in the DSM-IV symptom list for ODD), the ODD behaviors had median ages of onset between 5.0 and 8.0 years of age. In contrast, the "intermediate" CD behaviors had ages of onset between 8.0 and 10.5 years of age, and the "advanced" CD behaviors onset between 11.5 and 13.0 years of age. In one sense, these data reveal a continuum of ages of onset in the ODD and CD behaviors without clear natural breakpoints. However, if one keeps in mind the earlier caveat that we are proposing the distinction of developmental

**Table 1. Median Age of Onset Reported by Parent of Symptoms
of Oppositional Defiant Disorder and Conduct Disorder[a]**

| Median age | Oppositional defiant disorder | Conduct disorder |
| --- | --- | --- |
| 3.0 | Stubborn | |
| 3.5 | | |
| 4.0 | | |
| 4.5 | | |
| 5.0 | Defies adults, temper tantrums | |
| 5.5 | | |
| 6.0 | Irritable, argues | |
| 6.5 | Blames others | |
| 7.0 | Annoys others | |
| 7.5 | Spiteful | |
| 8.0 | Angry | Lies |
| 8.5 | | Fights |
| 9.0 | | Bullies, sets fires |
| 9.5 | Swears | Uses weapon |
| 10.0 | | Vandalizes |
| 10.5 | | Cruel to animals |
| 11.0 | | |
| 11.5 | | Physical cruelty |
| 12.0 | | Steals, runs away from home |
| 12.5 | | Truant, mugs |
| | | Breaks and enters |
| 13.0 | | Forces sex |

[a]This combines retrospective and prospective ages of onset over four annual assessments in the Developmental Trends Study.

levels for heuristic purposes when it is clear that the difference between levels is blurred rather than sharp, these data are fully consistent with the developmental levels model. On average, every ODD behavior (except swearing) emerged prior to, or at the same time as, the earliest "intermediate" CD behavior. Similarly, every "intermediate" CD behavior onset at least a full year earlier than the first "advanced" CD behaviors emerged.

Data on the age of onset of conduct problems in the Developmental Trends Study are examined in a different way in Figure 4. Unlike the data presented in Table 1, which combined retrospective and prospective data, the data in Figure 4 are based only on prospective data. Consistent with the developmental levels model, only 12.6% of behaviors at the ODD level emerged for the first time *after* the first year (when the boys were 7 to 12 years of age) of the 4-year prospective study (i.e., were present in Years 2, 3, or 4, but were not present in Year 1). In contrast,

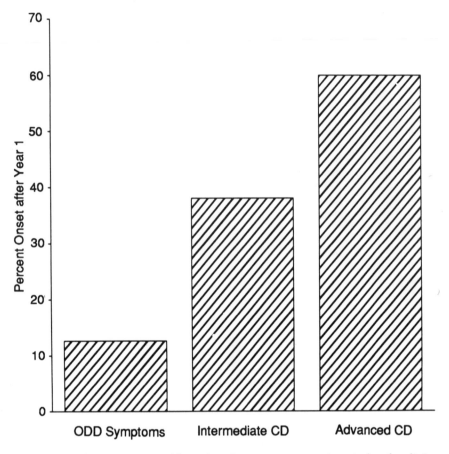

**FIGURE 4.** The percentage of boys in a four-year prospective study of a clinic-referred sample who first exhibit behaviors at the ODD, intermediate CD, and advanced CD levels after Year 1 (i.e., during Years 2 to 4).

38.1% of the "intermediate" CD behaviors emerged for the first time after Year 1, and 60% of the "advanced" CD behaviors emerged for the first time in Years 2 to 4. Such findings are strikingly consistent with the developmental levels model.

These findings from the Developmental Trends Study are consistent with parental reports of age of onset from the Pittsburgh Youth Study on a community sample of over 500 13-year old boys (Loeber, Stouthamer-Loeber, Van Kammen, & Farrington, 1990). The boys' low upper-age limit meant that very few boys exhibited the more serious CD behaviors, such as breaking and entering, running away from home, and forced sex, but the order of age of onset in this study closely paralleled the developmental levels model. Data from Le Blanc and Fréchette (1989) on the self-reports of an older sample of boys similarly indicated that many of the more serious CD behaviors continued to emerge after the age of onset of the less serious CD behaviors.

## Developmental Course of Behaviors

The developmental course of conduct problems, defined as changes in the prevalence of the behaviors with increasing age, can also be used to test the validity of the developmental levels model. However, as will become apparent, the developmental course of ODD behaviors and "intermediate" CD behaviors are similar, and the only clear difference in developmental course of these behaviors is between the "advanced" CD level and the two lower levels in the model. Several studies suggest that ODD and "intermediate" CD behaviors are common at early ages and then decline somewhat in prevalence with increasing age in most children (Achenbach & Edelbrock, 1981; Campbell, 1990; Greene et al., 1973; MacFarlane et al., 1962; Werry & Quay, 1971). In contrast, the behaviors at the "advanced" CD level increase in prevalence with increasing age. Importantly, data on the developmental course of conduct problems are similar for most behaviors for boys and girls in these studies.

The most convincing evidence on developmental course comes from prospective longitudinal studies. MacFarlane et al. (1962) found similar small decreases with age for both sexes in the prevalence of conduct problems that we have placed at the ODD and "intermediate" CD levels, with the greatest decline taking place during the elementary-school years. Similarly, Tremblay (1990), in a follow-up of a large community sample, found a decline in boys' oppositional behavior between first and second grades. A prospective epidemiologic survey in New Zealand by Anderson et al. (1987) similarly showed that parent-rated aggression decreased between ages 5 and 11 for children without a diagnosed disorder. It should be noted that the prevalence of some oppositional behaviors may drop during the elementary-school period, then increase again during adolescence (Kashani, Orvaschel, Rosenberg, & Reid, 1989; MacFarlane et al., 1962). More evidence on this phase of the developmental sequence of conduct problems is sorely needed.

In contrast to the decreasing prevalence of ODD and "intermediate" CD behaviors is the consistent finding that "advanced" CD behaviors increase in prevalence with increasing age in both sexes (Elliott,

Knowles, & Canter, 1981; Le Blanc & Fréchette, 1989; Loeber, 1985; Olweus, 1989). These increases are more pronounced when self-reports are used than when ratings rely on parental reports because many of the behaviors often are not noticed by parents as the youngsters conceal these acts (Loeber, 1985). This developmental increase in prevalence includes the more advanced nonaggressive CD behaviors, such as truancy, underage drinking, and running away, and more serious forms of aggression, including aggravated assault, rape, and homicide (Farrington, 1986; Le Blanc & Fréchette, 1989; Zimring, 1979).

A strong comparison of the developmental course of behaviors at the three putative developmental levels can be made using data from the Developmental Trends Study (Lahey et al., 1990; Frick et al., 1993) in which structured diagnostic interviews of the child, parent, and teacher in a group of 171 clinic-referred boys assessed each year for 4 years. For the purpose of this analysis, we divided the boys into three age cohorts on the basis of their age (7.0 through 8.11, mean = 8.0; 9.0 through 10.11, mean = 10.0; and 11.0 through 12.11, mean = 12.0). The number of behaviors at each level reported during each of the four annual assessments was analyzed in a 3 (Age Cohort) × 4 (Repeated Annual Assessments) mixed between and within analysis of variance to portray the developmental course of the three levels of conduct problems. This analytic strategy allows the distinction of the intertwined effects of increasing age from repeated annual assessments. Note in Figures 5 to 7 that, consistent with the developmental levels model, the prevalence of ODD behaviors is higher than that of "intermediate" CD behaviors, which is higher than for "advanced" CD behaviors at all ages.

The number of ODD symptoms reported during each of four annual assessments for boys in the Developmental Trends Study are presented in Figure 5. Data are presented separately for boys in three age cohorts who were an average of 8, 10, or 12 years old in the first year of the study. There was a statistically significant effect of Repeated Annual Assessments, $F (3,504) = 17.77$, $p < .0001$, on the number of ODD behaviors, but there was neither a significant effect of Age Cohort nor an Age Cohort × Repeated Annual Assessment interaction. This reflects a pattern in which, regardless of the child's age in Year 1, the number of ODD behaviors was highest in Year 1, declined in Year 2, then did not decline significantly after Year 2.

Comparable data on the developmental course of "intermediate" CD behaviors can be seen in Figure 6. Like ODD behaviors, there was a significant effect of Repeated Annual Assessments, $F (3,504) = 5.79$, $p < .001$, but there was neither a significant effect of Age Cohort nor an Age Cohort × Repeated Annual Assessment interaction. This reflects a simi-

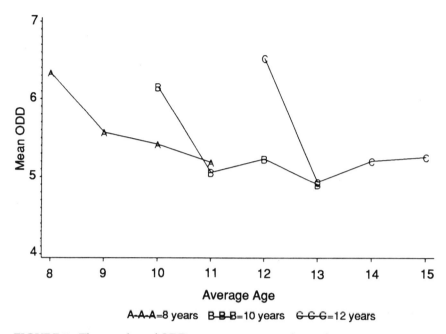

**FIGURE 5.** The number of ODD symptoms reported over four successive annual assessments in a prospective study of clinic-referred boys. The subjects are divided into three age cohorts who were an average of 8, 10, or 12 years old in the first year of the study.

lar pattern in which the number of "intermediate" CD behaviors was highest in Year 1, regardless of the child's age in Year 1, then declined somewhat in Year 2, then did not decline significantly after Year 2.

In contrast, the data presented in Figure 7 on the developmental course of "advanced" CD behaviors reveal a markedly different pattern. There was a significant effect of both Age Cohort, $F$ (2,168) = 8.00, $p <$ .0005, and Repeated Annual Assessments, $F$ (3,504) = 4.01, $p < .01$, but the interaction was not significant. As predicted by the model, "advanced" CD symptoms are more common in the oldest age cohort (mean age 12 years in Year 1) and tend to increase (after a decline from Year 1 to Year 2 in the 10-year-old cohort) around the time of puberty.

Several comments should be made about the analyses of developmental course shown in Figures 5 to 7. When age was distinguished from the effect of repeated assessments, our analyses yielded little evidence of true developmental declines in either ODD or "intermediate" CD behaviors. Rather, our data suggest that the declines from Year 1 to

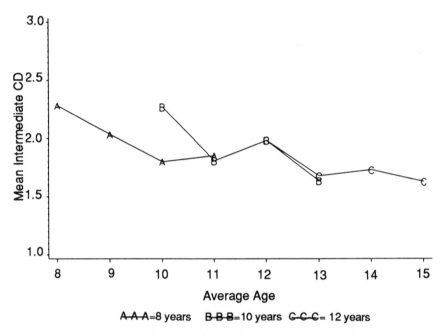

**FIGURE 6.** The number of intermediate CD symptoms reported over four successive annual assessments in a prospective study of clinic-referred boys. The subjects are divided into three age cohorts who were an average of 8, 10, or 12 years old in the first year of the study.

Year 2 are either an artifact of repeated measurement ("test–retest attenuation") or possibly reflect declines from transient peaks in misbehaviors in Year 1 that precipitated clinic referral of the child. It is not possible to determine the extent to which the conclusions of previous studies were influenced by similar nondevelopmental factors, raising questions about the developmental course of ODD and "intermediate" CD behaviors.

Regardless of the eventual outcome of this question, however, the data presented in Figures 5 to 7 strongly support the distinction between "advanced" CD and the two lower developmental levels in terms of changes in prevalence of behaviors with increasing age. Whether future studies suggest that ODD and "intermediate" CD behaviors do or do not decrease over increasing age in clinic-referred youths, it is clear that the developmental course of these two levels of conduct problems is quite different from that of the "advanced" CD behaviors.

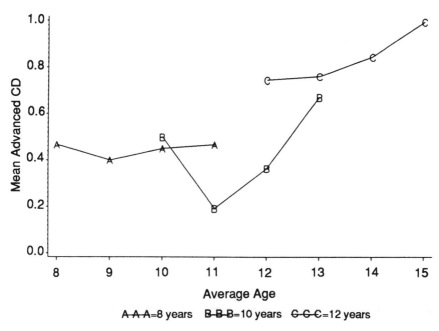

**FIGURE 7.** The number of advanced CD symptoms reported over four successive annual assessments in a prospective study of clinic-referred boys. The subjects are divided into three age cohorts who were an average of 8, 10, or 12 years old in the first year of the study.

## Seriousness Ratings and Severity of Impairment

We can also test the developmental levels model by asking whether ODD and CD behaviors are rated by adults as increasingly more serious at higher levels of developmental progression. Results from two studies of adults' ratings of the seriousness of ODD and CD behaviors conducted over 50 years apart show remarkable agreement among mental health professionals and teachers (Vidoni, Fleming, & Mintz, 1983; Wickman, 1928). Although these studies did not examine all ODD and CD behaviors, they indicate that nearly all ODD behaviors were judged as less serious than nearly all CD behaviors. There are several replications of Wickman's (1928) findings, reviewed by Beilin (1958), that buttress the not surprising notion that as children grow older their problem behaviors often escalate in seriousness.

It is also important to test the developmental model by comparing youths at the two levels of CD on socially significant measures of severity of impairment. However, if the developmental levels model is to be useful, two things must be demonstrated concerning severity. First, the youths at the "advanced" level must be more severely impaired than youths at the "intermediate" level. Second, the association of the levels with severity must be stronger than the association of the total number of symptoms of CD with measures of impairment. That is, the developmental levels model would be of little value if a simple count of the number of CD behaviors exhibited by the youth (at any level) provided the same information.

To answer this question, we analyzed data from the recently completed DSM-IV Field Trials for the Disruptive Behavior Disorders (Lahey et al., in press). This sample consists of 440 clinic-referred male and female children and adolescents ages 4 to 17 years drawn from 12 different psychiatry, psychology, and pediatrics clinics, and from a juvenile corrections system. Youths in the field trials sample at the "advanced" level of CD had more than three times the number of police contacts as youths at the intermediate level, a difference that was highly significant. The critical question is whether this difference simply reflects the fact that youths at the "advanced" level exhibited more CD behaviors. However, the difference between the two levels of CD was still statistically significant when the number of symptoms of CD was controlled using analysis of covariance. Indeed, virtually all of the variance in the prediction of the number of police contacts was accounted for by the developmental level of the youth rather than the total number of CD behaviors.

Because the developmental levels are necessarily confounded by age, another analysis of covariance was conducted to determine if the differences in police contacts that appear to be associated with the developmental levels are simply an artifact of the different ages of the youths at the two levels of CD. Again, the effect of levels was significant after age was controlled through covariance. Thus, consistent with the developmental levels model, the important determinant of impairment is not how many behaviors the youth exhibits, but *which* behaviors are exhibited. CD behaviors at the "advanced" level have far more serious consequences for the youth in terms of conflict with the legal system. Surprisingly, however, a comparison of boys classified at the three developmental levels using data from the Pittsburgh Youth Study did not find differences in the number of police contacts among the three levels.

## Developmental Sequencing of the Levels

We have marshalled considerable support for the distinction of three developmental levels of conduct problems in children and adolescents. However, we have not yet addressed the most critical hypothesis of the developmental model—the hierarchical sequencing of the levels. The differences that we have delineated thus far between the groupings of behaviors at the three putative levels of the model could equally be interpreted as suggesting that there are three *separate and unrelated* syndromes of conduct problems. That is, an alternative to our developmental model that is equally consistent with the data that we have presented thus far is that different youths develop these different groups of conduct problems. In order to fully explore the viability of the developmental levels model, it is necessary to demonstrate that behaviors at higher levels emerge in youths that have *already* developed the behaviors at the lower level(s).

It is stated in DSM-III-R that youths who exhibit CD will also exhibit ODD behaviors, suggesting a *hierarchical relation between ODD and CD:* "In Conduct Disorder all of the features of Oppositional Defiant Disorder are likely to be present; for that reason, Conduct Disorder preempts the diagnosis of Oppositional Defiant Disorder" (p. 57). In this light, the developmental levels model does not represent a radical departure from the conceptualization of ODD and CD in DSM-III-R. Recent evidence from the Developmental Trends Study suggests that the assumption of a hierarchical relation between ODD and CD is defensible. Walker et al. (1991) reported that 96% of clinic-referred boys aged 7 to 12 years who met DSM-III-R criteria for CD also met full criteria for ODD. Similarly, 84% of the clinic-referred youths with CD in the DSM-III-R Field Trials also met criteria for ODD (Spitzer, Davies & Barkley, 1991) and Faraone, Biederman, Keenan, & Tsuang (1991) reported that 96% of youths referred to an ADHD clinic who met criteria for DSM-III CD also met criteria for DSM-III ODD. These findings support the view that CD behaviors develop in youths who had begun exhibiting ODD behaviors at an earlier age. That is, these data are consistent with the view that two levels of CD are "developmentally stacked" on the ODD behaviors.

The possibility of a developmental progression from ODD to CD can be evaluated more fully using analyses of prospective data from the Developmental Trends Study (Hinshaw, Lahey, & Hart, 1993; Lahey et al., in press). In Year 1, 68 boys received a DSM-III-R diagnosis of CD (Lahey et al., 1990). During Year 2, 15 additional boys who had not met criteria for CD in Year 1 newly met CD criteria; of these 15 new cases, 13 (87%) had received a diagnosis of ODD in Year 1. During Year 3 and Year 4, 17 additional youths met criteria for CD for the first time, 14 of whom (82%) had received an ODD diagnosis during at least one preceding year. In this one prospective study of boys, then, ODD preceded the development of CD in the great majority of cases.

On the other hand, ODD does not always portend the later development of CD. In the Developmental Trends Study, 62% of the 68 boys with ODD in Year 1 who did not also meet criteria for CD at that time had not progressed to CD by the end of the fourth year of the investigation. About half (47%) of these youths with only ODD in Year 1 received a diagnosis of ODD at least one more time during Years 2 to 4 without progressing to CD, and 15% never met criteria for ODD or CD again beyond the first year. Examining the same data in a different way, however, we see that among the total of 135 youths who met criteria for ODD in Year 1 (65 who also already met criteria for CD in Year 1 and 68 who did not), 44 (33%) never met criteria for CD during any of the four annual assessments.

Thus, although nearly all boys with CD in Year 1 also met criteria for ODD in Year 1, and over 80% of boys who developed CD for the first time after Year 1 had previously met criteria for ODD, nearly two-thirds of boys with ODD during Year 1 who did not already exhibit CD did not subsequently develop CD. When considered along with the differences in the age of onset ODD and CD behaviors, the data from this one study of boys suggest that there is both a developmental and hierarchical relation between ODD and CD that is consistent with the developmental levels model. That is, it may be that childhood CD nearly always begins developmentally with ODD in boys, but not all boys with ODD progress to later CD. Confirmation of this tentative conclusion by other longitudinal studies is sorely needed, however, particularly studies including girls.

We have also analyzed data from the Developmental Trends Study to determine whether the serious CD behaviors are also developmentally "nested" within the "intermediate" CD behaviors. During each of the four annual assessments in the Developmental Trends Study, 72% to 88% of the boys who exhibited at least one "advanced" CD behavior exhibited at least two "intermediate" CD behaviors, and 62% to 70% of boys with one or more "advanced" behaviors exhibited three or more "intermediate" CD behaviors. These data strongly support the assumption of a developmental hierarchy among the three levels of conduct problems.

In addition, we have addressed the issue of the hierarchical developmental relationship between "advanced" and "intermediate" CD using data from the DSM-IV Field Trials for the Disruptive Behavior Disorders (Lahey et al., in press). We classified youths who met criteria for CD as being at the "advanced" level if they exhibited at least two of the following symptoms during the past year: forced sex, physical cruelty, use of a weapon, stealing without confrontation, stealing with confrontation, breaking and entering, and running away from home. We have conducted two tests of the assumption that the two levels of CD are developmentally sequenced. First, youths at the two levels of CD should differ in age at the time of assessment. In the field trials sample, youths at the two developmental levels of CD were significantly different in age, with the mean age of youths at the "intermediate" level being 10.5 years and the mean age at the "advanced" level being 12.0 years. Second, the developmental model also assumes that more severe behaviors are added to the less severe behaviors in the repertoire of youths with CD in accretionary fashion during the course of development. Therefore, the finding that the two levels of CD also differed in the total number of CD behaviors present in the past year also supports the developmental levels model.

## Comparison of the Correlates of ODD and CD

Given that ODD and CD appear to be related both hierarchically and developmentally, it is important to determine if ODD and CD are related to family history, impairment, persistence, and other diagnostically significant correlates in similar or different ways. If ODD is related to the same correlates as CD, but to a lesser extent, a stronger argument could be made that CD should be conceptualized as a more developmentally advanced form of ODD. On the other hand, one could argue more strongly that ODD and CD should be thought of as entirely distinct and unrelated syndromes if they have distinctly different correlates. Although ODD has been the subject of far fewer investigations than CD, a few recent studies have compared the two diagnoses on a range of relevant correlates.

### Socioeconomic Status and Family Psychopathology

Four studies have compared youths with ODD and CD on socioeconomic status and found no differences (Faraone et al., 1991; Frick et al., 1992; Rey et al., 1988; Schachar & Wachsmuth, 1990). Faraone et al. (1991) compared the family history of psychopathology of youths referred to an ADHD clinic who received DSM-III diagnoses of ODD, CD, or neither diagnosis. They found that the prevalence of APD in the parents of children with CD did not differ significantly from youths with ODD. However, when the frequency of either APD or childhood ODD was assessed in the parents, the prevalence was highest in the CD group, intermediate in the ODD group, and lowest in the clinic control group, with all comparisons being statistically significant. Similarly, the

prevalence of substance abuse or dependence was found to be significantly more common among the parents of youths with CD than either
youths with ODD or youths with neither diagnosis, with the latter
groups not differing at the .05 level.

Similarly, Frick et al. (1992) found that antisocial personality disorder (APD) was significantly more prevalent in the biological parents of
boys in the Developmental Trends Study with CD than ODD in Year 1,
but APD was significantly more prevalent in the biological parents of
boys with ODD than in the parents of clinic-referred boys with neither
ODD nor CD. Parental substance abuse was significantly more common
among the parents of boys with CD than in the clinic control group, but
the prevalence of substance abuse among the parents of boys with ODD
was intermediate and did not differ significantly from either the CD or
the clinic control groups. Schachar and Wachsmuth (1990) found that
prepubertal clinic-referred boys with DSM-III ODD displayed rates of
paternal psychopathology that were equal to boys with DSM-III CD, and
both groups showed greater parental psychopathology than a group of
clinic-referred boys with neither ODD nor CD. Although the prevalence
of specific parental diagnoses were not reported, Schachar and Wachsmuth (1990) reported that the most frequent diagnoses were substance
abuse and APD. The results of these studies are summarized in Table 2.

## Impairment

To provide a comparison of the impairment associated with DSM-III
ODD and CD, Rey et al. (1988) compared clinic-referred adolescents
with these diagnoses on the norm-referenced Child Behavior Checklist
(Achenbach & Edelbrock, 1983). The two diagnostic groups did not differ from one another on the Internalizing scale, but the CD group was
rated significantly higher than the ODD group on both the Externalizing
and the Total Behavior Problems scales. Schachar and Wachsmuth (1990)
reported that both DSM-III ODD and CD groups had more sibling and
peer relationship difficulties than the clinic control group, but the ODD
and CD groups did not differ from one another. However, the CD group
was rated by clinical interviewers as demonstrating less capacity for
enduring social relationships than the other two groups. Christ, Lahey,
Frick, Applegate, and Loeber (1991) compared boys in the Developmental Trends Study with DSM-III-R ODD, CD, or neither diagnosis on
sociometric measures and found no differences between ODD and CD.
The ODD and CD boys received more nominations as the child who is
"liked least," "meanest," and "fights most" than the clinic control
group, but the ODD and CD groups did not differ significantly. The

Table 2. Summary of Relations of Oppositional Defiant Disorder and Conduct Disorder to Family Variables, Comorbidities, and Impairment

| | | | |
|---|---|---|---|
| Socioeconomic status | | | |
| Rey et al. (1988) | CD[a] | ODD[a] | |
| Schachar & Wachsmuth (1990) | CD[a] | ODD[a] | CC[a] |
| Frick et al. (1993) | CD[a] | ODD[a,b] | CC[b] |
| Parental psychopathology | | | |
| Antisocial personality disorder | | | |
| Faraone et al. (1991) | CD[a,b] | ODD[a] | CC[b] |
| Frick et al. (1994) | CD[a] | ODD[b] | CC[c] |
| Substance abuse | | | |
| Faraone et al. (1991) | CD[a] | ODD[b] | CC[b] |
| Frick et al. (1993) | CD[a] | ODD[a,b] | CC[b] |
| General psychopathology | | | |
| Schachar & Wachsmuth (1990) | CD[a] | ODD[a] | CC[b] |
| Impairment | | | |
| Sibling and peer problems | | | |
| Schachar & Wachsmuth (1990) | CD[a] | ODD[a] | CC[b] |
| Social relatedness | | | |
| Schachar & Wachsmuth (1990) | CD[a] | ODD[b] | CC[b] |
| Peer-nominated aggression | | | |
| Frick et al. (1993) | CD[a] | ODD[a] | CC[b] |
| Peer rejection | | | |
| Frick et al. (1993) | CD[a] | ODD[a] | CC[b] |
| School suspensions | | | |
| Frick et al. (1994) | CD[a] | ODD[b] | CC[b] |
| Police contacts | | | |
| Frick et al. (1994) | CD[a] | ODD[b] | CC[b] |

Note. Diagnostic groups with different superscripts differ at the .05 level, with means or proportions labeled with [a] being significantly greater than means or proportions labeled with [b], and means or proportions labeled with [b] being significantly greater than means or proportions labeled with [c].

three groups did not differ in terms of "like-most" nominations, but the ODD and CD groups had more negative social preference scores ("like most" minus "like least") than the clinic control group, but did not differ from one another.

When the three diagnostic groups were compared on the number of police contacts and the number of disciplinary school suspensions, the CD group showed significantly more of both types of impairment than both the clinic control group and the ODD, with the ODD group not differing significantly from the clinic control group on either measure. Thus, it appears that the assumption of greater severity of CD than ODD is true in some areas of adjustment (police contacts and school suspensions), but not in others (peer and sibling relationships).

Overall, the evidence points to the diagnoses of ODD and CD having similar correlates, with those boys who have progressed to more frequent or serious disruptive behaviors being from families with more antisocial behavioral and other handicaps than those whose disruptive behavior remains at the ODD level. At present, no information is available on differences in the correlates of boys who have advanced from the "intermediate" to the "advanced" level of CD. And, as in other areas, little evidence is now available on possible differences in the correlates of the hypothesized levels of conduct problems in girls.

## Stability of Antisocial Behavior and the Levels of CD

We have described numerous ways in which the three hypothesized developmental levels of CD are different. We are encouraged to see that there is evidence that the course of development does appear to progress sequentially and hierarchically from the ODD level upward and that the levels differ in terms of statistical covariation, severity, and correlations with variables that may be of etiological significance. However, if the developmental levels model is to represent progress in our understanding of serious conduct problems, it must have validity beyond the mere description of the developmental sequences.

Perhaps the ultimate test of any developmental model is its ability to predict the course of future development. For this reason, we have conducted new analyses of the longitudinal Developmental Trends Study of clinic-referred boys to see if the distinction of developmental levels of CD *predicts* the persistence of CD over 4 years (Lahey, Loeber, Green, Applegate, Hart, Hanson, & Frick, 1993). Sixty-five boys who met DSM-III-R criteria for CD in Year 1, when they were 7 to 12 years of age, were divided into two groups on the basis of their persistence in CD over the next 3 years. The 51 boys who continued to meet criteria for CD again in at least Year 3 or Year 4 (35 of whom met criteria for CD during both Years 3 and 4) were said to exhibit "Persistent CD." In contrast, the 14 boys who met criteria for CD in *neither* Year 3 nor Year 4 were termed "Recovered CD." The two groups of boys with CD in Year 1 did not differ on the number of "intermediate" CD behaviors exhibited in Year 1, but the boys who "recovered" from CD exhibited significantly fewer "advanced" CD behaviors than with persistent CD.

It is important to add that the Persistent CD groups continued to exhibit significantly higher levels of both "intermediate" and "advanced" CD behaviors than the Recovered CD group into Year 4, which had fallen to low numbers of both "intermediate" and "advanced" CD by Year 4 that were not significantly different from boys who had never met criteria for CD. These findings reinforce the impression that clinically significant recovery from CD had occurred in the boys in the Recovered CD group. What is important is that the degree to which boys have penetrated to "advanced" CD predicted the persistence of CD over time. Stated differently, boys who meet criteria for CD but who have not progressed to the highest level of CD by the time of clinic-referral are not only unlikely to do so in the future, but they are likely to "drop down" the developmental pyramid out of the range of clinically significant CD in the future.

Similarly, Russo et al. (1992) compared three groups of boys from the Pittsburgh Youth Study (a group said to exhibit "advanced" CD, a group said to exhibit "intermediate" CD, and a group who met criteria for ODD) on the proportion of boys in each group who met criteria for "stable delinquency." Stable delinquency was defined in this study as committing at least one serious delinquent act during two or more years as assessed in the repeated longitudinal assessments. Although 28.2% of the ODD boys and 33.3% of the "intermediate" CD boys exhibited stable delinquency, a significantly higher proportion (61.5%) of boys classified as exhibiting "advanced" CD exhibited stable delinquency. Again, boys who had penetrated to the highest developmental level of CD were most likely to show stable serious antisocial behavior. This replicated finding provides strong support for the validity of the distinction between "intermediate" and "advanced" CD.

## Developmental Subtypes of CD

It is clear to all who study antisocial behavior in youths that CD is a heterogeneous diagnostic category (Farrington, 1987; Kazdin, 1987; Loeber, 1988). Subtypes of CD have been proposed, therefore, in an effort to capture differences in behavior, developmental trajectories, and assumed etiology. Subclassifications from earlier editions of the DSM and the ICD and from the field of developmental criminology have distinguished subtypes of CD on the basis of the capacity of the youth for maintaining social relationships, the presence or absence of aggression, and age of onset.

It is an important feature of our developmental levels model that we hypothesize that some youths will enter the developmental sequence *for the first time* in early to middle adolescence, without previously exhibiting conduct problems. We hypothesize that youths with *"adolescent-onset"* CD exhibit almost exclusively the nonaggressive behaviors of the "advanced" CD level and that this developmental subtype of CD is distinctly different from CD that onsets in childhood in a number of fundamental ways.

Loeber (1988) proposed the distinction between childhood and adolescent-onset forms of CD, which has been adopted as part of the DSM-IV definition of CD, based on a review of the developmental criminology and developmental psychopathology literatures. His review suggested that youths with adolescent-onset antisocial behavior tend to be less severe in their offending, particularly in exhibiting markedly less aggression, and have a better prognosis for desistance in offending (Loeber, 1982, 1988). Consistent with this distinction, Robins (1966) found that youths whose CD onset before age 11 were *twice* as likely to receive a diagnosis of APD (sociopathy) in adulthood as those with an onset after age 11.

More recently, Moffitt (1990) and McGee, Feehan, Williams, and Anderson (1992) provided important evidence on question of adolescent-onset CD using the Dunedin Multidisciplinary Health and Development Study. The identified a group of male and female youths in a longitudinal sample who exhibited significant antisocial behavior for the first time after age 11. Compared to a group of childhood-onset youths who had shown persistent oppositional and antisocial behavior since age 5, the adolescent-onset antisocial youths were less likely to be aggressive, had much less history of ODD in childhood, and were more likely to be female. Indeed, most females who ever met criteria for CD did so for the first time after age 11.

The distinction between childhood and adolescent-onset subtypes of CD also was tested in the DSM-IV Field Trials (Lahey et al., in press). Youths who had *no* CD behaviors with an age of onset before age 11 (classified as adolescent onset) exhibited markedly and significantly fewer symptoms of aggression against persons than youths whose first CD behaviors emerged before age 11 (childhood-onset CD). In addition, although only 15% of all youths who met criteria for childhood-onset CD were females, 50% of youths with adolescent-onset CD were females. These differences are consistent with the results of earlier studies and support the existence of at least two developmental subtypes based on age of onset, predominance of aggression, and gender ratio. If future studies confirm earlier indications of less persistence in adolescent-onset CD, this distinction will prove to be of considerable significance.

Given the marked differences between childhood- and adolescent-onset CD in terms of aggression, it is possible that subtyping CD on the basis of age of onset will subclassify youths with CD in much the same way as earlier subtyping schema based on aggression. That is, it is possible that youths with CD described as Undersocialized Aggressive or Solitary Aggressive in DSM-III and DSM-III-R onset during childhood for the most part, whereas youths described as Group Type or Socialized Nonaggressive generally onset in adolescence. If this turns out to be the case, the literature on the relationship of aggression to the persistence of CD will take on new meaning. For example, Henn et al. (1980) found in their 10-year follow-up of incarcerated juvenile delinquents that youths rated as physically aggressive were significantly more likely to commit violent acts including assault, murder, and rape as adults. Similarly, Stattin and Magnusson (1989) found high levels of aggression as early as age 10 to be highly predictive of persistent adult-male criminality, especially violent and destructive crime. These findings may reflect much greater persistence in youths who develop CD during childhood (and who are more aggressive).

## Areas for Future Elaboration of the Developmental Model

We have described a general model for the development of ODD and CD in this chapter. We expect to provide further tests of the tenets of this model in the future and plan to elaborate this model in a number of potentially important directions.

### Multiple Developmental Pathways

In delineating two subtypes of CD based on age of onset we have already suggested that there appear to be at least two distinct "developmental pathways" to adolescent CD. However, Loeber et al. (1994) have provided evidence that there appear to be more than one developmental pathway within childhood-onset CD. Youths who meet criteria for CD in childhood appear to develop oppositional, aggressive, and nonaggressive conduct problems in different predictable sequences that define separate pathways. One potentially important area for further elaboration of the developmental levels model, therefore, will be in the probable delineation of multiple pathways within the general framework visualized in the "developmental pyramid" (Figure 1).

### Importance of Comorbid Conditions

We strongly suspect that the developmental course and severity of ODD and CD are closely linked to coexisting conditions, such as maladaptive levels of anxiety, depression, and attention-deficit hyperactivity disorder (ADHD). Specifically, we currently have unpublished data from the Developmental Trends Study and the DSM-IV Field Trials that suggest that comorbid anxiety disorder is associated with aggression in a complex fashion that changes from childhood to adolescence, and data that suggest that ADHD is linked to both the age of onset and persistence of CD. Thus, we anticipate important elaborations of the developmental levels model in these areas in the future. In doing so, it will be interesting to attempt to link two concepts that are important in our thinking: (1) the association of comorbid disorders with differences in the topography (particularly aggressivity) and severity of CD and (2) the delineation of different developmental pathways. We may find that we are approaching the same concepts in different ways.

### Factors that Give Rise to, Maintain, and Interrupt the Development of ODD and CD

As progress is made in detailing the developmental progression of ODD and CD, we expect the developmental levels model to facilitate research on etiology, prevention, and treatment. Once we have a reasonably accurate view of the development of ODD and CD, it will be possible to identify factors associated with the initiation of the developmental sequence, the maintenance of (or desistance from) a given level of conduct problems, and the progression to higher levels of conduct problems. This information should turn out to be invaluable in the design of future strategies for the prevention and treatment of ODD and CD.

### Gender Differences in ODD and CD

As we have pointed out several times in this chapter, much less is known about ODD and CD in girls than in boys. The great majority of current information about CD and ODD stems from studies of males. The extent to which one can generalize any diagnostic schema based on current evidence to girls is, therefore, very questionable. Indeed, even among our currently sparse data on CD in girls, there are suggestions of key differences. It appears that CD onsets later in girls and that girls are markedly less aggressive than boys on the average. It is very important to continue to study ODD and CD in girls to determine if different developmental models are needed for girls.

### Summary

We have suggested a general heuristic framework for a developmental model of serious conduct problems in children and adolescents. We proposed that there are three developmentally sequenced levels of conduct problems that can be visualized in the "developmental pyramid" presented in Figure 1. During childhood, youths enter the developmental sequence with ODD behaviors, with some youths progressing to "intermediate" CD behaviors, and then to "advanced" levels of CD behaviors. We further hypothesize that youths who have penetrated to the "advanced" level of CD are most likely to exhibit the disorder persistently.

We supported the developmental levels model by reviewing evidence on statistical covariation among the behaviors that define each level, the age of onset of symptoms, the severity of impairment associated with the different levels, developmental sequencing of the levels, and the persistence of conduct problems in youths at the different levels. The ODD behaviors emerge earlier than the "intermediate" CD behaviors, and the "advanced" CD behaviors characteristically onset later than the "intermediate" CD behaviors. A large and consistent literature on the statistical covariation of ODD and CD behaviors is consistent with the developmental levels model. In factor-analytic studies, the ODD behaviors consistently load on a factor that is distinct from the factor on which the "advanced" CD behaviors load. However, fighting, bullying, lying, and other "intermediate" CD behaviors are associated with both ODD and CD in terms of statistical covariation. The distinction of "intermediate" CD behaviors from ODD behaviors was most clear when large numbers of factor-analytic studies were integrated using multidimensional scaling and when the association of behaviors with levels was directly tested using tentative a priori definitions of the three developmental levels.

We further addressed the validity of developmental levels model by examining evidence on the developmental sequencing of the levels. The evidence reviewed in this chapter suggests that ODD and CD are related both developmentally and hierarchically. That is to say, although many youths with ODD do not progress to CD, almost all youths with clinically significant CD whose symptoms began during childhood developed CD after ODD, while retaining the ODD behaviors. Furthermore, the small, existing literature comparing the two disorders suggests that ODD and CD are quite similar in terms of socioeconomic status, family history of psychopathology, and impairment. When differences emerged, they almost always suggested greater impairment and family history of antisocial behavior among youths with CD than ODD, but with youths with ODD showing more deviance than control subjects. These tentative findings suggest that it would be reasonable to conceptualize ODD and CD as two levels of severity within the same developmental continuum of serious conduct problems.

In addition, we presented evidence in support of the "advanced" level of CD that suggests that few youths who develop CD in childhood exhibit these serious behaviors without also exhibiting the less-severe CD behaviors at the "intermediate" level that tend to emerge much earlier in the developmental sequence. That is, "advanced" CD behaviors are developmentally nested within "intermediate" CD behaviors.

We further proposed that some youths enter the developmental sequence for the first time during adolescence and show a distinct gender ratio, a characteristically nonaggressive pattern of symptoms, and little ODD. Evidence from developmental criminology suggests that these youths often come into conflict with the police but that their prognosis is markedly better than for youths with childhood-onset CD. These youths appear to arrive at adolescent antisocial behavior through a distinct developmental pathway, and evidence is now emerging that additional distinct pathways may exist with the general childhood onset described in the developmental levels model.

Finally, we outlined some areas in which we expect the developmental levels model to be elaborated in the near future, including the probable distinction of multiple developmental pathways through the levels and the description of key interactions of anxiety, ADHD, and other dimensions of psychopathologies with the developmental progression of serious conduct problems. We also plan to relate the developmental levels to distal and proximal factors involved in the origins, maintenance, and cessation of serious conduct problem behaviors. When we have identified factors that change the course of the development of ODD and CD behaviors, we should be in a much better position to design preventive and treatment interventions. As frequently mentioned in this chapter, however, much remains to be learned about the development of conduct problems in girls that will inform our understanding of antisocial behavior in both girls and boys.

ACKNOWLEDGMENTS. The chapter was written with support from grants MH-42529 and MH-39158 from the National Institute of Mental Health and grant 86-JN-CX-0009 from the Office of Juvenile Justice and Delinquency Prevention, Office of Justice Programs, U.S. Department of Justice.

## References

Achenbach, T. M., & Edelbrock, C. S. (1979). The Child Behavior Profile: III. Boys aged 12–16 and girls aged 6–11 and 12–16. *Journal of Consulting Clinical Psychology, 47*, 223–233.

Achenbach, T. M., & Edelbrock, C. S. (1981). Behavioral problems and competencies reported by parents of normal and disturbed children aged four through sixteen. *Monographs of the Society for Research in Child Development, 46*, 1–82.

Achenbach, T. M., & Edelbrock, C. S. (1983). *Manual for the Child Behavior Checklist and Revised Child Behavior Profile*. Burlington, VT: University Associates in Psychiatry.

Achenbach, T. M., Edelbrock, C. S., & Howell, C. T. (1987). Empirically based assessment of the behavioral/emotional problems of 2- and 3-year-old children. *Journal of Abnormal Child Psychology, 15*, 629–650.

Achenbach, T. M., Conners, C. K., Quay, H. C., Verhulst, F. C., & Howell, C. T. (1989). Replication of empirically derived syndromes as a basis for taxonomy of child/adolescent psycho-pathology. *Journal of Abnormal Child Psychology, 17*, 299–320.

American Psychiatric Association. (1980). *Diagnostic and statistical manual of mental disorders* (3rd ed.). Washington, DC: Author.

American Psychiatric Association. (1987). *Diagnostic and statistical manual of mental disorders* (3rd ed. rev.). Washington, DC: Author.

Anderson, J. C., Williams, S., McGee, R., & Silva, P. A. (1987). DSM-III disorders in preadolescent children: Prevalence in a large sample from the general population. *Archives of General Psychiatry, 44*, 69–76.

Beilin, H. (1958). Teachers' and clinicians' attitudes toward the behavior problems of children: A reappraisal. *Child Development, 30*, 9–25.

Bird, H. R., Canino, G. et al. (1988). Estimates of the prevalence of childhood maladjustment in a community survey in Puerto Rico. *Archives of General Psychiatry, 45*, 1120–1126.

Campbell, S. B. (1990). *Behavior problems in preschool children: Developmental and clinical issues*. New York: Guilford.

Christ, M. A. G., Lahey, B. B., Frick, P. J., Applegate, B., & Loeber, R. (1991). *Correlates of peer rejection in clinic-referred boys*. Unpublished manuscript, University of Georgia.

Elliott, D. S., Knowles, B. A., & Canter, R. J. (1981). *The epidemiology of delinquent behavior and drug use among American adolescents, 1976–1978*. Unpublished manuscript. Boulder, CO: Behavior Research Institute.

Faraone, S. V., Biederman, J., Keenan, K., & Tsuang, M. T. (1991). Separation of DSM-III attention deficit disorder and conduct disorder: Evidence from a family genetic study of American child psychiatry patients. *Psychological Medicine, 21*, 109–121.

Farrington, D. P. (1986). Age and crime. In M. Tonry & N. Morris (Eds.), *Crime and justice* (Vol. 7, pp. 29–90). Chicago: University of Chicago Press.

Farrington, D. P. (1987). Epidemiology. In H. C. Quay (Ed.), *Handbook of juvenile delinquency* (pp. 33–61). New York: Wiley.

Fowler, P. C., & Parke, R. M. (1979). Factor structure of the pre-school behavior questionnaire in a normal population. *Psychological Reports, 45*, 599–606.

Frick, P. J., Lahey, B. B., Loeber, R., Stouthamer-Loeber, M., Christ, M. A. G., & Hanson, K. (1992). Familial risk factors to oppositional defiant disorder and conduct disorder: Parental psychopathology and maternal parenting. *Journal of Consulting and Clinical Psychology, 60*, 49–55.

Frick, P. J., Lahey, B. B., Loeber, R., Stouthamer-Loeber, M., Green, S., Hart, E. L., & Christ, M. A. G. (1990). Oppositional defiant disorder and conduct disorder in boys: Patterns of behavioral covariation. *Journal of Clinical Child Psychology, 20*, 202–208.

Frick, P. J., Lahey, B. B., Loeber, R., Tannenbaum, L., Van Horn, Y., Christ, M. A. G., Hart, E., & Hanson, K. (1993). Oppositional defiant disorder and conduct disorder: A meta-analytic review of factor analyses and cross-validation in a clinic sample. *Clinical Psychology Review, 13*, 319–340.

Glueck, S., & Glueck, E. T. (1968). *Delinquents and nondelinquents in perspective*. Cambridge, MA: Harvard University.

Greene, E. L., Langner, T. S., Herson, J. H., Jameson, J. D., Eisenberg, J. D., & McCarthy, E. D. (1973). Some methods of evaluating behavioral variations in children 6 to 18. *Journal of the American Academy of Child Psychiatry, 12,* 531–553.

Harrington, R., Fudge, H., Rutter, M., Pickles, A., & Hill, J. (1991). Adult outcomes of childhood and adolescent depression: II. Links with antisocial disorders. *Journal of the American Academy of Child and Adolescent Psychiatry, 3,* 434–439.

Henn, F. A., Bardwell, R., & Jenkins, R. L. (1980). Juvenile delinquents revisited: Adult criminal activity. *Archives of General Psychiatry, 37,* 1160–1165.

Hinshaw, S., Lahey, B. B., & Hart, E. L. (1993). Issues of taxonomy and comorbidity in the development of conduct disorder. *Development and Psychopathology, 5,* 31–49.

Kashani, J. H., Orvaschel, H., Rosenberg, T. K., & Reid, J. C. (1989). Psychopathy in a community sample of children and adolescents: A developmental perspective. *Journal of the American Academy of Child and Adolescent Psychiatry, 28,* 701–706.

Kazdin, A. E. (1987). Treatment of antisocial behavior in children: Current status and future directions. *Psychological Bulletin, 102,* 187–203.

Kohn, M. (1977). *Social competence, symptoms and underachievement in childhood: A longitudinal perspective*. Washington, DC: Winston.

Lahey, B. B., Applegate, B., Greenhill, L., McBurnett, K., Garfinkel, B., Newcorn, J., Jensen, P., Richters, J., Hynd, G. H., Ollendick, T., Barkley, R., Hart, E. L., Perez, D., Waldman, I., & Shaffer, D. (in press). *DSM-IV Field Trials for Oppositional Defiant Disorder and Conduct Disorder in Children and Adolescents. American Journal of Psychiatry.*

Lahey, B. B., Loeber, R., Stouthamer-Loeber, M., Christ, M. A. G., Green, S., Russo, M. F., Frick, P. J., & Dulcan, M. (1990). Comparison of DSM-III and DSM-III-R diagnoses for prepubertal children: Changes in prevalence and validity. *Journal of the American Academy of Child and Adolescent Psychiatry, 29,* 620–626.

Lahey, B. B., Loeber, R., Quay, H. C., Frick, P. J., & Grimm, J. (1992). Oppositional defiant and conduct disorders: Issues to be resolved for DSM-IV. *Journal of the American Academy of Child and Adolescent Psychiatry, 31,* 539–546.

Lahey, B. B., Loeber, R., Green, S. M., Applegate, B., Hart, E. L., Hanson, K. L., & Frick, P. J. (1994). *Four-year Longitudinal Study of Conduct Disorder in Boys: II. Background and developmental predictors of persistence*. Unpublished manuscript, University of Georgia.

LeBlanc, M., & Fréchette, M. (1989). *Male criminal activity from childhood through youth: Multilevel and developmental perspectives*. New York: Springer-Verlag.

Lindgren, S., Wolraich, M., Stromquist, A., Davis, C., Milich, R., & Watson, D. (1990, June). *Diagnostic heterogeneity in Attention Deficit Hyperactivity Disorder*. Paper presented at the fourth annual NIMH International Research Conference on the Classification and Treatment of Mental Disorders in General Medical Settings, Bethesda, MD.

Loeber, R. (1982). The stability of antisocial and delinquent child behavior: A review. *Child Development, 53,* 1431–1446.

Loeber, R. (1985). Patterns and development of antisocial child behavior. In G. J. Whitehurst (Ed.), *Annals of Child Development* (Vol. 2). Greenwich, CO: JAI.

Loeber, R., (1988). Natural histories of conduct problems, delinquency, and associated substance use. In B. B. Lahey & A. E. Kazdin (Eds.), *Advances in clinical child psychology* (Vol. 11, pp. 73–124). New York: Plenum.

Loeber, R., & Schmaling, K. B. (1985). Empirical evidence for overt and covert patterns of antisocial conduct problems: A meta-analysis. *Journal of Abnormal Child Psychology, 13,* 337–352.

Loeber, R., Green, S. M., Lahey, B. B., Christ, M. A. G., & Frick, P. J. (1992). Developmental sequences in the age of onset of disruptive child behaviors. *Journal of Child and Family Studies, 1*, 21–41.

Loeber, R., Keenan, K., Lahey, B. B., Green, S., & Thomas, C. (in press). Evidence for developmentally based diagnoses of ODD and CD. *Journal of Abnormal Child Psychology.*

Loeber, R., Lahey, B. B., & Thomas, C. (1991). The diagnostic conundrum of oppositional defiant disorder and conduct disorder. *Journal of Abnormal Psychology, 100*, 379–390.

Loeber, R., Stouthamer-Loeber, M., Van Kammen, W. B., & Farrington, D. P. (in press). *Childhood origins of antisocial behavior, substance use, and psychopathology.* New York: Cambridge University Press.

Loeber, R., Wung, P., Keenan, K., Giroux, B., Stouthamer-Loeber, M., & Van Kammen, W. B. (in press). Developmental pathways in disruptive child behavior. *Development and Psychopathology.*

MacFarlane, J. W., Allen, L., & Honzik, M. P. (1962). *A developmental study of the behavior problems of normal children between twenty-one months and fourteen years.* Berkeley: University of California Press.

McDermott, P. A. (1983). A syndrome topology for analyzing school children's disturbed social behavior. *School Psychology Review, 12*, 250–259.

McGee, R., Feehan, M., Williams, S., & Anderson, J. (1992). DSM-III disorders from age 11 to age 15. *Journal of the American Academy of Child and Adolescent Psychiatry, 31*, 50–59.

Moffitt, T. E. (1990). Juvenile delinquency and attention deficit disorder: Boys' developmental trajectories from age 3 to age 15. *Child Development, 61*, 893–910.

O'Donnell, J. P., & Van Tuinan, M. (1979). Behavioral problems of preschool children: Dimensions and congenital correlates. *Journal of Abnormal Child Psychology, 7*, 61–75.

Offord, D. R., Boyle, M. H., Racine, Y. A., Fleming, J. E., Cadman, D. T., Blum, H. M., Byrne, C., Links, P. S., Lipman, E. L., MacMillan, H. L., Grant, N. R., Sanford, M. N., Szatmari, P., Thomas, H., & Woodward, C. A. (1992). Outcome, prognosis, and risk in a longitudinal follow-up study. *Journal of the American Academy of Child and Adolescent Psychiatry, 31*, 916–923.

Offord, D. R., Boyle, M. H. et al. (1987). Ontario Health Study: II. Six-month prevalence of disorder and rates of service utilization. *Archives of General Psychiatry, 44*, 832–836.

Olweus, D. (1989). Prevalence and incidence on the study of antisocial behavior: Definition and measurements. In M. W. Klein (Ed.), *Cross-national research in self-reported crime and delinquency.* Dordrecht: Kluwer.

Quay, H. C. (1986a). Classification. In H. C. Quay, & J. S. Werry (Eds.), *Psychopathological disorders in childhood* (3rd ed.). New York: Wiley.

Quay, H. C. (1986b). Conduct disorders. In H. C. Quay, & J. S. Werry (Eds.), *Psychopathological disorders in childhood* (3rd ed.). New York: Wiley.

Reeves, J. C., Werry, J. S., Elkind, G. S., & Zametkin, A. (1987). Attention deficit, conduct, oppositional, and anxiety disorders in children: II. Clinical characteristics. *Journal of the American Academy of Child and Adolescent Psychiatry, 26*, 144–155.

Rey, J. M., Bashir, M. R., Schwarz, M., Richards, I. N., Plapp, J. M., & Stewart, G. W. (1988). Oppositional disorder: Fact or fiction? *Journal of the American Academy of Child and Adolescent Psychiatry, 27*, 157–162.

Robins, L. N. (1966). *Deviant children grow up: A sociological and psychiatric study of sociopathic personality.* Baltimore: Williams & Wilkins.

Robins, L. N., & Ratcliffe, K. S. (1979). Risk factors in the continuation of childhood antisocial behavior into adulthood. *International Journal of Mental Health, 7*, 96–115.

Russo, M. F., Loeber, R., Lahey, B. B., & Keenan, K. (in press). *Oppositional defiant and* conduct disorders: Validation of the proposed DSM-IV alternative diagnostic option. *Journal of Clinical Child Psychology.*

Schachar, R., & Wachsmuth, R. (1990). Oppositional disorder in children: A validation study comparing conduct disorder, oppositional disorder, and normal control children. *Journal of Child Psychology and Psychiatry, 31,* 1089–1102.

Spitzer, R. L., Davies, M., & Barkley, R. (1991). The DSM-III-R field trials for the disruptive behavior disorders. *Journal of the American Academy of Child Adolescent Psychiatry, 29,* 690–697.

Stanger, C., McConaughy, S. H., & Achenbach, T. M. (1992). Three-year course of behavioral/emotional problems in a national sample of 4- to 16-year-olds: II. Predictors of syndromes. *Journal of the American Academy of Child and Adolescent Psychiatry, 31,* 941–950.

Stattin, H., & Magnusson, D. (1989). The role of early aggressive behavior in the frequency, seriousness, and types of later crime. *Journal of Consulting and Clinical Psychology, 57,* 710–718.

Tremblay, R. (1990). [Prediction of child problem behavior]. Unpublished data, School of Psycho-Education, University of Montreal, Montreal, Quebec, Canada.

Verhulst, F. C., & van der Ende, J. (1992). Six-year developmental course of internalizing and externalizing problem behaviors. *Journal of the American Academy of Child and Adolescent Psychiatry, 31,* 924–931.

Vidoni, D. O., Fleming, N. J., & Mintz, S. (1983). Behavior problems of children as perceived by teachers, mental health professionals, and children. *Psychology in the Schools, 20,* 93–98.

Walker, J. L., Lahey, B. B., Russo, M. F., Frick, P. J., Christ, M. A. G., McBurnett, K., Loeber, R., Stouthamer-Loeber, M., & Green, S. M. (1991). Anxiety, inhibition, and conduct disorder in children: I. Relations to social impairment: I. *Journal of the American Academy of Child and Adolescent Psychiatry, 30,* 187–191.

Werry, J. S., & Quay, H. C. (1971). The prevalence of behavior symptoms in younger elementary school children. *American Journal of Orthopsychiatry, 41,* 136–143.

Werry, J. S., Reeves, J. C., & Elkind, G. S. (1987). Attention deficit, conduct, oppositional, and anxiety disorders in children: I. A review of research on differentiating characteristics. *Journal of the American Academy of Child Psychiatry, 26,* 133–143.

West, D. J., & Farrington, D. P. (1977). *The delinquent way of life.* London: Heinemann.

Wickman, E. K. (1928). *Children's behavior and teacher's attitudes.* New York: Commonwealth Fund.

Zimring, F. E. (1979). American youth violence: Issues and trends. In N. Morris & M. Tonry (Eds.), *Crime and justice: An annual review of research* (Vol. 1, pp. 67–107). Chicago: University of Chicago Press.

# 7

# Electrodermal Hyporeactivity and Antisocial Behavior

## DON C. FOWLES and ANN M. FURUSETH

## Introduction

Electrodermal hyporeactivity has been widely reported for individuals variously described as psychopathic, sociopathic, antisocial, delinquent, hyperactive, or aggressive. The present chapter will attempt to provide an overview of this hyporeactivity and its association with undersocialized behavior and to consider one of the major theoretical interpretations of these findings. Although the bulk of this literature is based on adult and late-adolescent (delinquent) populations, the continuity of antisocial behavior from childhood to adulthood and the assumption that electrodermal hyporeactivity reflects stable effects of temperament point to direct implications for childhood disorders involving antisocial behavior. In view of these implications, the paucity of electrodermal research with children is a deficiency that needs correcting. To that end, paradigms that have proved successful with children will be reviewed at the end of the chapter.

### Quay's Contributions

It is particularly apt to review this topic in a book dedicated to the work of Herbert Quay. The value of his contributions to the literature

DON C. FOWLES and ANN M. FURUSETH • Department of Psychology, University of Iowa, Iowa City, Iowa 15213.

*Disruptive Behavior Disorders in Childhood,* edited by Donald K. Routh. Plenum Press, New York, 1994.

reviewed here could hardly be exaggerated. These include (1) his early suggestion (Quay, 1965) that autonomic hyporesponsivity produces a lower than optimal level of arousal that in turn causes stimulation-seeking behavior, (2) his many contributions to delineating subgroups within the childhood disorders, including especially the early identification of factors or dimensions of psychopathic delinquency, neurotic delinquency, and subcultural delinquency (Quay, 1964; Peterson, Quay, & Tiffany, 1961) and the current distinction between Undersocialized Aggressive Conduct Disorder and Socialized Conduct Disorders (e.g., Quay, 1986, chap. 1), (3) his application of Gray's (e.g., 1987) concept of behavioral inhibition to understanding the etiology of developmental psychopathology (Quay, 1988a,b), and (4) his recent (Quay, 1990, 1993) proposal that electrodermal hyporeactivity reflects poor behavioral inhibition specifically in undersocialized aggressive conduct disorders. Thus, Quay's contributions have included both widely accepted diagnostic distinctions and highly influential theories of etiologies. In keeping with the dedication of this book to Quay's research, the theoretical discussion in the present chapter will be restricted to the deficient anxiety/poor behavioral inhibition explanation for electrodermal hyporeactivity, which is Quay's most recent proposal.

## Comments on the Nature of Electrodermal Activity

Before considering the clinical literature, a brief summary of the nature of electrodermal activity (EDA) is needed. EDA refers collectively to several types of measurements of the electrical activity across the epidermis on the palms of the hands and, occasionally, the soles of the feet. By applying a small external voltage (e.g., 0.5 volt) to the skin, one can measure the electrical conductivity of the epidermis, known as skin conductance, or the electrical resistance (the reciprocal of conductance). For technical reasons, skin-conductance measurements are often preferred (Venables & Christie, 1980). Far less often, electrodermal measurements include recordings of the endogenous potential across the epidermis. Skin-potential responses are mostly attributable to a large lumen negative potential associated with reabsorption of sodium chloride from the sweat in the duct (Fowles & Venables, 1970; Fowles, 1986). These measurements yield information about both *tonic level* (electrodermal level of EDL) and *phasic responses* (electrodermal responses or EDRs). In the older literature, EDRs were frequently called galvanic skin responses or psychogalvanic reflexes. Now the preferred terms are *skin-conductance response* (SCR), *skin-resistance response* (SRR), or *skin-potential response* (SPR), depending on the method of measurement (Venables &

Christie, 1980). Tonic levels are correspondingly designated as skin-conductance level (SCL), skin-resistance level (SRL), and skin-potential level (SPL).

All of the *phasic* measurements—collectively termed electrodermal responses (EDRs)—can be assumed largely to reflect activity of the *sweat glands*, which are innervated only by the sympathetic nervous system (SNS), albeit with cholinergic innervation in common with other exocrine glands (Fowles, 1986). As the sweat fills the epidermal portion of the sweat duct, it provides a low-resistance pathway through the skin, causing a phasic increase in conductance (a decrease in resistance) or an increase in surface negative potential (see Fowles, 1986, for an explanation). *Tonic-level* measurements, in contrast, include a substantial contribution from the *nonsudorific pathways* through the skin—that is, pathways not involving the sweat glands. Under resting conditions, *if the sweat glands have been inactive for a period of many minutes*, the sweat gland ducts will have emptied and will, therefore, contribute little to measures of EDL. Under activated conditions, the duct filling associated with EDRs contributes to standing levels, as well. Additionally, diffusion of sweat into the peritubular stratum corneum increases the conductivity of the nonsudorific pathway. Thus, tonic levels consist of a complex mixture of sudorific and nonsudorific contributions, but increases in response to experimental stimulation generally reflect prior and current sweat gland activity.

Because of the SNS innervation of the sweat glands and of the association of the SNS with the emergency response to stressful stimuli, electrodermal hyporeactivity has been attributed by many authors to a reduction in anxiety in a portion of antisocial individuals. This conclusion is made more credible if the hyporeactivity is seen in the face of aversive stimulation, such as the threat of an impending shock. It should be noted that only the sweat gland contribution to EDA has clear psychological importance. True resting levels, influenced largely or totally by nonsudorific components, have little or no psychological significance. Consequently, differences in EDL at rest have psychological significance only if they can be attributed to differences in the degree to which sweat glands are activated: The experimental situation itself constitutes a complex stimulus and in "resting" conditions we are observing a response to the experimental situation (Hare, 1970, p. 40).

Three different measures of EDA are common in the literature on antisocial behavior. First, the *amplitude* of EDRs to *discrete stimuli* presented briefly are called orienting responses (ORs) to neutral stimuli (tones or lights without meaning or significance) and signal ORs to stimuli with meaning or significance (e.g., the CS in a classical conditioning paradigm, the warning and imperative stimuli in a reaction time paradigm, slides of threatening objects, or any stimulus that is to be detected by the subject). Second, *counts* of EDRs during a period of time usually extending over minutes, such as a rest period or a period of threatened shock or a period of task performance, are called nonspecific EDRs. Third, readings of conductance, resistance, or potential taken at standard intervals during any experimental condition are called EDLs even though they will reflect contributions of EDRs to the overall tonic level. As noted above, all three are presumed to reflect sweat gland activity, but EDLs tend to be least sensitive, especially at rest, due to the strong nonsudorific component.

A fourth measure, the speed of recovery of the SCR (or SRR), is used much less frequently. Slow-recovery SCRs are consistent with a hyporeactivity hypothesis. They should *not* be interpreted according to either of the two popular theories in the literature: (1) Mednick's (1975) proposal that slow-SCR recovery mirrors the course of fear reduction in the central nervous system, or (2) the proposal that rapid recovery and slow recovery SCRs are produced by two different mechanisms with separate peripheral innervation, slow-recovery responses being said to reflect a defensive orientation and rapid-recovery responses a goal-directed orientation (Edelberg, 1970, 1972).

In view of the complexity of the peripheral mechanism of the electrodermal system, there has never been good evidence to support the Mednick hypothesis that recovery time of a single peripheral EDR reflects the course of central states of anxiety. The Edelberg hypothesis, on the other hand, was the subject of considerable research effort with some apparently positive findings. Nevertheless, it now appears unlikely that this hypothesis is valid (Edelberg, 1993; Edelberg & Muller, 1981; Fowles, 1986). Rather, the amount of prior sweat gland responding determines, at least to a significant degree, the speed of recovery: Slow-recovery SCRs reflect less prior sweat gland activity.

The factors influencing EDL, EDR amplitude, and EDR recovery time are complex, making these measures noisy or imperfect indices of the underlying sweat gland activity. Consequently, it is not unreasonable to see different aspects of EDA discriminate between groups in different studies. At least some degree of consistency can be inferred from the direction of the effects: Lessened sweat gland activity is associated with smaller EDRs, fewer nonspecific EDRs, lower SCL, and slower SCR recovery times. At the same time, the multiplicity of indices provides an opportunity for data snooping and Type I errors, making replication across studies critical.

## Empirical Findings

Many studies of EDA in antisocial individuals have employed adult prison inmates or adolescent delinquents selected as "primary psychopaths" on the basis of Cleckley's (e.g., 1950, 1964) concept of psychopathy, which closely resembles Quay's psychopathic delinquent. Others have employed the Gough and Peterson (1952) Delinquency (De) scale or its later version, the Gough Socialization Scale (So), which was incorporated into the California Psychological Inventory (Gough, 1960; Megargee, 1972). Many of the So-scale items overlap criteria used by Cleckley to select primary psychopaths (Schalling, Lidberg, Levander, & Dahlin, 1973).

Numerous reviews of EDA and antisocial behavior have been published, almost all of which have found some aspect of EDA to distinguish antisocial groups from controls. Because Hare's (1978a) review was one of the most comprehensive and because relatively few studies have been published since that date, his conclusions will be cited frequently in the present summary of the major findings. Following Hare's lead, the literature will be examined as a function of experimental conditions and type of EDA measure.

### EDL and Nonspecific EDRs: Resting Conditions

Hare (1978a) and Siddle (1977) reviewed findings for SCL and nonspecific EDRs under resting conditions. With respect to SCL, Hare reported that 6 studies found significantly lower SCLs and that the 10 that did not were in the direction of lower SC levels for psychopaths. Siddle (1977) noted that some of Hare's own studies showed significant differences but expressed a more negative view: "No firm conclusions can be drawn" (p. 203). Neither author found noteworthy support for differences in nonspecific EDRs at rest. Since these reviews, Schmidt, Solanto, and Bridger (1985) using conduct-disordered children versus normal controls and Delamater and Lahey (1983) using learning-disabled children (of whom 60% were also hyperactive) further subdivided on the basis of conduct disorder and tension–anxiety (from the Conners Teacher Rating Scale) both failed to find resting differences for either SCL or nonspecific EDRs. Raine, Venables, and Williams (1990, see p. 1004) found no differences in resting SCL among 15-year-old schoolboys as a function of concurrent antisocial behavior, although they did report fewer nonspecific EDRs at age 15 among boys who later became criminals than among those who did not.

It appears, therefore, that differences in the direction of less sweat gland activity among psychopaths may occasionally be found under resting conditions for SCL, but that the effect size is small. There is even less basis to infer differences in nonspecific fluctuations during rest. As suggested above, any such differences would reflect the subject's response to the experimental situation, and it appears that most experiments are not seen as stressful or stimulating enough to bring out differences between the two groups during the initial rest period.

## EDL and Nonspecific EDRs: Monotonous/Repetitive Stimulation

Repetitive or monotonous stimulation in the form of a series of low-to-moderate tones represents a slightly greater stimulation than resting levels. Psychopaths were found to show a declining SCL during 80-dB tones (following a balloon burst test) compared to a slight increase for nonpsychopaths (Hare, 1968a) and a smaller increase in SCL from rest to 93-dB tones (Schalling, Lidberg, Levander, & Dahlin, 1973; psychopaths defined within a criminal group by high scores on Gough's Delinquency scale). Although Hare (1968b) did not report results for nonspecific EDRs during the tones, Schalling et al. (1973) did find differences during tones. On the other hand, a number of studies employing a tone series either reported negative results or did not report any results for SCL and nonspecific EDRs (Borkovec, 1970; Raine & Venables, 1984; Schmidt, Solanto, & Bridger, 1985; Siddle, Nicol, & Foggitt, 1973). As in the resting-level results, with respect to SCL and nonspecific EDRs any effects seen with monotonous stimulation appear to be small and unreliable, and the Schalling et al. (1973) results can possibly be attributed to the use of relatively loud tones.

## EDL and Nonspecific EDRs: Stimulating/Stressful Conditions

More challenging experimental conditions have yielded more positive results. One study involving injection of adrenalin (Hare, 1972) and a second involving administration of shocks to other subjects (Dengerink & Bertilson, 1975) showed increases in SCL during the experiment in nonpsychopaths compared with stable records for psychopathic subjects. Even more to the point are seven studies (Hare, 1965b; Hare & Craigen, 1974; Hare, Frazelle, & Cox, 1978; Lippert & Senter, 1966; Schalling & Levander, 1967; Schalling, Levander, & Dahlin-Lidberg, 1975, Note 5 in Hare, 1978a; Tharp, Maltzman, Syndulko, & Ziskind, 1980) that showed smaller increases in EDA (levels, nonspecific fluctuations, or smaller anticipatory phasic responses) during a time period prior to an *anticipated* stressor. The anticipated stressor usually was electric shock (Hare, 1965b; Hare & Craigen, 1974; Lippert & Senter, 1966; Schmauk, 1970; Schalling, Levander, & Dahlin-Lidberg, Note 9 as reported on p. 100 by Schalling, 1978; Schalling & Levander, 1967), but also included a 120-dB fast-onset tone (Hare, Frazelle, & Cox, 1978), a 95-dB 1000-Hz tone (Tharp, Maltzman, Syndulko, & Ziskind, 1980), mental arithmetic (Schalling, Levander, & Dahlin-Lidberg, Note 9 as reported on p. 100 by Schalling, 1978); and social disapproval (Schmauk, 1970). In the Tharp et al. (1980) study, the psychopaths were noninstitutionalized subjects recruited from Gamblers Anonymous and required to have high ratings on impulsiveness, irresponsibility, superficiality of affect, inability to profit from past experience or punishment, and impairment of conscience. In the Hare, Frazelle, and Cox (1978) study, only the subjects that were rated as Cleckley psychopaths *and* had low-So scores showed lower skin-conductance-level increases and fewer nonspecific SCRs in anticipation of the aversive tones.

## EDRs to Signal Stimuli

In contrast to reliance on counts of nonspecific phasic responses and/or increases in SC levels as an indication of EDA response to threatened punishments, standard classical conditioning paradigms use individual EDRs to discrete stimuli (CSs). The CS acquires signal value by virtue of its association with the UCS. In the seminal study in this field, Lykken (1957) found that primary sociopaths showed smaller SCRs to the CSs with shock as the UCS. These results were replicated by Hare (1965b) and by Hare and Quinn (1971). Hare and Craigen (1974) found that psychopaths gave smaller SCRs to the onset of 10-second tones signaling shock at tone offset. Ziskind, Syndulko, and Maltzman (1977, cited by Tharp et al., 1980), reported deficient classical conditioning for psychopaths in two experiments: They either failed to establish differential conditioning (Experiment 1) or showed rapid habituation of a conditioned electrodermal response in spite of continued pairing with the aversive UCS. Raine and Venables (1981) examined classical conditioning as a function of socialization among 101 representative 15-year-old male schoolchildren. Antisocial behavior was assessed by teacher ratings on the Unsocialized-Psychopathic subscale of the Behavior Problem Checklist (Quay & Parsons, 1970) and by a self-report measure that was derived from a factor analysis of 18 standardized self-report scales. Although the initial analysis failed to find differences, when they divided the sample into high versus low social class, the expected association between poor conditioning and low socialization was found among high-social-class boys. The authors offered the plausible hypothesis that biological influences are stronger in the higher social classes where environmental influences toward antisocial behavior are minimized—a subtyping strategy that may well overlap with the traditional exclusion of subcultural delinquents (i.e., gang members) from those diagnosed as psychopathic.

Delamater and Lahey (1983) induced signal value by a reaction-time paradigm in which children (average age approximately 10 years) pressed a telegraph key as quickly they could following high-frequency tones (*signal* stimuli) but not low-frequency tones (*nonsignal* stimuli). The subjects were 36 children all of whom had been diagnosed as learning disabled by school psychologists and then were further subdivided into four groups on the basis of tension-anxiety and conduct problem scales on the Conners (1969) Teacher Rating Scale. There was a conduct problem × tension–anxiety crossover interaction in which among low-tension–anxiety children conduct problems were associated with smaller SCRs to the tones, whereas among high-tension–anxiety children conduct problems were associated with larger SCRs. This interaction was true for both signal tones ($p < .04$) and nonsignal tones ($p < .008$). The differences between high- and low-conduct problem children appeared to be greater among low-tension–anxiety children than among high-tension–anxiety children, and this pattern appeared especially true for the nonsignal tones. Although the initial selection of learning-disabled children differs from the other studies reviewed here, these results are of interest because they suggest a possibility that the association of antisocial behavior with electrodermal hyporeactivity may be limited to low-anxious antisocial children.

Schmauk (1970) reported SCR responding in the context of a mental maze task employed earlier by Lykken (1957). This maze consists of 20 choice points with four choices at each point, indicated by four levers. The correct choice advances the subject to the next choice point, whereas none of the three incorrect choices do so. One of the incorrect choices is punished—by shock in Lykken's original study but by shock, loss of money, or social punishment (the experimenter saying "wrong" in a disapproving tone), depending on the experimental condition in Schmauk's study. Of interest in the present context, Schmauk modified the task to require subjects to verbally indicate which of the four levers they would choose, but then to wait 5 seconds before pressing the lever. This strategy permitted recording of SCRs during the 5-second period of anticipation (autonomic anticipation), as well as following receipt of the consequences of lever presses (autonomic reactivity). It might be noted that the subjects were not given feedback before the 5-second period concerning the consequences of their choice, meaning that any responses in anticipation of punishment were in spite of their having chosen that lever in the hope that it was the correct response. The normal controls showed larger SCRs than the primary psychopaths in anticipation of shock and of social punishment but not in anticipation of loss of money—the differences between conditions being largely attributable to increased responding to loss of money (relative to the other punishments) among the primary psychopaths. No differences among groups were found for SCRs to the actual consequences of the lever pressing (including the receipt of the punishments). Thus, this study showed deficient SCR responding to the anticipation of shock and social punishment but not to anticipation of loss of money.

In most studies, the CS is given signal value via an experimental manipulation, but many stimuli have a preexisting significance to the subject. Mathis (1970; cited by Hare, 1978a) reported smaller SCRs to pictures of severe facial injuries. Hare and Quinn (1971) presented slides of nude females, which presumably have positively valenced significance—providing one of the few instances in the literature of an examination of responses to appetitive signal stimuli. There was a trend toward smaller responses to the slides of nudes for the psychopaths (0.73 microsiemens) than the nonpsychopaths (4.10 microsiemens), but this difference was not significant in the overall ANOVA including a third group of inmates that were neither clearly psychopathic nor clearly nonpsychopathic ($p > .10$). In the discussion of his paper, Borkovec (1970) comments that he found normal SCR reactivity in psychopaths to repeated pictures of a nude female, but he does not report details of the results. Thus, it may be the case that psychopaths show normal reactivity to positive affective or appetitive stimuli, although the minimal data available do not permit a clear conclusion in the case of SCRs. A study by Patrick using the eyeblink startle paradigm suggests that psychopaths show diminished reactivity to aversive stimuli but normal reactivity to appetitive stimuli (Lang, Bradley, Cuthbert, & Patrick, 1993).

## Summary

Classical conditioning studies with an aversive UCS appear to yield reasonably reliable differences in the direction of poor electrodermal conditioning among psychopaths. These studies focusing on individual phasic responses (usually the amplitude is of primary interest) to discrete CSs parallel those in which SCL and/or counts of nonspecific phasic responses are used to assess the response over longer periods in anticipation of an aversive stimulus. The specific electrodermal measure and even the precise time periods appear to be less important than the presence of an aversive stimulus. Indeed, comparison of the results for rest periods, monotonous stimulation, and the anticipation of painful or aversive stimuli suggests that the electrodermal hyporeactivity is only reliable during the anticipation of aversive (shock, loud tones) or stressful (mental arithmetic) stimuli. This hyporeactivity in anticipation of aversive stimuli is consistent with the traditional hypothesis that psychopaths show very little anticipatory fear to cues associated with painful stimuli (e.g., Hare, 1978a).

## SCRs to Nonsignal Stimuli

Many studies, especially those with children, employ a series of tones of low-to-moderate intensity to elicit an OR, which responds to the novelty of the initial stimuli in the series and then habituates rapidly. Two studies (Borkovec, 1970; Siddle, Nicol, & Foggitt, 1973) found smaller SCRs to the first tone for the psychopathic subjects. Schmidt, Solanto, and Bridger (1985) compared undersocialized aggressive conduct-disordered children (age approximately 10 years) with normal controls and found a smaller response to the first of eight 90-dB bell sounds but no differences to a preceding series of eight 75-dB tones. Possibly instructions prior to the bell series (the sounds "will not be really scary, but loud") intended to "induce mild anticipatory anxiety" (p. 655) created more anticipatory anxiety that facilitated responses in the control subjects than in the conduct-disordered children. In their study of learning-disabled children, Delamater and Lahey reported a trend ($p < .06$) for a main effect of conduct problem (smaller SCRs) during a series of 10 nonsignal tones, but there were no group differences in the response to two novel tones that followed the 10 identical tones—a negative finding that is inconsistent with the positive results for the initial tone (the most novel) in the studies above.

Raine and Venables (1984) rejected the hypothesis that antisocial behavior is associated with a smaller response to the first tone in a habituation series. Although acknowledging the positive results reported by Borkovec (1970) and Siddle et al. (1973), they cite six experiments (Blackburn, 1979; Hare, 1968b; Hinton, O'Neil, Dishman, & Webster, 1979—two failures; Hinton, O'Neil, Hamilton, & Burke, 1980; Lippert & Senter, 1966) plus their own with negative results, all of which examined the SCR to the first tone in a series of repetitive auditory orienting stimuli. Three additional studies (Goldstein, 1965; Hare, 1978b; Ziskind,

Syndulko, & Maltzman, 1978) used somewhat different stimulation paradigms or scoring methods and also found no differences. To this latter list might be added Hare, Frazelle, and Cox as reported in Hare (1978a, Note 1), who found no differences to 80-dB tones embedded in a series of varying intensity (and varying rise time).

In their own study, Raine and Venables (1984) found an association between antisocial behavior and number of SCRs to all nine tones—a procedure common in research on schizophrenia. Their subjects were those described for Raine and Venables (1981) above. The canonical correlation between the frequency of SCORs to the tones and the pooled assessments of antisocial behavior was 0.44 ($p < .001$), with antisocial boys showing fewer SCRs. In further analyses, these authors compare nonresponding among antisocial subjects and conclude that "it is specifically a 'schizoid' group of antisocials who are characterized by nonresponding" (Raine & Venables, 1984, p. 430; see also Raine, 1987); they emphasize a link between antisociality and psychosis proneness. Although the empirical basis for this proposal is not particularly strong (see Fowles, 1993), it does relate to Schalling's suggestion of a schizoid subtype as discussed below.

## The SCR Recovery Limb

A few investigators have reported that antisocial subjects show a slower return of their SCRs to baseline-conductance levels. For example, Siddle (1977) analyzed the recovery of the first SCR to a tone series from the Siddle et al. (1973) data and found slower recovery for the high-antisocial group compared to the low-antisocial inmates. Similarly, Hare (1978a) reviewed a modest amount of data supporting slower recovery SCRs in psychopathic or criminal subjects.

## The Socialization Scale in Noncriminal Populations

As noted above, Gough's So scale has been used to good effect in several studies with criminal populations. It is of considerable interest that, among college students who score low on the So scale, Waid and Orne (1982) have found electrodermal hyporeactivity to noxious (98-dB) noise bursts (Waid, 1976b), an unexpected loud hand clap (Waid, Orne, & Wilson, 1979), lie detection tests (Waid, Orne, & Wilson, 1979), and a verbal response conflict task modified from the Stroop Color-Word Interference Test (Waid & Orne, 1982). Note that the lie detection and modified Stroop tasks do not involve physically aversive punishments, thereby supporting the expansion of the hyporeactivity results beyond physical punishments.

## Theoretical Implications: Anxiety and Inhibition

One of the dominant theoretical approaches has been to view electrodermal activity as an index of conditioned anticipatory anxiety (e.g., Blackburn, 1983; Hare, 1970, chap. 6; Hare & Quinn, 1971; Lykken, 1957). For example, Hare (1970, chap. 6) cited Mowrer's two-factor theory of avoidance learning, in which fear responses are acquired through classical conditioning and then, in turn, serve to motivate both active and passive avoidance. Successful avoidance of either kind reduces the fear, thereby reinforcing the response. Passive avoidance (the avoidance of a response-contingent punishment by not making the response) is particularly important in this theory: It is a straightforward extrapolation to view the psychopath's impulsivity as a form of poor passive avoidance with regard to future (response-contingent) punishments. It is of importance to the later discussion that the anxiety in question involves *anticipatory* fear responses and feelings of *apprehension* (p. 81, emphasis added). Hare points out further that in approach–avoidance situations, in which both rewards and punishments may be expected as a result of some action, the poor-anxiety conditioning/poor-passive-avoidance hypothesis accounts for the psychopath's inability to resist temptation. In the examples given, psychopaths are prone to charge excessive amounts on credit cards and to cash bad checks, due to their poor capacity for responding to (by resisting temptation) the future negative consequences.

Hare (1978a) cited several studies in which heart rate increases in the anticipation of noxious stimuli were *greater* for criminal psychopaths than controls. This state of affairs precluded a simple autonomic hyporesponsivity hypothesis and required some explanation for the specificity of heart rate and electrodermal activity. In order to explain the dissociation between heart rate and electrodermal activity, Fowles (1980) modified the traditional anxiety interpretation. This proposal drew on Obrist's (1976) active coping hypothesis and Gray's (e.g., 1987) motivational theory.

Gray (e.g., 1987) hypothesizes two motivational systems, one concerned with behavioral activation and one with behavioral inhibition. The Behavioral Activation System (BAS) activates behavior in response to conditioned stimuli for response-contingent reward (simple reward paradigm) or for relieving nonpunishment (safety cues signaling the absence of an expected punishment in an active avoidance paradigm). The Behavioral Inhibition System (BIS) inhibits behavior that would otherwise occur in response to conditioned stimuli for response-contingent punishment (approach–avoidance conflict paradigm) or frustrative nonreward (the absence of expected reward in an extinction paradigm). Activity in the BAS is associated with positive affect (hope, relief), whereas that in the BIS is associated with negative affect (fear or anxiety, frustration). The various anxiolytic drugs (alcohol, barbiturates, minor tranquilizers) reduce the efficacy of the BIS. The BIS is viewed as the neurophysiological substrate for anxiety. Several authors (Blackburn, 1983; Gray, 1970; Fowles, 1980; see especially Trasler, 1978; Quay, 1990, 1993) have proposed that psychopathic behavior can be seen as reflecting a quantitative weakness of the BIS. This hypothesis accounts for impulsivity (as poor passive avoidance and poor extinction), as well as for reduced anxiety in response to cues for potential punishment or failure. It differs from the earlier learning theory formulation in that classical conditioning is not involved in learning via the BIS (instrumental learning is), behavioral inhibition/passive avoidance is a direct consequence of BIS activity, and active avoidance is relatively unaffected by BIS deficits.

Obrist (1976) found that attempts to actively cope with an impending aversive stimulus (by making some response) produce cardiac acceleration, whereas passively accepting the punishment is associated with cardiac deceleration, or at least an absence of acceleration. Drawing on Obrist's work as well as the widely accepted cardiac-somatic coupling hypothesis, Fowles (1980) proposed that heart rate is more strongly tied to the BAS (reward incentives, active avoidance, or active coping) than to the BIS. At the same time, he argued that electrodermal activity appears to reflect the emotional response to threats of punishment and, at least in that sense, could be used to assess the BIS reaction to such threats. Thus, the diminished electrodermal activity seen in psychopaths faced with threats of punishment were consistent with the weak BIS hypothesis, and the failure of heart rate to follow this pattern was attributed to its independence of the BIS. The greater cardiac acceleration in anticipation of punishment was attributed to a dominance of active avoidance tendencies (BAS) over inhibitory processes associated with passively accepting the punishment. The attractive features of this proposal were that it accounted for the divergent electrodermal and heart rate patterns while retaining the original link between deficient anxiety and impulsivity—albeit in the context of a different theory of motivation. The post hoc quality of the explanation for the cardiac acceleration is a weakness, although it is not unreasonable in view of data on animals and humans facing an impending punishment, where both cardiac acceleration and deceleration can be seen, with deceleration emerging as animals stop struggling to escape and as human subjects become resigned to the punishment.

## Two Types of Anxiety

It now appears that a significant modification of Fowles's proposal is required. Barlow (1988) argues forcefully for two types of anxiety, one preparatory and one acute. *Anxiety* or *anxious apprehension* prepares the organism to cope with the challenges and stresses of everyday life. Barlow views this preparatory anxious apprehension as the process underlying Generalized Anxiety Disorder. It consists of negative affect, high arousal, perceptions of helplessness or uncontrollability of future events, and worry (pp. 235, 247). *Fear* is a massive *alarm reaction* to potentially life-threatening situations, which Barlow equates with Cannon's well-known fight-or-flight response (1929, pp. 3–4, 158). Panic attacks are viewed as (false) alarm reactions. In contrast to the traditional view of the fight/flight response as a reaction only to a life-threatening event (a "true alarm"), Barlow concludes that this same reaction can occur without such an event, in which case it is a "false alarm." Thus, false alarms or panic attacks include a sudden burst of anxiety accompanied by somatic symptoms and by a fear of dying and/or losing control.

Fowles (1992) argued that Barlow's anxious apprehension is parallel to Gray's BIS and that Barlow's alarm reaction parallels Gray's fight/flight system. Gray's fight/flight system has heretofore been neglected, because, according to Gray, it responds to unconditioned stimuli for punishment. With Barlow's concept of false alarms, it is reasonable to consider that the fight/flight system is clinically relevant. Needless to say, to the extent that Barlow's delineation of two types of anxiety in adult psychopathology is valid, the concept of anxiety in childhood disorders requires careful scrutiny.

In the context of antisocial behavior, Schalling (1978) distinguished two kinds of anxiety: psychic anxiety versus somatic anxiety. Psychic anxiety consists of "worry, anticipatory anxiousness, slow recuperation after stress, sensitivity, insecurity, and social anxiety" (p. 88)—features that closely resemble Barlow's anxious apprehension, which as noted above may relate to BIS functioning. Somatic anxiety consists of "autonomic disturbances, vague distress and panic attacks, and distractibility" (p. 88)—features that point to a similarity to Barlow's alarm reaction or Gray's fight/flight system. A muscular tension scale tended to be associated with somatic anxiety, consistent with mobilization for vigorous physical activity in the fight/flight system. Noting controversy over whether or not psychopaths are anxious, Schalling (1978, p. 89) concludes from her own work that they "may have high and low anxiety, depending on what aspect or component is measured. They tend to have more vague distress and panic, more cardiovascular symptoms and muscular tenseness, but less worry and anticipatory concern than non-psychopaths have." That is, psychopaths tend to be low on psychic anxiety but high on somatic anxiety and muscular tension. Additionally, somatic anxiety was positively correlated with impulsivity and other psychopathy-related scales "in various groups" (p. 88)—presumably of normal and criminal samples. This perspective suggests that the traditional theory of deficient anxiety in psychopaths relates to BIS function and refers to the anticipatory response to threats of aversive events and not to the somatic anxiety/alarm reaction associated with a fight/flight system reaction. Further, it suggests that in some way the state of arousal associated with somatic anxiety may actually facilitate impulsivity. Such a hypothesis is more complex than the traditional view that low anxiety facilitates impulsivity. Perhaps this hypothesis could help to clarify the orthogonality of scales that appear to measure behavioral inhibition and scales that measure neuroticism or anxiety or negative affect (e.g., Fowles, 1987, 1992; Tellegen, 1985)—that is, somatic anxiety/alarm reactions may contribute significantly to negative affect factors and be independent of BIS functioning.

## Detached versus Impulsive Subtypes?

Schalling (1978) cited Mayer-Gross, Slater, and Roth (1954) for the existence of two subgroups within the psychopaths identified by Cleckley ratings or low So scores: (1) the Unstable Drifters or *impulsiveness syndrome*, characterized by impulsiveness, stimulus seeking, high somatic anxiety, an easygoing style, leading aimless lives, inability to learn from experience, and indifference to their own future and past; and (2) the Cold and Emotionally Callous or *detachment syndrome*, characterized by low empathy, detachment (a lack of close, warm, interpersonal relations), a lack of concern for others, poverty of affect and suspiciousness, and high scores on the Eysenck Psychoticism Scale. Following Mayer-Gross et al., Schalling suggests that the detachment syndrome is related to a schizoid personality type that is found in excess among the relatives of schizophrenics. Finally, Schalling calls attention to developmental theories that argue that the development of conscience does not depend solely on anxiety-mediated avoidance learning.

Rather, internalization of social norms is strongly facilitated by warm attachments (perhaps especially with the same-sexed parent). This important perspective points to a possible etiology of antisocial behavior that has nothing to do with deficient response to cues for punishment but rather has a basis in early attachments. The implication appears to be that the absence of warm attachments could happen to a perfectly normal child as a result of external factors or could happen as a result of a child's inability to form warm attachments due to genetic loading for a schizoid personality.

Although the link is not made as explicit by Schalling as the juxtaposition above would suggest, these proposals appear to imply two etiological paths to psychopathic behavior: one by way of poor attachments leading to a failure of socialization with the core feature of indifference to others; the second by way of difficulty in inhibiting behavior that leads to future punishments and nonrewards with the core feature of impulsivity. This picture might at least be put forth as a tentative hypothesis derived from Schalling's review.

On the other hand, it is not at all clear how mutually exclusive these features are. For example, Fowles (1980) suggested that poor attachments might be secondary to impulsivity, reflecting conflict with the social environment as a result of impulsivity—a suggestion consistent with the impact of impulsive behavior on parents and with peer rejection secondary to impulsivity. Similarly, there may be an impulsivity component associated with the detachment syndrome, especially in view of its association with high scores on the Eysenck Psychoticism scale (see Fowles, 1993). In spite of this ambiguity, these are interesting subtypes to pursue.

## Electrodermal Activity and Developmental Disorders

The complexities of extending the findings reviewed here downward in age can be seen by considering Quay's attempts to apply the Gray model to developmental disorders. At a behavioral level, behavioral excess can be taken to reflect an overactive BAS or an underactive BIS, but it is difficult to distinguish between the two. Similarly, behavioral deficits can be attributed to an underactive BAS or an overactive BIS. Quay (1988a,b) observed that both attention-deficit disorder and conduct-disorder children manifest difficulty in withholding inappropriate responses. On the basis largely of pharmacological considerations, he proposed that attention-deficit disorder children suffer from an underactive BIS and that conduct-disordered children suffer from an overactive BAS. However, partially on the basis of electrodermal findings Quay (1990, 1993) emphasized a possible contribution of a BIS deficiency to undersocialized aggressive conduct disorder. In contrast, other authors have noted EDA hyporeactivity in connection with hyperactivity (e.g., Cohen & Douglas, 1972; Dykman, Ackerman, Clements et al., 1971; Hastings & Barkley, 1978; Satterfield & Dawson, 1971; Zahn, Abate, Little, & Wender, 1975) and attention-deficit disorder (see Satterfield's comment following Quay's 1988b article). In view of possible diagnostic confusion associated with these older studies, especially with respect to probable comorbid conduct problems, Quay's (1990, 1993) interpretation of the literature must be considered the more likely. Nevertheless, enough uncertainty remains to warrant examination of electrodermal responding in attention-deficit disorder, particularly in view of the strong association with impulsivity.

It should be emphasized that at a theoretical level it is Gray's motivational systems that are the primary constructs and that they relate directly to behavior. The proposal that EDA may usefully index the reaction of the BIS under some conditions (e.g., threats of punishment) is not to say that EDA universally indexes BIS activity (EDA is subject to many influences—see Fowles, 1986). The primary contribution of EDA is to assist in attributing impulsivity to too much BAS or too little BIS—that is, if impulsive individuals show deficient EDA in response to threats of punishment and nonreward, the impulsivity is more readily attributed to a deficient BIS.

In encouraging the application of the present review to developmental disorders, it may be useful to highlight the issues raised. These include at least three major issues: stimulus conditions, subtypes, and the effects of two types of anxiety on behavior and electrodermal activity. With respect to stimulus conditions, more reliable differences have been obtained with more stimulating conditions. These conditions most often involve a manifest threat of punishment—an unpopular paradigm for research with children. The few studies with younger subjects tend to employ nonsignal tones. It is not clear whether responses to threats of punishment versus those to nonsignal tones reflect a similar or different underlying processes. It does seem advisable for future research to assess responses to both nonsignal stimuli and more threatening stimuli. Even though shock may not be a suitable stressor, other stressors such as mental arithmetic or the anticipation of dental work might be. Additionally, it would be of considerable interest to see whether hyporeactivity is found with stimulating conditions other than the anticipation of threat. For example, it is a simple matter to give stimuli signal value in the context of a reaction-time paradigm. It is also easy to create positive

signal value for stimuli by associating them with money or other rewards.

The previous suggestion of possible differences between impulsive
and detached psychopaths merits consideration as subtypes within the
solitary aggressive type of conduct disorder in children. Such subtypes
might relate differentially to peer interactions and academic performance.

The implications of the two types of anxiety have not been worked
out in the present review, and they probably are quite complicated. The
possibility that somatic anxiety might promote impulsivity in children
with weak inhibitory controls suggests that, in some cases, an impulsive
child might have both low psychic anxiety (and an associated weak
inhibitory capacity) and high somatic anxiety—and might well help to
account for the comorbidity of conduct disorder and negative affect. The
implications of this combination for electrodermal measures is unclear:
Will high somatic anxiety increase or low psychic anxiety decrease electrodermal responding? Hopefully, paradigms involving the *anticipation*
of punishment will somewhat selectively reflect psychic anxiety with its
future orientation, but this possibility remains to be confirmed.

## Electrodermal Measures in Younger Children

Most theories of psychopathy assume an important contribution of
temperament that should be manifest in childhood. Although the vast
majority of studies on EDA have employed adult criminals or adolescent
delinquents, there is much to be gained by extending this research to
children. Assessments in children might facilitate diagnostic improvements, early detection, and even preventive interventions. In particular,
it would be useful to examine EDA among children with Oppositional
Defiant Disorder, which has an age of onset around 8 years. Because
relatively little research has been reported with electrodermal measures
in younger children (Shields, 1983), it may be useful to review some of
the more effective paradigms that have been employed—by way of
encouraging more attempts in this area.

In an early study, Wechsler, Crabbs, & Freeman (1930) reported that
children aged 2 to 4 years gave the largest responses to loud sounds
(doorbell, Klaxon) and the threat of loss of balance (chair tipping), intermediate responses to turning lights on or off, and minimal responses to
verbal stimuli (e.g., "Look there" and "You are a brave boy"). In a
massive study Venables (1978) reported responses to six 75-dB orienting
tones among 1,800 three-year-old subjects and among smaller samples
($N = 128$) of 5-, 10-, 15-year-old subjects. The proportion who responded

(at all) to the tones were 43.8%, 74.4%, 86.9%, and over 95% (comparable to adults) as age increased from 3 to 15 years. Clearly, very young children do not respond fully to nonsignal stimuli of low intensity, but the sensitivity of this paradigm increases with more intense stimuli and with increasing age.

Grim (1967) assessed SCR amplitudes among first-graders, sixth-graders, and adults in response to the visual imperative stimulus in a reaction-time (RT) paradigm with irregularly presented preparatory intervals of 3, 5, 10, 15, and 20 seconds. The procedure was presented as a game to the children. All groups showed an increase in the amplitude of SCRs as the preparatory interval increased from 5 to 20 seconds (which Grim interpreted as a correlate of sustained attention), but there were no effects of age. Thus, first-graders showed the same differential responding to longer preparatory intervals seen in adults. Zahn et al. (1975) also employed a reaction-time paradigm with normal children and children diagnosed as minimally brain dysfunctioned recruited from grades one through six. Although the focus of the report was on differences between these groups, it was clear that the normal children showed appropriate electrodermal responses to the RT imperative stimuli. Age effects were not mentioned, suggesting that there were no obvious deficiencies in the responses of younger children. Cohen and Douglas (1972) compared SCRs to the warning stimulus (tone) in an RT task versus a nonsignal tone series for hyperactive and normal children aged 5.8 to 11.4 years. The normal children showed an increase in SCL from a nonsignal tone series to the RT task and larger SCRs to the initial signal stimuli (warning stimuli) than to initial nonsignal tones (hyperactive children did not show these responses to the increased task demands). Again, age effects were not mentioned, suggesting that the younger children showed responses similar to those of the older children. Interestingly, these authors cited a dissertation by Cohen (1970) in which normal children (but not hyperactive children) showed an increase in the frequency of SCRs to the warning stimuli when rewards were given for especially fast RTs. Delamater and Lahey's (1983) use of an RT paradigm with learning-disabled 10-year-olds has been described earlier. Based on several studies, therefore, it appears that even relatively young children respond sensitively in a reaction-time task.

Two studies have attempted to assess preexisting signal value in children. Lieblich (1970) compared eight 3- and sixteen 4-year-old children's SCRs to their own name versus other names. Although the design and results were complex, it appeared that significant differential responding was obtained to the child's name and his/her parents' names relative to names with less significance to the child—that is, even these young children showed larger responses to stimuli with signal value. Furuseth, Fowles, and Beeghly (1990) employed a word association task to assess the SCRs to three categories of signal stimuli: fear-related (e.g., snake), drug-related (e.g., cigarettes), and attachment (e.g., Mom, Dad, best friend) among children recruited from the community. Younger children (8 to 10 years old) failed to respond differentially to these significant stimuli compared to neutral stimuli; but older children (11 to 14 years) produced significantly larger SCRs to all three categories. More recently, Furuseth (1993) demonstrated that 8- to 10-year-old children do respond to visual stimuli with either negative or positive valence, although the results appear stronger for negatively valenced stimuli.

In summary, several studies have documented the efficacy of an RT paradigm in eliciting responses among children 6 years old or older. The word association task has the potential for assessing reactions to a broad range of stimuli, but to date it is limited to children of approximately 11 years and older. Preliminary data indicate that visual stimuli with negative valence elicit SCRs in 8- to 10-year-old children. Although visual stimuli do not have the flexibility associated with verbal stimuli, they may be successful in assessing the affective reaction to negatively valenced stimuli at ages relevant to the onset of Oppositional Defiant Disorder. Additionally, even younger children have been found to respond to a variety of stimuli: loud sounds, loss of balance, turning lights on and off, the parent's name, and the child's own name. Weaker stimuli, such as nonsignal tones are less effective. In view of this success, it seems likely that the eccrine sweat gland system is psychologically responsive even in 3- to 4-year-olds, and that the major consideration is to find effective stimuli for children so young.

# References

Barlow, D. H. (1988). *Anxiety and its disorders.* New York: Guilford Press.

Blackburn, R. (1979). Cortical and autonomic arousal in primary and secondary psychopaths. *Psychophysiology, 16,* 143–150.

Blackburn, R. (1983). Psychopathy, delinquency and crime. In A. Gale & J. A. Edwards (Eds.), *Physiological correlates of human behavior* (Vol. 3, pp. 187–203). New York: Academic Press.

Block, J. (1957). A study of affective responsiveness in a lie-detection situation. *Journal of Abnormal and Social Psychology, 55,* 11–15.

Borkovec, T. D. (1970). Autonomic reactivity to sensory stimulation in psychopathic, neurotic, and normal juvenile delinquents. *Journal of Consulting and Clinical Psychology, 35,* 217–222.

Brown, R. F. (1988). *Probability learning and psychophysiological reactivity in psychopathic (un-*

*dersocialized aggressive) preadolescent males.* Unpublished doctoral dissertation, University of Miami, Coral Gables, FL.

Cannon, W. B. (1929). *Bodily changes in pain, hunger, fear and rage* (2nd ed.). New York: Appleton-Century-Crofts.

Cleckley, H. (1950). *The mask of sanity* (2nd ed.). St. Louis: Mosby.

Cleckley, H. (1964). *The mask of sanity* (4th ed.). St. Louis: Mosby.

Cohen, N. J. (1970). *Psychophysiological concomitants of attention in hyperactive children.* Unpublished doctoral dissertation, McGill University.

Cohen, N. J., & Douglas, V. I. (1972). Characteristics of the orienting response in hyperactive and normal children. *Psychophysiology, 9,* 238–245.

Conners, C. K. (1969). A teacher rating scale for use in drug studies with children. *American Journal of Psychiatry, 127,* 884–888.

Delamater, A. M., & Lahey, B. B. (1983). Physiological correlates of conduct problems and anxiety in hyperactive and learning-disabled children. *Journal of Abnormal Child Psychology, 11,* 85–100.

Dengerink, H. A., & Bertilson, H. S. (1975). Psychopathy and physiological arousal in an aggressive task. *Psychophysiology, 12,* 682–684.

Dykman, R. A., Ackerman, P. T., Clements, S. D. et al. (1971). Specific learning disabilities: An attentional deficit syndrome. In H. R. Myklebust (Ed.), *Progress in learning disabilities* (Vol. 2, pp. 56–93). New York: Grune & Stratton.

Edelberg, R. (1970). The information content of the recovery limb of the electrodermal response. *Psychophysiology, 6,* 527–539.

Edelberg, R. (1972). Electrodermal recovery rate, goal-orientation, and aversion. *Psychophysiology, 9,* 512–520.

Edelberg, R. (1993). Electrodermal mechanisms: A critique of the two-effector hypothesis and a proposed replacement. In J.-C. Roy, W. Boucsein, D. Fowles, & J. Gruzelier (Eds.), *Progress in electrodermal research* (pp. 7–29). London: Plenum Press.

Edelberg, R., & Muller, M. (1981). Prior activity as a determinant of electrodermal recovery rate. *Psychophysiology, 18,* 17–25.

Fowles, D. C. (1980). The three arousal model: Implications of Gray's two-factor learning theory for heart rate, electrodermal activity, and psychopathy. *Psychophysiology, 17,* 87–104.

Fowles, D. (1986). The eccrine system and electrodermal activity. In M. G. H. Coles, S. W. Porges, & E. Donchin (Eds.), *Psychophysiology: Systems, processes, and applications.* (Vol. 1, pp. 51–96). New York: Guilford Press.

Fowles, D. (1987). Application of a behavioral theory of motivation to the concepts of anxiety and impulsivity. *Journal of Research in Personality, 21,* 417–435.

Fowles, D. (1992). A motivational approach to anxiety disorders. In D. G. Forgays, T. Sosnowski, & K. Wrzesniewski (Eds.), *Anxiety: Recent developments in self-appraisal, psychophysiological, and health research* (pp. 181–192). Bristol, PA: Hemisphere/Taylor & Francis.

Fowles, D. C. (1993). Electrodermal activity and antisocial behavior: Empirical findings and theoretical issues. In J.-C. Roy, W. Boucsein, D. Fowles, & J. Gruzelier (Eds.), *Progress in electrodermal research* (pp. 223–238). London: Plenum Press.

Fowles, D., & Venables, P. H. (1970). The effects of epidermal hydration and sodium reabsorption on palmar skin potential. *Psychological Bulletin, 73,* 363–378.

Fox, R., & Lippert, W. W. (1963). Spontaneous GSR and anxiety level in sociopathic delinquents. *Journal of Consulting Psychology, 27,* 368.

Furuseth, A. (1993). *Children's orienting responses to relatively permanent sets of significant stimuli.* Unpublished doctoral dissertation, University of Iowa, Iowa City, IA.

Furuseth, A. M., Fowles, D. C., & Beeghly, J. (1990). The signal-OR in externalizing disorders. In J. Gruzelier & A. Crider (Chairs), *Individual differences in electrodermal response*. Symposium presented at the Fifth International Conference of Psychophysiology, Budapest, Hungary, July 9–13, 1990.

Goldstein, I. B. (1965). The relationship of muscle tension and autonomic activity to psychiatric disorders. *Psychosomatic Medicine, 27,* 39–52.

Gough, H. G. (1960). Theory and measurement of socialization. *Journal of Consulting Psychology, 24,* 23–30.

Gough, H. G., & Peterson, D. R. (1952). The identification and measurement of predispositional factors in crime and delinquency. *Journal of Consulting Psychology, 16,* 207–212.

Gray, J. A. (1970). The psychophysiological basis of intraversion-extraversion. *Behavior Research and Therapy, 8,* 249–266.

Gray, J. A. (1987). *The psychology of fear and stress* (2nd ed.). Cambridge, England: Cambridge University Press.

Grim, P. F. (1967). Sustained attention comparison of children and adults using reaction time set and the GSR. *Journal of Experimental Child Psychology, 5,* 26–38.

Hare, R. D. (1965a). Acquisition and generalization of a conditioned fear response in psychopathic and non-psychopathic criminals. *Journal of Psychology, 59,* 367–370.

Hare, R. D. (1965b). Temporal gradient of fear arousal in psychopaths. *Journal of Abnormal Psychology, 70,* 442–445.

Hare, R. D. (1968a). Detection threshold for electric shock in psychopaths. *Journal of Abnormal Psychology, 73,* 268–272.

Hare, R. D. (1968b). Psychopathy, autonomic functioning, and the orienting response. *Journal of Abnormal Psychology, Monograph Supplement 73,* no. 3, 1–24.

Hare, R. (1970). *Psychopathy.* New York: Wiley.

Hare, R. D. (1972). Psychopathy and physiological responses to adrenalin. *Journal of Abnormal Psychology, 79,* 138–147.

Hare, R. D. (1978a). Electrodermal and cardiovascular correlates of psychopathy. In R. D. Hare & D. Schalling (Eds.), *Psychopathic behavior: Approaches to research* (pp. 107–144). New York: Wiley.

Hare, R. D. (1978b). Psychopathy and electrodermal responses to nonsignal stimulation. *Biological Psychology, 6,* 237–246.

Hare, R. D., & Craigen, D. (1974). Psychopathy and physiological activity in a mixed-motive game situation. *Psychophysiology, 11,* 197–206.

Hare, R. D., Frazelle, J., & Cox, D. N. (1978). Psychopathy and physiological responses to threat of an aversive stimulus. *Psychophysiology, 15,* 165–172.

Hare, R. D., & Quinn, M. J. (1971). Psychopathy and autonomic conditioning. *Journal of Abnormal Psychology, 77,* 223–235.

Hastings, J. E., & Barkley, R. A. (1978). A review of psychophysiological research with hyperkinetic children. *Journal of Abnormal Child Psychology, 6,* 413–447.

Hemming, J. H. (1981). Electrodermal indices in a selected prison sample and students. *Personality and Individual Differences, 2,* 37–46.

Hinton, J., O'Neil, M., Dishman, J., & Webster, S. (1979). Electrodermal indices of public offending and recidivism. *Biological Psychology, 9,* 297–310.

Hinton, J., O'Neil, M., Hamilton, S., & Burke, M. (1980). Psychophysiological differentiation between psychopathic and schizophrenic abnormal offenders. *British Journal of Social and Clinical Psychology, 19,* 257–269.

Hirschfeld, R. (1978). Review of "Psychoticism as a Dimension of Personality," by H. J. Eysenck & S. B. G. Eysenck. *Psychiatry, 41,* 411–412.

Lang, P. J., Bradley, M., Cuthbert, B. N., & Patrick, C. J. (1993). Emotion and psychopathology: A startle probe analysis. In L. J. Chapman, J. P. Chapman, & D. C. Fowles (Eds.), Models and methods of psychopathology (pp. 163–199). New York: Springer Publishing Company.

Levander, S. E., Schalling, D. S., Lidberg, L., Bartfai, A., & Lidberg, Y. (1980). Skin conductance recovery time and personality in a group of criminals. Psychophysiology, 17, 105–111.

Lieblich, I. (1970). Manipulation of contrast between differential GSRs in very young children. Psychophysiology, 7, 436–441.

Lippert, W. W., & Senter, R. J. (1966). Electrodermal responses in the sociopath. Psychonomic Science, 4, 25–26.

Lykken, D. T. (1957). A study of anxiety in the sociopathic personality. Journal of Abnormal and Social Psychology, 55, 6–10.

Mathis, H. I. (1970). Emotional responsivity in the antisocial personality. PhD dissertation, George Washington University, Washington, DC.

Mayer-Gross, W., Slater, E., and Roth, M. (1954). Clinical psychiatry. London: Cassel.

Mednick, S. A. (1975). Autonomic nervous system recovery and psychopathology. Scandinavian Journal of Behavior Therapy, 4, 55–68.

Megargee, E. I. (1972). The California Psychological Inventory handbook. San Francisco: Jossey-Bass.

Nikula, R. (1991). Psychological correlates of nonspecific skin conductance responses. Psychophysiology, 28, 86–90.

Obrist, P. A. (1976). The cardiovascular-behavioral interaction as it appears today. Psychophysiology, 13, 95–107.

Peterson, D. R., Quay, H. C., & Tiffany, T. L. (1961). Personality factors related to juvenile delinquency. Child Development, 32, 355–372.

Quay, H. (1964). Personality dimensions in delinquent males as inferred from the factor analysis of behavior rating. Journal of Research in Crime and Delinquency, 1, 35–37.

Quay, H. (1965). Psychopathic personality as pathological stimulus-seeking. American Journal of Psychiatry, 122, 180–183.

Quay, H. C. (1986). Conduct disorders. In H. C. Quay & J. S. Werry (Eds.), Psychopathological disorders of childhood (3rd ed., pp. 35–72). New York: Wiley.

Quay, H. C. (1988a). Attention deficit disorder and the behavioral inhibition system: The relevance of the neuropsychological theory of Jeffrey A. Gray. In L. M. Bloomingdale & J. A. Sergeant (Eds.), Attention Deficit Disorder: Criteria, cognition, intervention (pp. 117–125). Oxford: Pergamon.

Quay, H. C. (1988b). The behavioral reward and inhibition systems in childhood behavior disorder. In L. M. Bloomingdale (Ed.), Attention deficit disorder: Research in treatment, psychopharmacology & attention (Vol. 3, pp. 176–186). New York: Spectrum.

Quay, H. C. (1990). Electrodermal responding, inhibition, and reward-seeking in undersocialized aggressive conduct disorder. Paper presented at the annual meeting of the American Academy of Child and Adolescent Psychiatry, Chicago, Illinois, October 14.

Quay, H. C. (1993). The psychobiology of undersocialized aggressive conduct disorder: A theoretical perspective. Development and Psychopathology, 5, 165–180.

Quay, H. C., & Parsons, L. B. (1970). The differential classification of the juvenile offender. Washington, DC: Bureau of Prisons.

Raine, A. (1987). Effect of early environment on electrodermal and cognitive correlates of schizotypy and psychopathy in criminals. International Journal of Psychophysiology, 4, 277–287.

Raine, A., & Venables, P. H. (1981). Classical conditioning and socialization—A biosocial interaction. *Personality and individual differences, 2*, 273–283.

Raine, A., & Venables, P. H. (1984). Electrodermal nonresponding, antisocial behavior, and schizoid tendencies in adolescents. *Psychophysiology, 21*, 424–433.

Raine, A., Venables, P. H., & Williams, M. (1990b). Relationships between N1, P300 and contingent negative variation recorded at age 15 and criminal behavior at age 24. *Psychophysiology, 27*, 567–575.

Rotenberg, M. (1975, August). Psychopathy, insensitivity, and sensitization. *Professional Psychology,* 175–180.

Satterfield, J. H., & Dawson, M. E. (1971). Electrodermal correlates of hyperactivity in children. *Psychophysiology, 8*, 191–197.

Schalling, D. (1978). Psychopathy-related personality variables and the psychophysiology of socialization. In R. D. Hare & D. Schalling (Eds.), *Psychopathic behavior: Approaches to research* (pp. 85–106). New York: Wiley.

Schalling, D., Cronholm, B., Asberg, M., & Espmark, S. (1973). Ratings of psychic and somatic anxiety incidents—Interrater reliability and relations to personality variables. *Acta Psychiatrica Scandinavica, 49*, 353–368.

Schalling, D., & Levander, S. (1967). *Spontaneous fluctuations in skin conductance during anticipation of pain in two delinquent groups differing in anxiety proneness.* Reports from the Psychological Laboratories, The University of Stockholm, No. 306. Cited by Schalling (1978), p. 100 (in Hare & Schalling, see Trasler, 1978).

Schalling, D., Levander, S., & Dahlin-Lidberg, Y. (1975). *A note on the relation between spontaneous fluctuations in skin conductance and heart rate, and scores on the Gough Delinquency scale.* Unpublished manuscript, University of Stockholm. Cited by Hare (1978a) as Note 5.

Schalling, D., Lidberg, L., Levander, S. E., & Dahlin, Y. (1973). Spontaneous autonomic activity as related to psychopathy. *Biological Psychology, 1*, 83–97.

Schmauk, F. J. (1970). Punishment, arousal, and avoidance learning in sociopaths. *Journal of Abnormal Psychology, 76*, 325–335.

Schmidt, K., Solanto, M. V., & Bridger, W. H. (1985). Electrodermal activity of under-socialized aggressive children: A pilot study. *Journal of Child Psychology and Psychiatry, 26*, 653–660.

Shields, S. A. (1983). Development of autonomic nervous system responsivity in children: A review of the literature. *International Journal of Behavioral Development, 6*, 291–319.

Siddle, D. A. T. (1977). Electrodermal activity and psychopathy. In S. A. Mednick & K. O. Christiansen (Eds.), *Biosocial bases of criminal behavior* (pp. 199–211). New York: Gardner Press.

Siddle, D. A. T., Nicol, A. R., & Foggitt, R. H. (1973). Habituation and over-extinction of the GSR component of the orienting response in anti-social adolescents. *British Journal of Social and Clinical Psychology, 12*, 303–308.

Tellegen, A. (1985). Structures of mood and personality and their relevance to assessing anxiety, with an emphasis on self-report. In A. A. Tuma and J. D. Maser (Eds.), *Anxiety and the anxiety disorders* (pp. 681–706). Hillsdale, NJ: Lawrence Erlbaum.

Tharp, V. K., Maltzman, I., Syndulko, K., & Ziskind, E. (1980). Autonomic activity during anticipation of an aversive tone in noninstitutionalized sociopaths. *Psychophysiology, 17*, 123–128.

Trasler, G. (1978). Relations between psychopathy and persistent criminality—Methodological and theoretical issues. In R. D. Hare & D. Schalling (Eds.), *Psychopathic behavior: Approaches to research* (pp. 273–298). New York: Wiley.

Venables, P. H. (1978). Psychophysiology and psychometrics. *Psychophysiology, 15,* 302–315.

Venables, P. H., & Christie, M. J. (1980). Electrodermal activity. In I. Martin & P. H. Venables (Eds.), *Techniques in psychophysiology* (pp. 3–67). New York: John Wiley & Sons.

Waid, W. M. (1976a). Skin conductance response to punishment as a predictor and correlate of learning to avoid two classes of punishment. *Journal of Abnormal Psychology, 85,* 498–504.

Waid, W. M. (1976b). Skin conductance response to both signalled and unsignalled noxious stimulation predicts level of socialization. *Journal of Personality and Social Psychology, 34,* 923–929.

Waid, W. M., & Orne, M. T. (1982). Reduced electrodermal response to conflict, failure to inhibit dominant behaviors, and delinquency proneness. *Journal of Personality and Social Psychology, 43,* 769–774.

Waid, W. M., Orne, M. T., & Wilson, S. K. (1979). Effects of level of socialization on electrodermal detection of deception. *Psychophysiology, 16,* 15–22.

Wechsler, D., Crabbs, L. M., & Freeman, R. G. (1930). Galvanic responses of preschool children. *Journal of Genetic Psychology, 38,* 203–222.

Zahn, T. P., Abate, F., Little, B. C., & Wender, P. H. (1975). Minimal brain dysfunction, stimulant drugs, and autonomic nervous system activity. *Archives of General Psychology, 32,* 381–387.

Ziskind, E., Syndulko, K., & Maltzman, I. (1977). Evidence for a neurologic disorder in the sociopath syndrome: Aversive conditioning and recidivism. In C. Shagass, S. Gershon, & A. I. Friedhoff (Eds.), *Psychopathology and brain dysfunction* (pp. 255–265). New York: Raven Press.

# 8

# Endogenous Opioids, Childhood Psychopathology, and Quay's Interpretation of Jeffrey Gray

MARKUS J. P. KRUESI, HENRIETTA L. LEONARD, SUSAN E. SWEDO, SUSAN N. NADI, SUSAN D. HAMBURGER, JAMES C. S. LIU, and JUDITH L. RAPOPORT

## Introduction

One of Herbert C. Quay's many contributions to our evolving understanding of childhood psychopathology was his 1983 extension of the theories of Jeffrey A. Gray to children with disruptive behavior disorders (DBD) (Quay, 1988). Quay (1988) placed three broad-band child-

MARKUS J. P. KRUESI • Institute for Juvenile Research, Department of Psychiatry, University of Illinois at Chicago, Chicago, Illinois 60612.    HENRIETTA L. LEONARD and SUSAN E. SWEDO • National Institute of Mental Health (NIMH), Child Psychiatry Branch, Bethesda, Maryland 20892.    SUSAN N. NADI • National Institute of Neurological and Communicative Orders and Stroke, Laboratory of Neurophysiology, Bethesda, Maryland 20892.    SUSAN D. HAMBURGER • NIMH, Child Psychiatry Branch, Bethesda, Maryland 20892.    JAMES C. S. LIU • University of Medicine and Dentistry of New Jersey, Piscataway, New Jersey 08854.    JUDITH L. RAPOPORT • NIMH, Child Psychiatry Branch, Bethesda, Maryland 20892.

*Disruptive Behavior Disorders in Childhood,* edited by Donald K. Routh. Plenum Press, New York, 1994.

hood disorders—attention-deficit disorder with hyperactivity, conduct disorder, and anxiety-withdrawal disorder—within Gray's model of a Behavioral Activation System (BAS) and a Behavioral Inhibition System (BIS) (Gray, 1972, 1973, 1979, 1982).

The BAS was posited to modulate signals of reward and of non-punishment ("relief"), whereas the BIS was thought to be responsible for modulation of threats of punishment, fear in passive avoidance, and frustration in extinction paradigms. Gray offered chemical descriptions and anatomic locations for these symptoms. The BAS was said to correspond to the pathways identified by the rewarding effects of electrical intracranial self-stimulation. The pathways were described as catecholaminergic. The BIS is located in the medial and lateral septal regions and their connections to the hippocampus. This septohippocampal system was described as primarily noradrenergic.

Quay suggested that childhood disorders resulted from an imbalance of the BIS and BAS. Attention-deficit disorder was viewed as the product of a deficient BIS both because of the well-known poor performance of ADD children in situations that require withholding of responses (suggesting deficient behavioral inhibition) and because evidence did not appear to support reward oversensitivity. Support invoked by Quay included observations that follow:

- Amphetamine augments self-stimulation in the (noradrenergic) medial forebrain bundle (Olds & Fobes, 1981) thus increasing BAS activity.
- However, the noradrenergic BIS is also expected to be activated by amphetamine. And amphetamine does improve passive avoidance or inhibitory behavior in attention deficit disorder. Therefore, amphetamine effects on the BIS must outweigh those on the BAS.
- Antianxiety agents, which have a negative effect on only the Behavioral Inhibition System, appear to worsen behavior in attention deficit disorder.

Conversely, conduct disorder was hypothesized by Quay to be most closely related to reward oversensitivity or an overactive BAS. His reasoning was:

- Severe conduct disorder children and adult psychopaths are recognized as deficient in withholding responses.
- Amphetamine, which is an agonist to both the BAS Activation and the BIS, improves passive avoidance but does not improve conduct disorder behavior (Campbell et al., 1982). Thus, facilitating *both* systems does not improve conduct disorder.

- Yet, haloperidol and propranolol, which antagonize the BAS, as evidenced by their properties of decreasing brain self-stimulation and antagonizing dopamine and norepinephrine, appear to decrease conduct disorder behavior. (Campbell et al., 1982).

Internalizing or anxiety-withdrawal disorders were said to be prototypes for an overactive BIS. Hypothesized performance of those children with internalizing disorders in learning paradigms emphasized the polarity with those who had conduct disorders and/or attention-deficit disorder. Those with internalizing disorders were predicted to do better under conditions of punishment, whereas the externalizers, particularly those with conduct disorder, would perform best under conditions of reward.

Subsequent investigations have supported Quay's hypothesis of reward oversensitivity in conduct disorder. Conduct-disordered individuals are oversensitive to reward even in the face of ever-declining odds of reward and increasing odds of punishment. Response perseveration following adoption of a response set for reward has been documented as a behavioral characteristic of adult psychopaths (Newman, Patterson, & Kosson, 1987), adolescents with undersocialized conduct disorder (Shapiro, Quay, Hogan, & Schwartz, 1988), children with conduct disorder (Daugherty & Quay, 1991), and preschoolers with seriously disruptive behavior (Kalantari, Yule, & Gardner, 1990). Further, in a task involving mixed incentives (rewards and punishments), adolescent psychopaths were found to be overresponding to the reward contingencies (Scerbo et al., 1990).

Reward can also be viewed as the omission of punishment or relief of a noxious state. One noxious state that might be construed as a form of punishment is guilt. Obsessive compulsive disorder (OCD) and antisocial or disruptive behavior disorders (DBD) appear to occupy opposite ends of the spectrum of guilt (Winslow & Insel, 1990). Obsessives are plagued with ruminative doubts and unreasonable guilt nearly constantly, whereas psychopaths appear to be guilt free. Further support for constitutional dichotomy comes from studies of child and adolescent patients, in which significant differences were found in CSF 5-HIAA concentrations (Kruesi et al., 1990a), CSF somatostatin concentrations, and perhaps in body habitus (Kruesi et al., 1990b) among age, race, and sex-matched pairs of DBD and OCD patients. These patients also were highly significantly different on measures of aggression and of obsessive traits providing support for behavioral polarity, as well.

One neurochemical system long associated with reward, pain relief, and analgesia is the opioid system. Electrical brain stimulation para-

digms and classical clinical observations of opiates' reinforcing properties and abuse potential demonstrated the opioid role in reward response (Olds & Travis, 1960). Subsequently, studies demonstrated that
intracranial self-stimulation altered endogenous brain opioid peptides
(Stein, 1985). When schedules of intermittent reinforcement are used,
opiate antagonists reliably reduce responding of rats in electrical brain
stimulation paradigms. This is consistent with a modulatory effect of
endogenous opiate systems on reward (for review, see Schaefer, 1988).

We sought to test the following hypothesized relationships:

1. Quay's hypothesized differences in terms of reward sensitivity
   or freedom from punishment (guilt) between internalizers and
   those with conduct disorder/attention-deficit disorder predict a
   difference in guilt between our groups with more guilt experienced in the OCD group.
2. The relationship between opioids and intracranial self-
   stimulation set forth by Gray's Behavioral Activation System predicts that there would be a difference in CSF opioid immunoreactivity between these two patient groups.
3. If differences in guilt exist between the two groups as hypothesized above and if endogenous opioids are associated with relief
   from guilt (reward), then we would predict interaction between
   guilt and opioid concentration.

## Subjects and Methods

Twenty-eight children and adolescents with disruptive behavior disorders (DBD) and 36 with obsessive compulsive disorder were studied.
They ranged in age from 6 to 19 years. Most had been part of previous
studies of relationships between cerebrospinal fluid neurochemistry and
psychiatric disorders in children and adolescents (Kruesi et al., 1985,
1990a,b; Swedo et al., 1992). For the DBD group, inclusion criteria were a
diagnosis of at least one DSM-III diagnosis (attention-deficit disorder,
conduct disorder, or oppositional disorder) from the spectrum now referred to as disruptive behavior disorders (DBD). DBD diagnoses were
made after clinical as well as structured interviews, the Diagnostic Interview for Children and Adolescents (DICA) (Herjanic & Campbell, 1977)
and Diagnostic Interview for Children and Adolescents—Parent Version
(DICA—P) (Herjanic & Reich, 1982), of child and parent(s) respectively.
None of the DBD children had present or past histories of OCD by
structured interviews of the parent(s) and child. The 38 obsessive

compulsive-disordered patients had LP's performed under identical conditions. All OCD cases met DSM-III criteria for severe primary OCD on the basis of interviews by two child psychiatrists (H. L. and J. L. R.). Exclusion criteria for both groups were any medical and/or neurologic disorders, IQ less than 80, and/or psychosis.

All patients were evaluated as inpatients at the National Institute of Mental Health. The study was approved by the National Institutes of Health Research Review Committee, and children and parent(s) gave informed assent and consent, respectively.

## Behavior Ratings

Guilt status was determined by patient and parent reports to the DICA and DICA-P (Herjanic & Campbell, 1977; Herjanic & Reich, 1982) question that asked: "When you [he] do something wrong, do you feel guilty or bad about it even if no one finds out?" Those answering "yes" were defined as those experiencing guilt. The absence of guilt or remorse has often been seen as part of being undersocialized. Socialization has been theoretically linked to endogenous opiate systems (Panksepp et al., 1980).

We used three additional measures to assess the empathy or socialization of our subjects. The I-6 Questionnaire for children and adolescents was completed by the patients and age-normed scores on the Empathy subscale recorded (Eysenck, Easting, & Pearson, 1984). A Socialization rating derived from the DICA and DICA-P interviews (details available upon request) was scored from child and parent reports. T-scores from the Total Social Competence scale of the parent-completed Child Behavior Checklist (Achenbach & Edelbrock, 1983) were also measured.

### Procedure for Lumbar Puncture

All patients were medication-free for a minimum of 3 weeks and on a low monoamine diet for 3 days prior to lumbar puncture (LP). Subjective and objective side effects of the procedure have been described elsewhere (Kruesi et al., 1988). All remained at bedrest from midnight the night before, except for being allowed to get up once to void. All were at bedrest for a minimum of 1 hour prior to LP. LPs were performed between 9:00 A.M. and 10:30 A.M. with the patient in the lateral decubitus position. The L4-L5 interspace was preferentially used.

## Methods for the Determination of Enkephalins and Beta Endorphin

Met- and Leu- enkephalins and beta endorphin were determined by a double antibody radioimmunoassay. The cerebrospinal fluid was deproteinized with 5% trichloroacetic acid (TCA) and centrifuged.

The acid was subsequently removed by extraction with water-saturated ethyl ether, and the extracts were dried in a Savant rotary evaporator. The pellets were resuspended in the assay buffer that was composed of 0.05 M potassium-sodium phosphate, 0.1% triton X-100, 0.1 bovine serum albumin, 0.01% sodium azide at pH-7.4. The standard peptides for the assay were purchased from Sigma Biochemicals. The $I_{125}$ tracers were purchased from New England Nuclear. The antibody and second antibody were purchased from Peninsula Laboratories.

The assays for both enkephalins and endorphins were carried out as follows: The standard curve and the unknowns were incubated with the antibody and buffer at 4 °C 16 to 24 hours. At this point the incubation was continued at 4 °C following the addition of the radioactive tracer for an additional 16 to 24 hours. The incubation was stopped by the addition of the second antibody (goat antirabbit antiserum) and 20% polyethylene glycol. The samples were incubated at room temperature for 2 hours, and the pellets were separated by spinning at 3000 rpm in a Beckman centrifuge. The pellets were counted in a Micromedic 4/200 gamma counter. The concentration of the CSF samples were calculated based on the standard curve. The sensitivity of the assay for enkephalins was 10 pg and endorphin 25 pg. The interassay variation was 4.2%.

## Statistical Analyses

Chi-square analysis was used to assess whether the proportion of those answering "yes" to the guilt question in the DBD group was greater than that in the OCD group. To assess whether the lumbar CSF concentrations of the three opiate peptides differed between groups, T-tests were carried out using SAS (SAS Institute, 1985). If the concentration of an opioid peptide differed between groups, then analysis of variance was used to assess whether concentrations differed within diagnostic groups by guilt status, and two-way analysis of variance (using SAS) was carried out to assess whether a guilt × group interaction existed. Pearson product moment correlations were carried out to assess the strength of relationships between opioid peptide concentrations and measures of socialization or empathy.

## Results

As predicted, parent, child, and combined reports consistently demonstrated a greater percentage of those with OCD than those with DBD experienced guilt. These results are summarized in Table 1.

Of the three opioid peptide immunoreactivities measured in CSF, only beta-endorphin concentration significantly differed between the two groups ($t = 2.05$, $p < .05$). Significantly lower concentrations of beta endorphin were observed in the DBD group, as shown in Table 2.

Within each of the two groups there was not a significant interaction between beta-endorphin concentration and guilt status (for DBD group, $f = 1.24$, $df = 1,26$, $p = ns$; for OCD group, $f = 3.57$, $df = 1,32$, $p = .07$). However, as shown in Figure 1, two-way analysis of variance did show a significant interaction between guilt status, diagnosis, and beta-endorphin concentration.

Correlational analyses performed within diagnostic groups to assess the strength of relationships, if any, between opioid concentrations and socialization measures found limited relationships, but a fairly consistent picture. As seen in Table 3, no significant correlations were found

**Table 1. Guilt: Response to DICA—P Question—DBD vs. OCD**

At least one source reported guilt

|  | No | Yes |
|---|---|---|
| DBD | 15 | 12 |
| OCD | 5 | 29 |
| $\chi^2 = 10.6$ |  | $p = .001$ |

Child report only

|  | No | Yes |
|---|---|---|
| DBD | 12 | 15 |
| OCD | 3 | 25 |
| $\chi^2 = 7.88$ |  | $p = .005$ |

Parent report only

|  | No | Yes |
|---|---|---|
| DBD | 10 | 18 |
| OCD | 2 | 15 |
| $\chi^2 = 3.10$ |  | $p = .08$ |

Table 2. Concentrations of Opioid Peptide Immunoreactivity (pg/ml) in CSF,
Comparison between DBD and OCD Groups

|     | n | Beta-endorphin mean (SD) | Met-enkephalin mean (SD) | Leu-enkephalin mean (SD) |
| --- | --- | --- | --- | --- |
| DBD | 28 | 0.88  (.5) | 9.8   (2.9) | 3.1   (1.1) |
| OCD | 36 | 1.19 (0.7) | 10.6  (3.9) | 3.3   (1.4) |
| t |  | 2.05 | 0.93 | 0.60 |
| df |  | 61.1 | 62.0 | 62.0 |
| p |  | 0.04 | 0.34 | 0.55 |

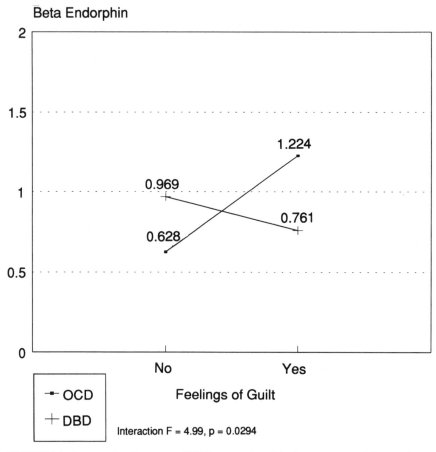

FIGURE 1. Interaction between CSF beta-endorphin immunoreactivity and experiencing feelings of guilt in subjects with obsessive compulsive disorder (OCD) and in subjects with disruptive behavior disorders (DBD).

**Table 3. Correlations of Socialization Measures with CSF Beta-Endorphin—OCD Group**

|  | n | r | p |
|---|---|---|---|
| CBCL[a]—social | 28 | −.12 | ns |
| I6[b]—empathy | 30 | −.27 | ns |
| DICA[c]—socialized | 25 | .25 | ns |
| DICA-P[d]—socialized | 16 | .22 | ns |

Correlations of socialization measures with CSF beta-endorphin—DBD group

|  | n | r | p |
|---|---|---|---|
| CBCL[a]—social | 25 | .19 | ns |
| I6[b]—empathy | 26 | .50 | .009 |
| DICA[c]—socialized | 26 | .45 | .02 |
| DICA-P[d]—socialized | 26 | .01 | ns |

[a]CBCL = Child Behavior Checklist—social competence.
[b]I6 = I6 Impulsive Questionnaire.
[c]DICA = Diagnostic Interview for Children and Adolescents.
[d]DICA—P = Diagnostic Interview for Children and Adolescents—Parent.

for the OCD group. For the DBD group, two measures, empathy and socialization, from the child's report showed significant positive correlations such that higher CSF beta-endorphin concentrations were associated with empathy and socialization. However, parental reports did not demonstrate such a relationship.

## Discussion

Two of the three hypotheses were supported by the results of this investigation. As suggested by Quay's work, beta-endorphin immunoreactivity was significantly lower in the DBD group compared to the OCDs, and the DBDs were significantly less likely to feel guilt. The present findings also add support to other studies demonstrating a biological polarity between the disorders (Kruesi et al., 1990a,b; Swedo et al., 1992; Winslow & Insel, 1990). A significant interaction was found between guilt status, beta endorphin, and diagnosis, but relationships within each diagnostic group between guilt and beta-endorphin were nonsignificant.

The relatively higher CSF beta-endorphin concentrations in patients with OCD have some consistency with results from studies of adults with anxiety disorders. Obsessive Compulsive Disorder is classified as an Anxiety Disorder in DSM-III-R (APA, 1987) and shares many biologic and behavioral similarities with the anxiety disorders, such as panic disorder. A Swedish study found adults with panic disorder have significantly higher CSF beta-endorphin-like immunoreactivity on and off antidepressants than normals (Erikkson et al., 1989). An independent study in this country, found elevated CSF beta endorphin in alcoholics with panic disorder compared to normal controls and alcoholics without panic disorder (George et al., 1990). However, a third study failed to find significant differences in CSF beta endorphin between panic disorder patients and controls (Lepola et al., 1990).

Panksepp et al. (1980) hypothesized a relationship between endogenous opioids and social behavior; he drew analogies between the behavior of opiate addicts and that of autistic children. Subsequent studies, in species such as goldfish (Kavaliers, 1989), rats (Dokla & DeFillipis, 1989), and prairie voles (Shapiro et al., 1989), have offered support for endogenous opioid involvement in socially affiliative behavior. The positive correlations within the DBD group between the child's reports of socialization and empathy are consistent with this possibility.

Results from administration of opiate antagonists on a variety of psychiatric disorders and on brain-endogenous opioid concentrations in intracranial self-stimulation paradigms offer additional perspectives for interpreting our results. Naloxone, an opioid antagonist, caused symptomatic worsening when administered double blind to two adults with OCD (Insel & Pickar, 1983) but naloxone has also been reported to obliterate OCD symptoms in Tourette's syndrome (Sandyk, 1987). Combat veterans with post-traumatic stress disorder, another anxiety-spectrum disorder, develop naloxone-reversible analgesia when exposed to PTSD-provoking stimuli (van der Kolk, Greenberg, Orr, & Pitman, 1989). Naloxone does not produce panic attacks or alter the panic-producing properties of lactate infusion (Leibowitz et al., 1984). However, in another study, naloxone administration did impair the beneficial treatment effects of systematic desensitization in simple phobia (Hunt, Adamson, Egan, & Carr, 1988). The van der Kolk and Hunt studies suggest the common denominator may be opioid mediation of conditioned fear responses.

Study of endogenous opioids in childhood psychopathology has largely focused upon autistic (Campbell et al., 1989) and/or self-injurious behavior (Davidson, Kleene, Carroll, & Rockowitz, 1983; Herman, Hammock et al., 1987). Endogenous opioid species have, to the best of our knowledge, not been investigated in childhood DBD. The significant positive correlations between empathy and socialization reports and beta-endorphin concentrations in DBD but not OCD children may represent strain or genetic differences between the two groups. This is analogous to findings of opioid involvement in social affiliative behavior of prairie but not montane voles (Shapiro, Meyer, & Dewsbury, 1989). The presence of significant correlations in the DBD group but not the OCD group along with the significant interaction seen in Figure 1 suggest the possibility that the endogenous pharmacodynamics of the endorphin system may differ in these two patient groups. Opiate antagonist trials in each group would expand our understanding.

There are a number of limitations to this study, and these results should be considered preliminary. As has been noted in our previous CSF studies (Kruesi et al., 1990a,b; Swedo et al., 1989), without a normal control group it is only possible to report the relative contrast in concentrations. It is not possible to tell whether either group has higher, lower, or the same concentrations as a group of normal children.

Our guilt measure may not truly assess the behavioral activation system. If "guilt" on the DICA represents fear in passive avoidance rather than relief from punishment, differences are still expected between our groups. In Quay's interpretation, given the polarity of our groups, differences in fear in passive avoidance are expected. As discussed elsewhere, opioid modulation of fear has also been proposed (Hunt et al., 1988). Future studies that assess relationships between clinical "guilt" and performance in learning paradigms would be informative. Similarly, opiate-antagonist challenges to antisocials during varied learning paradigms would also expand our understanding. These proposed investigations represent a continuation of the provocative application by Quay of Gray's theory to childhood psychopathology.

## References

Achenbach, T. M., & Edelbrock, C. (1983). *Manual for The Child Behavior Checklist and Revised Child Behavior Profile.* Burlington, VT: University of Vermont.

American Psychiatric Association (APA). (1987). Committee on Nomenclature and Statistics. *Diagnostic and Statistical Manual of Mental Disorders* (3rd ed., rev.). Washington, DC: Author.

Campbell, M., Cohen, J. L., & Small, A. A. (1982). Drugs in aggressive behavior. *Journal of American Academy of Child Psychiatry, 21,* 107–117.

Campbell, M., Overall, J. E., Small, A. M. et al. (1989). Naltrexone in autistic children: An acute open dose range tolerance trial. *Journal of American Academy of Child Psychiatry, 28,* 200–206.

Daugherty, T. K., & Quay, H. C. (1991). Response perseveration and delayed responding in childhood behavior disorders. *Journal of Child Psychological Psychiatry, 32,* 453–461.

Davidson, P. W., Kleene, B. M., Carroll, M., & Rockowitz, R. J. (1983). Effects of naloxone on self-injurious behavior: A case study. *Applied Research in Mental Retardation, 4,* 1–4.

Dokla, C. P. J., & DeFillipis, J. K. (1989). Naloxone reduces social locomotor activity in rats. *Society for Neuroscience Abstracts, 15,* 844.

Eriksson, E., Westberg, P., Thuresson, K., Modigh, K., Kman, R., & Widerlon, E. (1989). Increased cerebrospinal fluid levels of endorphin immunoreactivity in panic disorder. *Neuropsychopharmacology, 2*(3), 225–228.

Eysenck, S. B. G., Easting, G., & Pearson, P. R. (1984). Age norms for impulsiveness, venturesomeness and empathy in children. *Personality and Individual Differences, 5*, 315–321.

George, D. T., Adinoff, B., Ravitz, B., Nutt, D. J., DeJong, J. Berrettini, W., Mefford, I. N., Costa, E., & Linnoila, M. (1990). A cerebrospinal fluid study of the pathophysiology of panic disorder associated with alcoholism. *Acta Psychiatrica Scandinavica, 82*, 1–7.

Gray, J. A. (1972b). The psychophysiology nature of introversion-extraversion: A modification of Eysenck's theory. In V. D. Neblitsin and J. A. Gray (Eds.), *Biological bases of individual behavior* (pp. 108–205). New York: Academic Press.

Gray, J. A. (1982). *The neuropsychology of anxiety: An enquiry into the functions of the septohippocampal system.* New York: Oxford University Press.

Gray, J. A. (1973). Casual theories of personality and how to test them. In J. R. Royce (Ed.), *Multivariate analysis and psychological theory* (pp. 409–463). New York: Academic Press.

Gray, J. A. (1979). A neuropsychological theory of anxiety. In C. E. Izard (Ed.), *Emotions in personality and psychopathology* (pp. 303–335). New York: Plenum Press.

Herjanic, B., & Campbell, W. (1977). Differentiating psychiatrically disturbed children on the basis of a structured interview. *Journal of Abnormal Child Psychology, 5*, 127–134.

Herjanic, B., & Reich, W. (1982). Development of a structured psychiatric interview for children: Agreement between child and parent on individual symptoms. *Journal of Abnormal Child Psychology, 10*, 307–324.

Herman, B. H., Hammock, M. K. et al. (1987). Naltrexone decreases self-injurious behavior. *Annals of Neurology, 222*, 550–552.

Hunt, D. D., Adamson, R., Egan, K., & Carr, J. E. (1988). Opioids: Mediators of fear or mania. *Biological Psychiatry, 23*, 426–428.

Insel, T. R., Pickar, D. (1983). Naloxone administration in obsessive-compulsive disorder: Report of two cases. *American Journal of Psychiatry, 140*, 1219–1220.

Kalantari, M., Yule, W., & Gardner, F. (1990, January 25). *Oversensitivity to reward in persistent conduct disordered pre-school children.* Paper presented at 2nd Annual Meeting of the Society for Research in Child and Adolescent Psychopathology, Costa Mesa, CA.

Kavaliers, M. (1989). Day-night rhythms of shoaling behavior in goldfish: Opioid and pineal involvement. *Physiological Behavior, 46*, 167–172.

Kruesi, M. J. P., Linnoila, M., Rapoport, J. L., Brown, G. C., & Petersen, R. (1985). Carbohydrate craving, conduct disorder and low CSF 5-HIAA. *Psychiatry Research, 16*, 83–86.

Kruesi, M. J. P., Swedo, S. E., Coffey, M. L., Hamburger, S. D., Leonard, H., & Rapoport, J. L. (1988). Objective and subjective side effects of research lumbar punctures in children and adolescents. *Psychiatry Research, 25*, 59–63.

Kruesi, M. J. P., Swedo, S. E., Leonard, H. L., Rubinow, D. R., & Rapoport, J. L. (1990b). CSF-somatostatin in childhood psychiatric disorders: A preliminary investigation. *Psychiatry Research, 33*, 277–284.

Kruesi, M. J. P., Rapoport, J. L., Hamburger, S., Hibbs, E., Potter, W. Z., Lenane, M., & Brown, G. L. (1990a). CSF monoamine metabolites, aggression and impulsivity in disruptive behavior disorders of children and adolescents. *Archives of General Psychiatry, 47*, 419–426.

Leibowitz, M. R., Gorman, J. M., Fyer, A. J., Dillon, D. J., & Klein, D. F. (1984). Effects of naloxone on patients with panic attacks. *American Journal of Psychiatry, 141*, 995–997.

Lepola, U., Jolkkonen, J., Pikanen, A., Riekkinen, P., & Rimon, R. (1990). Cerebrospinal fluid monoamine metabolites and neuropeptides in patients with panic disorder. *Annals of Medicine, 22,* 237–239.

Newman, J. P., Patterson, M., & Kosson, D. (1987). Response preservation in psychopaths. *Journal of Abnormal Psychology, 96,* 145–148.

Olds, J., & Travis, R. P. (1960). Effects of chlorpromazine, pentobarbital, and morphine on self-stimulation. *Journal of Pharmacological Experimental Therapeutics, 128,* 397–404.

Olds, M. E., & Fobes, J. C. (1981). The central basis of motivation: Intracranial self-stimulation studies. In M. R. Rosenzweig & L. W. Porter (Eds.), *Annual Review of Psychology* (pp. 523–574). Palo Alto, CA: Annual Reviews, Inc.

Panksepp, J., Herman, B. H., Vilberg, T., Bishop, P., & DeEskinazi, F. G. (1980). Endogenous opioids and social behavior. *Neuroscience and Biobehavioral Reviews, 4,* 473–487.

Quay, H. C. (1988). The behavioral reward and inhibition system in childhood behavior disorder in attention deficit disorder. In Lewis M. Bloomingdale (Ed.), *New research in attention, treatment, and psychopharmacology* (Vol. 3, pp. 176–186). New York: Pergamon Press.

Sandyk, R. (1987). Naloxone obliterates obsessive-compulsive disorder in Tourette's syndrome. *International Journal of Neuroscience, 35,* 93–94.

SAS Institute. (1985). *User's Guide: Statistics, Version 5.* Cary, NC: Author.

Schaefer, G. J. (1988). Opiate antagonists and rewarding brain stimulation. *Neuroscience and Biobehavioral Reviews, 12,* 1–17.

Shapiro, S. K., Quay, H. C., Hogan, A. E., & Schwartz, K. P. (1988). Response perseveration and delayed responding in under socialized aggressive conduct disorder. *Journal of Abnormal Psychology, 97,* 371–373.

Shapiro, L. E., Meyer, M. E., & Dewsbury, D. A. (1989). Affiliative behavior in voles: Effects of morphine, naloxone, and cross-fostering. *Physiological Behavior, 46,* 719–723.

Stein, E. A. (1985). Effects of intracranial self-stimulation on brain opiate peptides. *Peptides, 6,* 67–73.

Swedo, S. E., Leonard, H. L., Kruesi, M. J. P., Rettew, D. C., Listwak, S. J., Berrettini, W., Stipetic, M., Hamburger, S., Gold, P. W., Potter, W. Z., & Rapoport, J. L. (1992). Cerebrospinal fluid neurochemistry of children and adolescents with obsessive compulsive disorder. *Archives of General Psychiatry, 49,* 29–32.

Scerbo, A., Raine, A., O'Brien, M., Chan, C. J., Rhee, C., & Smiley, N. (1990). Reward dominance and passive avoidance learning in adolescent psychopaths. *Journal of Abnormal Child Psychology, 18*(4), 451–463.

van der Kolk, B. A., Greenberg, M. S., Orr, S. P., & Pitman, R. K. (1989). Endogenous opioids, stress-induced analgesia, and post-traumatic stress disorder. *Psychopharmacology,* Bulletin 25, Vol. 25, No. 3, pp. 417–421.

Winslow, J. T., & Insel, T. R. (1990, August). Neurobiology of obsessive compulsive disorder: A possible role for serotonin. Laboratory of Clinical Science, NIMH, Bethesda, MD. *Journal of Clinical Psychiatry, 51*:8 (Supple): 27–31.

# Author Index

# Subject Index